Wavy-Haired READER

GW00720512

◆ I wish to:
recommend for future inclusion ❑   criticise ❑

name of outlet/service: _____

address: _____

comment: _____

_____

_____

◆ I wish to:
recommend for future inclusion ❑   criticise ❑

name of outlet/service: _____

address: _____

comment: _____

_____

_____

◆ Do you have any comments about this guide?

_____

_____

_____

_____

Please complete overleaf.

Please help us learn about our readers:

full name/title:

_____

address: postcode:

_____

Where did you first hear of / see this guide?

_____

Did you get the guide:
on impulse in a shop ❑   as a gift ❑
          on recommendation from a friend ❑
       on recommendation from another source ❑ specify:

_____

Do you normally live:
in Cambridge city ❑   near Cambridge ❑
    elsewhere ❑ if so, specify from which place/country:

_____

Which one best describes your status:
       a long-time resident of the Cambridge area ❑
          a new resident of the area ❑ a tourist ❑
studying in Cambridge ❑   other ❑ (please specify):

_____

Are you:
   a homemaker ❑ employed full-time ❑ part-time ❑
   self-employed ❑ unemployed ❑ student ❑ retired ❑
Are you:
single ❑   living with a partner/married ❑
What is your age:
below 20 ❑   20-35 ❑   36-45 ❑
46-55 ❑   56-65 ❑   66+ ❑
Are you:
in rented accommodation ❑   a home owner ❑
in hotel or college rooms ❑   other ❑ (specify):

_____

Tick here if you do not want to receive information about
our other publications: ❑

Please return this form to:

**Wavy-Haired Reader
PO Box 311
Cambridge CB4 3FG
England**

Cambridge

a user's guide

written and edited by
Neal E. Robbins
with additional research
and writing by

2001-2002 EDITION

Nicholas Best, Jane Bower,
Kate Burdett, John Gaskell,
Jan Gilbert, Penny Hancock,
Collette Nichols & Edward Yoxall.
Maps by Ian Agnew

in association with

 **UNIVERSITY OF CAMBRIDGE**

FREE UPDATES

Every effort is made to ensure that Wavy-Haired Reader guides are up-to-date and accurate at publication. In addition, free updates are posted on our website:

www.wavy-hairedreader.com

You can also find out about our other publications and, in future, obtain more special offers, discounts and many other services online.

THE IDEAL CORPORATE GIFT

Looking for the ideal membership or corporate gift? Something that lasts all year? Look no further. The next edition of this guide will be available for bulk, pre-publication purchases with a custom-printed first page and embossed hard cover.

For information contact us by e-mail:

info@wavy-hairedreader.com

**by fax: 01223 527603
or phone: 01223 462233**

This edition was first published in February 2001 by
The Wavy-Haired Reader Ltd
PO Box 311, Cambridge CB4 3FG, UK
Copyright © The Wavy-Haired Reader Ltd
Wavy-Haired Reader® is an imprint of The Cambridge Insider®
ISBN 0-9537183-2-8

Advertising, sales and marketing by BC Publications,
16 Market Place, Diss, Norfolk. For information:
phone 01379 64200, fax 01379 650480.
Printed by Pensord, Pontllanfraith, Blackwood NP12 2YA.
Cover design by Harris Design Associates, Cambridge.
Cover page pictures (left side from top): The Glassworks Health Club
(N Robbins); WAGN train (WAGN); bicyclist (N Robbins);
chemistry student (Univ of Camb Press and Publ); family along River
Cam (N Robbins). Title page (from left) nos 1 Cambridge graduates
and 4 (Folk Festival) by Findlay Kember; 2 (football girl) courtesy of
Cambridge City Council Sports Development Team; 3 (Trinity College
porter) by anon.

COMMENTS FROM READERS:

ON THE 'CAMBRIDGE PROFILE' CHAPTER:

'I found the text excellent and very informative. I learned a lot through being able to see Cambridge from the viewpoint of a resident!'

MIKE PETTY, WRITER, LECTURER & RESEARCHER ON CAMBRIDGESHIRE & THE FENS

'It reads very well, capturing the city's split personality nicely while being easy to read.'

SUE ELLIOT, CAMBRIDGE JOURNALIST

ON THE 'EMPLOYMENT' CHAPTER:

'Comprehensive. Should be a good source of advice for job-seekers coming into the area.'

KEITH McDONALD, MANAGER, DISTRICT JOBCENTRE

ON THE 'LEISURE' CHAPTER:

'It looks very good and the contents are excellent.'

MARGARET BADCOCK, TOURISM MANAGER, CAMBRIDGE TOURIST OFFICE

ON THE 'SHOPPING' CHAPTER:

'A great guide to mainstream shopping.'

KATE PATERSON, AUTHOR, CAMBRIDGE SECRETS

Photo courtesy of University of Cambridge

Photo by Findlay Kember

Photo courtesy of Arm Ltd

This book is about living in Cambridge and the surrounding villages and towns – especially the areas including Ely, Newmarket, Saffron Walden, Royston, Huntingdon and St Ives. If you have roots in the region or plan to set some down, whether for a matter of months or a lifetime, you'll find the guide makes life a lot easier and more enjoyable.

Newcomer or native, you'll benefit from the coverage of housing, shopping, jobs, transport, health, education, fun and activities – all organised in an easy-to-use, readable format with maps and pictures. Just arrived? You can start from the basics of where to live and how to get settled. A resident of long standing? We put at your fingertips what until now most people have had to learn the hard way. This book has all you need to get on with your life – and a lot more of interest that you might not have known about.

Think of this User's Guide as an A-to-Z answer to all your questions about living well in and around Cambridge.

Take housing. What do houses typically cost? What's the rent for a one-bedroom? How about education? What school options are there? What private secondaries serve

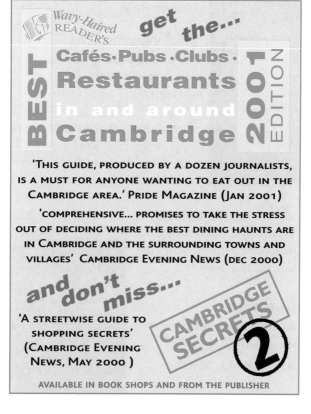

the area? Take health. What are the hospitals like? Take shopping. Where can you get the best pot plants? Where's a good place to buy a computer? Take jobs. What can you expect to find in this area? How about sport? Where can you learn to row on the river Cam? What are the fitness clubs like? Take transport. What's the easiest way to Heathrow? How do you get involved with volunteer groups or choose a church? It's all here.

The information was gathered by journalists who know the area well and give you the benefit of local experience.

The information was gathered by journalists who know the area well and give you the benefit of local experience. They write as if to a friend, with wit, warmth and frankness.

All efforts were made to ensure that the information is accurate and complete. But things do change. So an update is posted on our website (www.wavy-hairedreader.com) for anything in the guide that we come to learn may have changed since publication. You are invited to check this at any time and to investigate other services available online.

We also hope you give us your opinions by contacting us through the website, by e-mail (info@wavy-hairedreader) or by returning the reply form at the beginning of the book.

Neal E. Robbins

ACKNOWLEDGEMENTS

The publishers wish to acknowledge the generous sponsorship of the University of Cambridge, whose support made possible the months of writing and research required to produce this book. We are also grateful for support provided by ARM Ltd, who wish to welcome with these pages their many new employees.

Naturally any errors or shortcomings that may have crept into the book remain the sole responsibility of the author.

Our special thanks to second readers of the chapters:

Margaret Badcock, Tourism Manager, Cambridge City Council

Julie Bailey, Childcare Coordinator, University of Cambridge

Tony Croft, Chief Engineer, Cambridge City Council

Sue Elliot, reporter and feature writer

John Frost, Head of Revenue Cambridge City Council

Chris Jakes, Cambridge Central Library

Debbie Kay, Sports Development Team, Cambridge City Council

Kate Lancaster, Press Office, Papworth Hospital

Ruth Lynn, Assistant City Manager, Cambridge City Council

Heather McDonough, photography instructor, and her students at Anglia Polytechnic University: Jane Moorwood, Daniel Porter, Adam Ananayo, Robert Parr, Adam Cleaver Bastian Roden, Jenny Wilson and Ben Beechey

Keith McDonald, Jobcentre Manager, Peterborough

Jane Meggitt, Head of Communications, Addenbrooke's NHS Trust

Sarah Noel, Cambridge Enterprise Agency

Kate Paterson, author of *Cambridge Secrets2*

Mike Petty, writer, lecturer and researcher on Cambridgeshire and the Fens

Nick Redmayne, Redmayne Arnold and Harris estate agents

Campbell Ross-Bain, Environment and Transport, Cambridgeshire County Council

Wilma Smith, Manager, Cambridge Lea Hospital

Hilary Spiers, Cambridgeshire Health Authority

Peter Studdert, Director of Planning, Cambridge City Council

Kim Taylor, Head Teacher, Lady Adrian School

Elfreda Tealby-Watson, Appeal Manager, Q103 FM Appeal

Val Watson and Gill White, Cambridgeshire Careers Guidance

And thanks to other writers who contributed – Bill Davidson, Katie Martin, Ellee Seymour and Angela Singer – and especially indexer and proofreader Louise Tucker.

...and to the many people named and unnamed who generously gave of their time to help us gather information and pictures for the guide.

CHAPTER 1
CAMBRIDGE PROFILE

Photo by Bastian Roden

Life in Cambridge sometimes leads one to ask, 'Why am I here?' It doesn't matter if you are that Cambridge rarity, someone born and raised locally, an established resident or the greenest newcomer. There will be moments when you will doubt why you put up with the ludicrous expense of housing, maddening traffic and jostling Saturday crowds. Should all that ever get you down, return to this page. There are many remedies.

A stroll along the Backs, widely-held as the most beautiful walk in Europe, is one cure. Or ask a punt chauffeur to forget his spiel and say absolutely nothing while he takes you through that blissful stretch of honeyed stones from Magdalene down to Queens'. Listen to the evening choirs of King's, St John's and Clare; sit down to the Footlights Revue or take a shawl to an open-air Shakespeare production and warm to a glass of mulled wine; for those ready to stretch their legs, there is the walk from Newnham through Grantchester Meadows, the land of Byron or, according to taste, Pink Floyd.

> There will be moments when you will doubt why you put up with the ludicrous expense of housing, maddening traffic and jostling Saturday crowds. Should all that ever get you down, return to this page. There are many remedies.

And? The cattle on Coe Fen within a cow pat's throw of the very centre; the Council's Midsummer Common fireworks viewed from Castle Hill; the opening day of first-class cricket at Fenners; the sight of Ely Cathedral, the 'Ship of the Fens' rising from the morning mist; Anglesey Abbey in spring; finding yourself lost in the Iron Age embankments of the Wandlebury Ring; increasingly good restaurants; those steamy, July evening horse-race meetings at Newmarket, full of live music and champagne, the quietly freezing ones over the jumps at Huntingdon on Boxing Day; Trinity Street on its May Ball night teeming with young masters of the universe in evening dress.

At this point cynical old hands will say: 'Yeah, ok for some.' True, there are, undeniably, pockets of deprivation in the region as there are in every area of the world. Yet living here, regardless of the state of your wallet, can be full of moments that will change your life. If you are ready to throw yourself into one of the world's most beautiful melting pots you will find your mind stretched, your arguments confounded, your senses dazzled.

End of the advertisement, because here are the thorny questions which most people want answered…

ARE THE NATIVES FRIENDLY?

'No' is the short answer. Apologies to that minority of residents who always make an effort to welcome newcomers

Cover picture: The Great Gate, Gonville and Caius College.

and, if you have just moved in next to a delightful couple who are forever bringing round cups of tea and advising you of bus times, the answer might seem perverse. But the experience of most new arrivals to Cambridge is of opening the door of a freezer.

The Cambridge coolness towards new residents is wholly understandable and can be partly explained by the constant presence of so many short-stay incomers and tourists. On the street where you live experience may have shown that there is little immediate incentive to invest in long-term relationships. But, the locals will tell you, if you're here for a good stretch, then let us know and you might be surprised what warmth can be conjured from our frozen hearts.

Remember too that, even counting its longer-stay residents, this is overwhelmingly a city of outsiders, people from elsewhere who have been sent by their national employers, banks, stores and building societies for example, to work here, usually as a promotion. Don't forget that, in addition, there are around 30,000 transient Cambridge residents: university students, language school students and tourists. But what is sometimes assumed to be local aloofness can be explained by the worldly character that Cambridge has acquired. Think of it as the trade-off

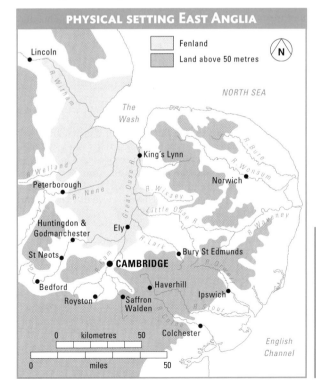

PHYSICAL SETTING EAST ANGLIA

Fenland
Land above 50 metres

N

Lincoln

R. Witham

NORTH SEA

The Wash

R. Bure
R. Wensum

King's Lynn

Welland

Peterborough
R. Nene

Great Ouse R.

R. Wissey

Little Ouse R.

Norwich

R. Waveney

Huntingdon & Godmanchester

Ely

R. Lark

St Neots

Bury St Edmunds

CAMBRIDGE

R. Stour

Bedford

Haverhill

Royston

Saffron Walden

Ipswich

Colchester

English Channel

0   kilometres   50

0   miles   50

between cosmopolitanism and neighbourliness. This is less true in the smaller villages, particularly those towards the Fens where the remoter communities tend to be more inclusive.

ANY FUN TO BE HAD HERE?

Tons of it. It is easier to say what one can't do – mountain climbing for example – rather than what one can. Some teenagers will whinge, as they do everywhere, because there isn't a bowling alley – though one is proposed – or a 10,000-seater rock stadium or that King's lawn hasn't been turned into a skating park. Yet there is plenty for them too. For this always will be a place with a huge population bulge in the 16-25 age group.

The number of clubs, bars and restaurants has increased rapidly in the last decade reflecting the prosperity of the region. But they mostly belong to national chains and while these are very welcome they don't distinguish the area from other well-heeled towns. What does distinguish the area – apart from museums (see the panel page 18) and breathtaking sites like Ely Cathedral, the Wren Library and King's College Chapel (not often a teenager's idea of fun, admittedly) – is the quality of the arts, rich well beyond what one might expect for the size of the region's population. Much of it – theatre, concerts, exhibitions, discussions, lectures – is university-based. But there is also cinema and some well-supported theatre and dance which are 'town'. For sport there is athletics, tennis, football, rowing, rugby (even rugby league), cricket, fishing, boating, speedway and boxing and, of course, Newmarket, the European HQ of horse-racing and home of the National Horse-racing Museum.

Something for everyone?

Yes. The majority of events draw town and gown alike, but some generalisations can be made: Warner's multiplex cinema in the Grafton Centre caters mostly for town, the Arts Picture House, which metamorphosed from the old Arts Cinema, attracts a university crowd. The tiny Abbey Stadium, home to Cambridge United football team, draws some students but you are unlikely to find any dons screaming their heads off in the Allotment End. They save that for the Bumps, where college rowing teams compete to become Head of the River (top of a league system). The races are mostly a university attraction, although town rowing has its own strong tradition. It's largely gown too at Grange Road, home of the university's rugby union.

May Balls, the June celebrations hosted by the colleges and open to the public, require a book to themselves but, as a loose generalisation, the higher the ticket price the more likely is it that your fellow revellers, say at Trinity, will be older, richer and more formally attired than at the determinedly cheap ones, King's for example.

MICHELLE SPRING – CRIME NOVELIST

When I walk around Cambridge, certain things always seem to catch my attention. I'm really fascinated by the combination of nature and the urban in Cambridge: the visual contrast between the green idyllic setting of the Backs with the stark Victorian terraces off Mill Road or the ponies on Stourbridge Common, and the plush ancient buildings of the historic centre. The interpenetration of town and country is incredible – on a punt you can move from the city bridges to the deep countryside of Granchester in only minutes. The contrast is breathtaking! I particularly love the trees in the city, and one of the times of year that I love best is the autumn, when the leaves are changing colour and you begin to smell smoke in the air. I absolutely relish Guy Fawkes Night (5 November). To me it is just thrilling. At 7 o'clock in the evening, when it's pitch black outside, you find yourself heading towards Midsummer Common, and it really does seem as if the whole world is walking there too. Everybody is outside, and in good spirits, happy and excited, while in the distance you can see the glow of the fireworks and the bonfire, and you can hear the music playing at the funfair. In fact, Bonfire Night in Cambridge always has the sensation to me of being like a medieval fair – it has a very wonderful and ancient quality about it. It is good-natured, and it is uplifting to be out on a dark night with such a large crowd of people – to enjoy the occasion so much and still feel completely safe. The atmosphere and drama of Bonfire Night on Midsummer Common and Cambridge and its surroundings continue to be a very real inspiration to me.

Photo by Neil E. Robbins

Author Michelle Spring set a series of her crime novels in Cambridge where she has lived for 30 years. Originally from Canada, her works include best-selling books such as In the Midnight Hour, Nights in White Satin *and* Standing in the Shadows.

Come summer, the students gone, the City Council takes over with its 'Summer In The City' programme geared towards children. Much of it takes place in the grounds of Cherry Hinton Hall, also home to the one event with a truly global appeal: the Cambridge Folk Festival, tickets for which sell out very quickly although there is usually a Thursday night event reserved for locals who must produce proof of their residence.

WHERE DID IT ALL BEGIN?

Long before fleeing academics arrived from Oxford in 1209 and started a university, Cambridge existed as a Roman camp. Where the Via Devana from Colchester to Chester crossed the river (the bridge on Bridge Street by Magdalene College) the Romans established a 25-acre settlement up around Castle Hill, where William the Conqueror would later build a castle.

The town – Cambridge was only made a city by Royal Charter in 1951 – was also the junction of the Via Devana and the Roman road which ran from the Norfolk coast via the Fens down to Cirencester and Bath. Trade flourished. When the fair on Stourbridge Common was established, the town's name became familiar throughout Europe as home to the biggest market in the known world, renowned particularly for its sale of wool.

By the 18th century the town was severely overcrowded. This was eventually relieved when surrounding fields were made available for housing. Population growth gained impetus from the opening of Cambridge railway station in 1845 – some distance from the town centre at the insistence of the University which refused to have trains running within a mile of its buildings. Horse-drawn trams, then buses, brought visitors into town.

In the 20th century Cambridge expanded rapidly. Industries grew out of the University's two needs: for printing (which was met by the existing Cambridge University Press) and for scientific equipment, particularly that demanded by the Cavendish Laboratory, the University's Physics Department, which, to this day, is the source of so much local prosperity. Cambridge Instruments and Pye (later taken over by Philips) began as suppliers to the Cavendish but became well-established on the world stage.

In 1975 the Cambridge Science Park was opened by Trinity College and was a huge success inspiring imitations throughout Europe. It has become probably Europe's most successful centre for high-tech industry and among the largest. Within a decade of its founding, there was a rapid growth in the region of small and medium-sized companies – including some notable failures – but, the trend established, Cambridge became a by-word for high-tech in Britain.

700 YEARS OF SCHOLARLY SOUVENIRS

In its 700 years of educating and nurturing some of the world's most eminent talents, it is not surprising that the University of Cambridge has been rewarded with many handsome souvenirs from its scholars, notably Darwin's specimens brought back from his voyages on the Beagle.

Many of these treasures are made available to the public through the University's museums and collections, and those that aren't, such as specimens at The Herbarium, can often be seen by appointment or by a pleading letter from the true enthusiast. With the exception of the Botanic Garden, all operate a free admission policy. You can also find out about the treasures from the experts and academics through workshops, lunchtime gallery talks and tours.

A Fitzwilliam Museum gallery

Photo courtesy of Fitzwilliam Museum

The Fitzwilliam Museum in Trumpington Street has art and antiquities of international importance from Ancient Greece, Egypt and Rome. Pottery, glass, furniture, armour, clocks, fans, rugs, coins, medals, illuminated manuscripts... all these and works by Titian, Rubens, Van Dyck, Canaletto, Hogarth, Gainsborough, Constable, Monet, Degas, Renoir, Cézanne and Picasso.

The Museum of Archaeology and Anthropology ('the Ark & Anth') holds important collections from the South Seas, West Africa and the Northwest coast of North America and photographic collections from the 19th and 20th centuries. It also holds important collections relating to Cambridge and the region. The Museum of Classical Archaeology ('the Ark') holds more than 600 casts of almost all the major pieces of classical sculpture, one of the largest collections of plaster casts of Greek and Roman statues in the world.

The Whipple Museum of the History of Science is a collection of scientific equipment from the Middle Ages to the present, with displays ranging from the earliest 'pocket' calculators to astrolabes and microscopes. The Sedgwick Museum of Earth Sciences is the University's oldest museum and some would say its most sensuous, containing one million fossils, some more than 3 billion years old. The University Museum of Zoology is another to have benefited from Darwin but also has a near-comprehensive collection of British birds.

> ### Singletons the Thing
>
> Cambridge itself is very much a city of singletons with more than one third of households having one occupier and another third with just two-person occupancy. Families are a minority here and always have been; colleges refused to allow dons (or, as they are more correctly called, 'fellows') to marry until the 1880s. As a result larger houses – fewer than 10% of dwellings are detached – command a premium beyond what might normally be expected.

HOW BIG IS IT?

The boundaries of Cambridge do not extend very far, about two miles from the city centre which is home to around 800 businesses taking in Trumpington to the south and Cherry Hinton to the southeast. Beyond the northeastern boundary is Milton, with Histon just beyond the northern edge. The commuting area extends well beyond these and other local villages, even to Milton Keynes and King's Lynn. The area is sometimes grouped under 'East Midlands,' or as 'Mid Anglia' by the Cambridge Evening News, but usually under 'East Anglia' in which region it is now assuming a central economic role, usurping that of Norwich, though lacking that city's importance as a media centre.

Within the city boundaries lives a population of around 130,000 – with an ethnic make up of 94% White, 1.7% Indian/ Pakistani/ Bangladeshi, 1.2% Black, 1% Chinese, 2% others – out of a county population of just over 500,000. There is little doubt that the number would be much higher if more land for development were available but green belt restrictions limit housing in the area. The modern village of Bar Hill has absorbed some of the demand, the newly-built Cambourne will absorb more. Meanwhile populations in surrounding towns continue to grow. St Neots is now 28,000, Newmarket 18,000, Ely 13,000, Royston 15,000 and Huntingdon, 18,000.

IS CAMBRIDGE SAFE?

Cambridge police advise against taking short cuts through parks or poorly-lit alleyways after dark and to avoid takeaway outlets at around pub closing time. But there are no no-go areas within the region, police say. Cambridge has more vagrants than the average city which leads to a heightened perception of crime. But in reality Cambridge's problems are no worse than other university/tourist spots such as Bath, Canterbury and York, all recognised by vagrants as a 'soft touch.' The regional crime rate is encouragingly low: 7,017 offences per 100,000 population compared to 9,785 nationally.

Although the city centre is reasonably well lit, and now extensively covered by CCTV cameras, robberies in the region have increased in line with the national trend, crim-

RULE ONE: GET A GOOD BIKE LOCK

Crime figures are inflated by a large number of cycle thefts in the Cambridge area, a problem which may eventually be reduced by the introduction of secure cycle parks. The use of stronger tubular metal 'D' locks rather than the plastic coiled wire locks, which are quickly severed by pincers, is recommended.

Bicycle theft takes the form of opportunist thefts, unlocked bikes taken from outside shops and houses; drunken thefts, late night requisitioning of a bike, and systematic theft by organised gangs, including the stripping of school cycle racks, which has become more common as more sophisticated models come on the market.

The police have a specialist cycle unit and the city squad also has regular auctions where recovered, but unclaimed, stolen bikes are offered at bargain prices.

inals now preferring to steal ready cash from purses and wallets rather than 'fence' goods stolen in burglaries. Similarly other crime statistics have tended to mirror fluctuations throughout the UK.

Safety on the roads, however, is not good, partly as a result of the frustrations created by congestion. The region has a bad record for fatal and serious road accidents. The rate per 100,000 of population in the region is 74 compared to 66 nationally. Much of this can be blamed on the A14, which runs from Newmarket over the north of Cambridge to Huntingdon, linking up with the M1 and M6. Consisting of just two lanes for the most part, it has become the major artery from Europe to the Midlands, Wales, Scotland and the North and has become notorious for accidents. Barely a week goes by without yet another serious accident or fatality on the road. Its record is appalling, a matter of political concern and one that ought to be taken seriously by anyone living in the region or passing through it.

Motorists, particularly in Cambridge, need to be aware of cyclists. Pedestrians, even in areas which appear to be intended as traffic-free, are always at risk from cyclists threading their way through, and from service vehicles.

WHAT'S IT LIKE FOR SHOPPING?

Heaven if you want clothes, books or a mobile phone. A bag of stone-ground flour, a packet of nails or a ball of wool might take more hunting down, but you can get them too.

The market square, Market Hill, is still accepted as the heart of Cambridge despite retail developments in other parts of the city. In the early 1970s, to the bitter regret of many locals, the adjacent Petty Cury area – an intricate web of narrow streets, with haberdashers and ironmongers, charm and curious old buildings – was pulled down to be replaced by the Lion Yard, so very full of …shops selling jeans, records and shoes. The opening of the Grafton Centre in the late 1970s, now home to about 80 retailers, came at the expense of many homes in the 'Kite' (so-called because of the shape of the area) and was fiercely opposed at the time.

Now, along with the surrounding streets, it offers 115,000 square feet of shopping compared to the historic centre's 70,000. Supermarket shopping, however, is confined to just Sainsbury's in the centre, although there is also a Marks and Spencer's food hall. Most of the major supermarkets are represented outside the centre, the most recent addition being Waitrose, off Trumpington Road, with a Tesco planned for the gas works site off Newmarket Road. Market stalls, more than 100 of them, offer a wide range of goods, from Monday to Saturday, with a Sunday craft market and a Farmers' Market selling mostly organic produce.

Today Cambridge as a shopping centre serves 500,000 people. Retail space in the city centre commands rentals which are among the most expensive 5% in the United Kingdom. According to Bidwells estate agents, Cambridge is the fifth most 'in-demand' city centre. Petty Cury draws tenants paying £150,000 per 1,000 square feet while Lion Yard tenants pay £115,000.

HOW'S THE ECONOMY DOING?

Working in the offices of ARM Ltd in Fulbourn Road, Cherry Hinton, were, at the last count, 25 people who have become paper millionaires in a company which has blossomed from a bright idea to a techno-stock darling. Shares once worth a few pence have since been traded at £50 each as the world has come to appreciate what its designs for super-efficient, low-power chips can do to extend the battery life of laptop computers and mobile phones in two booming markets.

PRODUCTIVITY UP, SALARIES SO-SO

The region as a whole is economically more active than most. Gross Domestic Product per head is 14% higher than the national average – but pay is slightly less than the national average for both men and women. The average man in April 1999 earned £436 a week gross (£440.70 nationally) and the average woman £323.90 (£325.60 nationally). Despite this, the average weekly household income was higher at £451 compared to £430 nationally.

The rate of employment for the region in Spring 1999 was 78.1% compared to 73.6% for the UK generally. The percentage of households receiving Income Support or Family Credit was 11% (15% nationally).

Government figures, Regional Trends September 2000.

Significantly, when the company was recently asked how it intended to progress, its response was not that of the traditional blue chip company (for by now it had entered the FTSE 100) intent on consolidating its market or inventing a smaller/bigger/faster/cheaper version of what it already does. Instead it raised the prospect of going into car air-bags.

Lateral thinking is very much alive in the Cambridge area. Invention has become so rife that when people talk of 'service industries' the description extends beyond the usual round of cleaners, gardeners, plumbers and builders to patent lawyers, venture capital companies and intellectual copyright specialists. Their agents no longer fly in by private jet to Cambridge Airport but have set up their own offices here.

> 'Cambridge faces a great future and enormous challenges but it has to solve the problems of too many private cars and too little affordable housing. It is a centre of excellence for education, research and high-tech and yet has pockets of severe poverty and homelessness. These problems can only be resolved with the cooperation of the residents.'
>
> *Evelyn Knowles, councillor and Mayor*

Photo courtesy of Cambridge City Council

Many of the new service industries are to be found alongside 'start-ups' in the Westbrook Centre and Orwell House, both off Milton Road, Robert Davies Court on Nuffield Road, Ronald Rolph Court off Wadloes Road and Barnwell Business Park off Barnwell Road. All aim to provide flexibility for small businesses and start-ups between 400 square feet and 1,500 square feet.

The biggest growth area is to the west of the city centre where the University is expanding its High Cross Research Park on some 75 acres by the M11. Current occupants include Schlumberger Cambridge Research, British Antarctic Survey and the Computer Aided Design Centre. The physical science and engineering faculties will eventually be relocated to a new campus adjoining this site.

Last, but not least, tourism has doubled in the past 20 years with more than 3.5 million visitors annually, mainly drawn to Cambridge because of the colleges. They buy around £200 million of local goods and services.

GROWING PAINS AND FUTURES

Cambridge is a victim of its own success. Over the last 20 years growth in high-tech industries has increased population, which is pushing up house prices, straining amenities and clogging roads. The area is adapting, but slowly and in ways that keep a heated development debate going in the press, at a hot-house called Cambridge Futures and, not least, in City Council chambers. All the time, a flock of shopping, leisure and transport projects responding to the needs are in the pipeline, and, if all goes well, will be completed by 2005:

● The city centre itself will be transformed by the construction of a Grand Arcade shopping complex with a new upgraded Robert Sayles (John Lewis) store, 50 shops, more parking, restaurants and entertainment.

● The railway station will have a £1 million makeover.

● The popular Park and Ride, now used by 18,000 people a month to avoid city-centre parking hassles, will grow by construction of new sites and expansion.

● Addenbrooke's Hospital has expansion plans for new bed space, for a £340 million biomedical science park, new link roads and a new railway station.

● A £30 million leisure park, including cinema, bowling alley, flats and parking linked to the railway station is on the way for the old Cattle Market.

● New supermarkets coming include a 70,000 sq ft Asda in the old Beehive Centre and Tesco at the old gasworks.

● Cambridge United Football club is putting £4.2 million into a stadium expansion to 10,000 seats.

● The Junction, a youth entertainment venue, has a £5 million refurbishment and expansion on the way.

● Expansions at Coral Park, off Newmarket Road, and on the old cement works, near Coldham's Lane are adding industrial distribution areas, hotels, swimming pools, restaurants and shopping.

Photo courtesy of Chapman Taylor Architects

Artist's conception of the future Grand Arcade

WHERE IS THE UNIVERSITY?

...is usually the first question asked by visitors to Cambridge, particularly those coach passengers who only have one hour to digest its 1200 years of history. They do not want to know that the city now has two, the new one being on East Road, Anglia Polytechnic University, formerly 'the tech'.

As far as the University of Cambridge is concerned, residents prefer to point visitors' cameras at the Senate House on King's Parade. That is where the Council of the University, the body that deals with administration and policy, holds its meetings. In fact, the physical University sprawls out across the city. It is the institution that creates and maintains the laboratories, the Faculties and departments of art, law, mathematics and the others – where the academics and students work. It awards degrees and organises the courses. But the university is not the same as the colleges. With budgets largely discrete from the University, the colleges are self-governing, financially independent bodies that select and give academic guidance to the students. They provide some of the teaching as well as food, accommodation and a social centre for dons and students.

Why so many colleges?

Several reasons: for example, Pembroke was founded by the French widow of the Duke of Pembroke in the hope that French and English students could live together in peace. Corpus Christi was founded by townsmen for townsmen. Trinity Hall and Magdalene were founded for student monks; Girton, New Hall and Newnham for the higher education of women. Churchill is a national memorial to Sir Winston and is expected to reflect his concern for the country's need for scientists and technologists.

There are also four post-graduate colleges: Darwin and Wolfson; Lucy Cavendish (women) and St Edmund's College; two teacher-training colleges: Homerton and Hughes Hall, and four theological colleges which do not come under the University's jurisdiction: Ridley Hall and Westcott House (Anglican), Westminster College (United Reformed Church) and Wesley House (Methodist).

University history in a nutshell...

The first Cambridge college was founded in 1284 and called Peterhouse as it was next to St Peter's Church (now St Mary the Less); there is no 'College' after the name. The second and third colleges to be built – King's Hall (1317) and Michaelhouse (1324) were joined by Henry VIII's collegiate merger of 1546 to form Trinity College which is the largest by student population and, as one of the country's biggest land-owners, is also the wealthiest.

Today, counting the four theological ones, there are 35 colleges, the most recent founded by the late Sir David

ALLAN BRIGHAM - STREET SWEEPER & HISTORIAN

Cambridge – the high-tech city grafted onto the university city – may have a lot of people with Porsches and designer clothes, but most people who work here have ordinary jobs; they are the army of service industry people like me who don't have anything to do with the University academics or Silicon Fen. They scrape a living – surviving by taking two jobs – doing the nightshift at Sainsbury's.

Photo by Philip Mynott

None of the guys who I work with could afford to live in Cambridge these days. I bought my house 20 years ago but the cheapest house now costs £100,000. To supplement their wages, half the people in my street have foreign students staying with them at times. This is one of the things I like about Cambridge. Where else would you find ordinary working class homes with students from Croatia, Italy or Brazil?

The trouble with being invisible is that you are easily overlooked. When I put on my orange street sweeper jacket on even I become invisible! Yet I attract all the prejudices that go with the job, though I'm doing an essential, unpleasant task – sweeping up the rubbish, everyone else's crap. It's ironic. Without the majority of ordinary working people, prosperous Cambridge wouldn't function.

The challenge is to develop Cambridge in a way that recognizes everyone's need to have an opportunity to live here and share what the city has to offer. Cambridge has an exciting future. It is becoming the focal point for the east of England. It's a beautiful city. The greenery – the trees, the gardens, the parks and commons – makes Cambridge an attractive place to live. The countryside comes right into the heart of the city. If Cambridge expands the areas of greenery need to be preserved.

If the people who clean the streets and offices, staff the shops, work as clerical staff and technicians can't afford to live here too, they'll end up in Fenland ghettos, outside the best areas. That is the threat. It would mean more people sitting in traffic jams on the A14, complaining about the price of fuel, resentment, exclusion and a real underclass.

Allan Brigham, a resident of Cambridge for 20 years, lives in the Mill Road area of Cambridge and is a road sweeper, tour guide and local historian.

Robinson, a businessman who first made his fortune locally through the sale of bicycles, then cars, then nationally through Robinson Rentals, hiring out televisions. Robinson College was opened by the Queen in 1981 when her presence, it was wrongly thought, would be enough to tempt Sir David out of his life as a recluse.

and town-gown relations...

Until recently there was a huge imbalance between the sexes in Cambridge as most of the university population was male. Local girls were in great demand to make up numbers at parties and discos causing much resentment among the local youth who saw their potential girlfriends being spirited away by often rich and privileged students.

'Grad-bashing' was a phenomenon which began in the 1950s. During the early 60s Rag Week was an unstructured sequence of undergraduate japes which riled local youths and again fisticuffs ensued. The taking over of Rag Week as a co-ordinated charity event by the Students' Union combined with the presence of many more young women in Cambridge have eased most tensions though, as elsewhere, the mixture of large numbers of young men and alcohol sometimes leads to predictable results.

Town-gown rivalry has a long history, dating back to riots in 1249. Mayors would refuse to take the oath to uphold the University's privileges in the town. Town-gown rivalry went to the highest level with Sir William Cecil, Chancellor of the University and Secretary of State, in the 1550s dispute with Lord North, High Steward of the town.

But today arguments are rare. Although one sometimes senses a rivalry, the University is much less the elitist, distant institution it once was. City and University – whose fates are increasingly intermingled – cooperate widely on development and policy, and the University has learned to make itself more accessible to the town and, indeed, the world.

What about the University today?

Although each college employs its own staff, the University itself is still the region's biggest employer, providing 9,000 jobs. The University's main teaching hospital, Addenbrooke's, employs 5,000 people and is a world leader in medical research. The science parks set up by Trinity and St John's colleges have flourished. The St John's Innovation Centre, opened across the road near the Milton A14 access in 1987, promotes the expansion of small and start-up technology-based enterprises. The University is at the heart of the 'Cambridge Phenomenon', sometimes known as 'Silicon Fen' with its core of expertise leading to research collaborations and spin-off companies. It also runs a 'think-tank', Cambridge Futures, which aims to consider how Cambridge will develop over the next 50 years.

The University, which has long provided cultural town-gown links through its museums, has programmes for local

The
ATRIUM
Club

01223 522522

Not only is The Atrium the best gym in town, it is the ONLY affordable fitness club

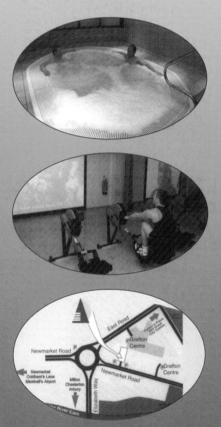

The biggest gym in East Anglia, Sauna Cabin, Aerobics, Step & Circuit classes, Turkish Steamroom, Jacuzzi Spa, Individual Health check, plus much more...

adults and children as part of its contribution towards community education. The Board of Continuing Education provides day schools in local and regional centres, residential courses at Madingley Hall, advanced courses for industry and business, international summer schools, day courses for local solicitors and residential courses for magistrates.

The School of Education organises maths and science activities for children. STIMULUS links University students with local schools whose pupils ask for help on IT projects. AskNRICH is an online maths club. The University's National Science Week, among the biggest in the country, attracted 33,000 visits in March 2000. The University Library puts on regular exhibitions of its many treasures and the University's Kettle's Yard gallery promotes modern art.

University students are recruited by Student Community Action whose services include Bridge, a body which offers holidays for underprivileged children.

WHO RUNS LOCAL GOVERNMENT?

Cambridge City Council is based at the Guildhall on the market square. Although it runs most city functions, it is the Cambridgeshire County Council, at Shire Hall on Castle Hill, which is in charge of transport and education in both the county and the city. The City Council teeters between Labour and Liberal Democrats, but is currently controlled by Liberal Democrats with an overall majority of four. It has its next elections in May 2002.

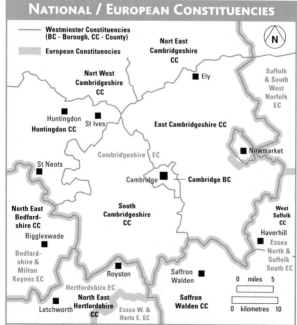

NATIONAL / EUROPEAN CONSTITUENCIES

Westminster Constituencies (BC - Borough, CC - County)

European Constituencies

Nort East Cambridgeshire CC

Nort West Cambridgeshire CC

Ely

Suffolk & South West Norfolk EC

Huntingdon
Huntingdon CC

St Ives

East Cambridgeshire CC

Newmarket

St Neots

Cambridgeshire EC

Cambridge

Cambridge BC

North East Bedfordshire CC

South Cambridgeshire CC

West Suffolk CC

Biggleswade

Haverhill

Bedfordshire & Milton Keynes EC

Royston

Saffron Walden

Essex North & Suffolk South EC

Hertfordshire EC

North East Hertfordshire CC

Letchworth

Essex W. & Herts E. EC

Saffron Walden CC

0 miles 5

0 kilometres 10

The County Council is invariably dominated by Conservatives, and Conservative support can be generalised as being focused on Huntingdon, parliamentary seat of the last Tory prime minister, John Major, and galvanised with returns from the more remote villages in the north of the county. Liberal Democrat voters tend to be concentrated in Cambridge with Labour winning its seats from less prosperous wards in the city. The County Council now has 33 Conservatives, 16 Lib Dems, and 10 Labour members.

South Cambridgeshire Council, based in Hills Road, is the district council for the area outside the Cambridge City limits and includes areas such as Fen Ditton, Milton, Impington, Girton, Cherry Hinton and the Science Park. 'South Cambs' council is not run by any one political party and one in four of its councillors are not members of any party. Outside the city there are also parish councils.

Who votes and how?

The City Council has 42 councillors representing the 14 wards which make up the city area. Each ward elects three councillors, one each year, and they each serve four years in office. In the fourth year there are County Council elections when 14 councillors are elected to represent the city's interests on the county council.

The Government has not been blind to the growth in prosperity of the region over recent years and appears to believe that the people of Cambridgeshire can afford to pay more from their own pockets to fund services.

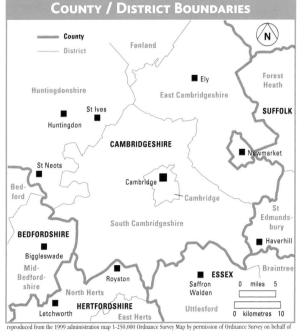

COUNTY / DISTRICT BOUNDARIES

In successive recent years, Cambridgeshire received less than any other county in cash per head of population. Education is particularly hard-hit, its poor national funding regarded locally as a scandal. To give schools their first modest budget increase for seven years, the Council is providing almost £5 million more than the Government provides.

The result is that Council Tax in 2000-2001 has risen by almost three times the rate of inflation – 8.5% – to pay for it.

What does local government do?

● education

Almost 60% of the county's budget is spent on education. It is responsible for educating 77,250 pupils in its 255 schools. Although at primary school level one third of classes have more than 30 pupils, exam results in later years are well above national averages and Government targets.

● environment and transport

The council is responsible for maintaining more than 4,000 kms of roads and 3,860 kms of footways, 53,700 streetlights and 1,500 bridges. It also disposes of 220,000 tonnes of domestic waste at a cost of £9 million a year. The Fire Service deals with more than 12,000 emergencies a year.

● libraries and heritage

This county council department provides 40 libraries and seven mobile libraries and, from every library, provides access to computer-based information.

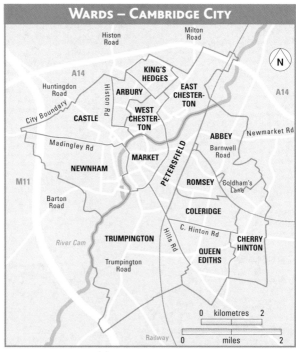

WARDS – CAMBRIDGE CITY

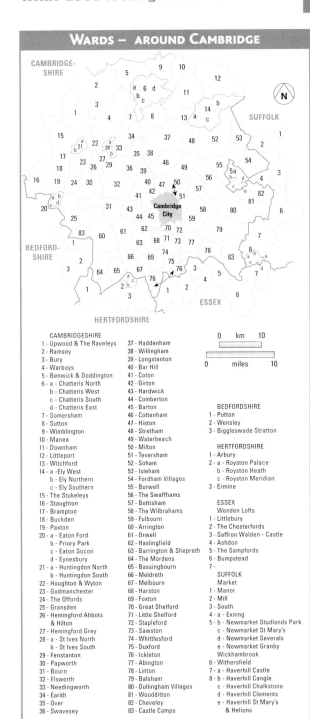

WARDS – AROUND CAMBRIDGE

CAMBRIDGE-SHIRE

SUFFOLK

N

Cambridge City

BEDFORD-SHIRE

ESSEX

HERTFORDSHIRE

0   km   10

0   miles   10

CAMBRIDGESHIRE
1 - Upwood & The Raveleys
2 - Ramsey
3 - Bury
4 - Warboys
5 - Benwick & Doddington
6 - a - Chatteris North
    b - Chatteris West
    c - Chatteris South
    d - Chatteris East
7 - Somersham
8 - Sutton
9 - Wimblington
10 - Manea
11 - Downham
12 - Littleport
13 - Witchford
14 - a - Ely West
    b - Ely Northern
    c - Ely Southern
15 - The Stukeleys
16 - Staughton
17 - Brampton
18 - Buckden
19 - Paxton
20 - a - Eaton Ford
    b - Priory Park
    c - Eaton Socon
    d - Eynesbury
21 - a - Huntingdon North
    b - Huntingdon South
22 - Houghton & Wyton
23 - Godmanchester
24 - The Offords
25 - Gransden
26 - Hemingford Abbots
    & Hilton
27 - Hemingford Grey
28 - a - St Ives North
    b - St Ives South
29 - Fenstanton
30 - Papworth
31 - Bourn
32 - Elsworth
33 - Needingworth
34 - Earith
35 - Over
36 - Swavesey

37 - Haddenham
38 - Willingham
39 - Longstanton
40 - Bar Hill
41 - Coton
42 - Girton
43 - Hardwick
44 - Comberton
45 - Barton
46 - Cottenham
47 - Histon
48 - Stretham
49 - Waterbeach
50 - Milton
51 - Teversham
52 - Soham
53 - Isleham
54 - Fordham Villages
55 - Burwell
56 - The Swaffhams
57 - Bottisham
58 - The Wilbrahams
59 - Fulbourn
60 - Arrington
61 - Orwell
62 - Haslingfield
63 - Barrington & Shepreth
64 - The Mordens
65 - Bassingbourn
66 - Meldreth
67 - Melbourn
68 - Harston
69 - Foxton
70 - Great Shelford
71 - Little Shelford
72 - Stapleford
73 - Sawston
74 - Whittlesford
75 - Duxford
76 - Ickleton
77 - Abington
78 - Linton
79 - Balsham
80 - Dullingham Villages
81 - Woodditton
82 - Cheveley
83 - Castle Camps

BEDFORDSHIRE
1 - Potton
2 - Wensley
3 - Biggleswade Stratton

HERTFORDSHIRE
1 - Arbury
2 - a - Royston Palace
    b - Royston Heath
    c - Royston Meridian
3 - Ermine

ESSEX
Wenden Lofts
1 - Littlebury
2 - The Chesterfords
3 - Saffron Walden - Castle
4 - Ashdon
5 - The Sampfords
6 - Bumpstead
7 -

SUFFOLK
Market
1 - Manor
2 - Mill
3 - South
4 - a - Exning
5 - b - Newmarket Studlands Park
    c - Newmarket St Mary's
    d - Newmarket Severals
    e - Newmarket Granby
Wickhambrook
6 - Withersfield
7 - a - Haverhill Castle
8 - b - Haverhill Cangle
    c - Haverhill Chalkstone
    d - Haverhill Clements
    e - Haverhill St Mary's
       & Helions

CAMBRIDGE PROFILE

ADDITIONAL INFORMATION

Books

● **literary Cambridge**

There is a wealth of fiction featuring Cambridge as a backdrop. Heffers and Waterstone's sometimes have displays of them. They include novels by C.P. Snow, P.D. James, Elizabeth George, Jill Paton Walsh's *Imogen Quy* mysteries, Michelle Spring's *Laura Principal* series.

● **history, archaeology and architecture**

Archaeology of Cambridgeshire, vols 1 & 2, by Alison Taylor (Cambs County Council) 1997 & 1998.

Cambridge Architecture, by Tim Rawle, Deutsch, 1985.

Cambridge: the Hidden History, by Alison Taylor (Tempus) 1999.

Cambridge Observed: An Anthology, by Charles Moseley and Clive Wilmer, Colt Books, 1998.

Cambridge: the Shaping of the City, by Peter Bryan, Peter Bryan publisher, 1999.

Cambridge Street Names: their Origin and Association, by Gray and Stubbings, Cambridge University Press, 2000.

Memory Lane Cambridge, by Mike Petty, Breedon, 1999.

The River Cam by E. N. Willmer, Burlington Press, 1979

● **University of Cambridge**

Cambridge University Press has a range of books about Cambridge and the University. A taster:

Cambridge University Library: The Great Collections, edited by Peter Fox, 1998.

Cambridge Commemorated: an Anthology of University Life, by Laurence & Helen Fowler 1984.

A History of the University of Cambridge, four volumes or *The Concise History of the University of Cambridge* by Elisabeth Leedham-Green, 1996.

The following books concern contributions made by Cambridge characters in academic disciplines:

Cambridge Contributions, edited by Sarah J Ormrod, 1998.

Cambridge Minds, edited by Richard Mason, 1998.

CAMBRIDGE BY ANY OTHER NAME...

'Cam' is the name of the river, which flows under the 'bridge' by Magdalene College on Bridge Street. Until relatively recently, the bridge was the last road crossing of the river before it enters the sea near King's Lynn.

In A.D. 890 the settlement appears in the Anglo-Saxon Chronicle as Grantebrycge, the river then being known as the Granta, later to become Grantabridge. By the 11th century it was Cantebrigge and via Caunbrigge and Caumbrigge eventually became known as Cambridge by the Elizabethan period.

Photo courtesy of Cambridgeshire Collection

A view from market square to the old Petty Cury, 1880

Cambridge Women: Twelve Portraits, edited by Edward Shils and Carmen Blacker 1996.

(Lifestyle and tourist guides are listed in the 'Leisure' chapter, page 178-180)

Key general information sources

● tourist information centres

Cambridge Tourist Information Office, The Old Library, Wheeler Street, Cambridge CB2 3QB (01223 322640)

www.tourismcambridge.com

(See page 180 for a full list of regional tourist offices)

● news media and internet

A good place for an internet look at Cambridge is the University of Cambridge's 'local area information' page (see below). Also try:

The Cambridge Evening News, the region's newspaper, Winship Road, Milton CB4 6PP (01223 434434)

www.cambridge-news.co.uk

Adhoc, www.adhoc.co.uk, and its free *City* magazine, has what's on, property, jobs and restaurants etc.

Cambridge (UK) Web Guide. Has everything from history and politics to public services, tourism and leisure: www.gwydir.demon.co.uk/cambridgeuk/   Similar   is www.e-cambridge.co.uk

(See 'Household Services' page 68 for a full list of news media and 'Leisure' page 178-180 for 'What's On' listings.)

● University of Cambridge sources

University of Cambridge, central number: 01223 337733. For information about the University itself: www.cam.ac.uk and for general local area information: www.cam.ac.uk/CambArea/index.html

Enjoying the market square today

Key government information sources

● **Cambridge city/district/county**

Cambridge City Council, Guildhall, Cambridge CB2 3QJ (01223 457000) www.cambridge.gov.uk and Cambridge On-Line City: www.colc.co.uk and e-mails to: Guildhall.Reception@cambridge.gov.uk

Cambridgeshire County Council, Shire Hall, Castle Hill, Cambridge CB3 OAP. (01223 717111):
   www.cambridgeshire.gov.uk

South Cambridgeshire District Council, 9/11 Hills Road, Cambridge CB2 1PB (01223 443000)
   www.scambs.gov.uk

● **area district councils**

East Cambridgeshire, The Grange, Nutholt Road, Ely, Cambs CB7 4PL (01353) 665555

Huntingdonshire Pathfinder Hse, St Mary's St, Huntingdon, Cambs PE29 3TN (01480 388388)

North Hertfordshire, Gernon Road, Letchworth, Herts, SG6 3JF (01462 474000)

Essex (Uttlesford) London Road, Saffron Walden, Essex CB11 4ER (01799 510510)

Suffolk (Forest Heath) College Heath Road, Mildenhall, Suffolk IP28 7EY (01638 719000)

St Edmundsbury, Borough Office, Angel Hill, Bury St Edmunds IP33 1XB (01284) 763233

Mid Bedfordshire The Limes, Dunstable St, Ampthill, Beds NK45 2JU (01525 402051)

Public libraries

The Cambridge Central Library, 7 Lion Yard, Cambridge CB2 3QD (01223 712000) is the largest of the public libraries in a system with 32 branches. For further information: www.cambridgeshire.gov.uk/library

(The full list of libraries is in the index to the city and regional maps on the inside covers of this book)

CHAPTER 2
A PLACE TO LIVE

Photo courtesy of Cambourne

It's never easy finding somewhere to live in Cambridge. Even allowing for differences in personal taste, there is never enough of the right sort of housing to go round. The whole area is a victim of its own success and likely to remain so for the foreseeable future. Even computer millionaires can't buy the lavish homes they can afford because that kind of home is in very short supply around Cambridge. The place just wasn't planned with so many different needs in mind.

The choices often seem unsatisfactory, but compromise is unavoidable if you want to live in Europe's No 1 growth spot for high-tech development

Yet don't despair. The process may be stressful, but you'll get there in the end. This chapter will help you on your way. Whether you're looking to rent or buy a small flat or a large family home, it will take you through the whole business, from deciding what kind of accommodation is best to weighing up the pros and cons of town versus country. It will show you the pitfalls – the major ones, anyway – and put you in touch with people who can tell you more. And it will try and tell you something about prices following years of dramatic increases.

DECIDING WHERE TO LIVE

This is the biggest question of all. In Cambridge itself, close to the colleges and shops? More sedately, in the suburbs? Or somewhere out in the Fens, where everything is black at night but also calm and peaceful, with room to turn round and a lot more garden for your money? It's your call, and the choice is not easy.

The key for most people, families especially, is the chronic shortage of family houses in the city itself. Most Cambridge homes are Victorian or Edwardian (pre-1914), with small or non-existent front gardens, tiny rear gardens, and no garage at all. For a city expanding as fast as Cambridge, that means that families often decide to live elsewhere even if they don't really want to, adding to the commuter traffic as they come in every day to work or go to school.

The result is that a lot of people end up living in the outlying villages or on modern housing estates outside the city. Some even live in another town altogether, settling in Ely or Newmarket where the pressures on the infrastructure aren't as severe as in Cambridge. The choices often seem unsatisfactory, but compromise is unavoidable if you want to live in Europe's No 1 growth spot for high-tech development. Once you've accepted that, you'll find it easier to decide which of the options will suit you best.

Cover picture: Typical house on the Village Green at Cambourne.

LIVING IN CAMBRIDGE ITSELF

The different residential areas are listed below, each with their own particular character. An important consideration in choosing between them is your daily journey to work (and your children's, if they go to school). The city looks fairly compact on the map, but it's actually a nightmare to drive around. Traffic regularly achieves gridlock and simple journeys sometimes take for ever. It's often easier to walk to work if you can, or else slip through the traffic on a bike – anything, rather than drive a car. Think about that (and see the chapter on transport, page 71) before deciding which part of the city best meets your particular needs:

Newnham

Convenient for: university, private schools, city centre.

This is very up-market, full of academics and affluent professionals. Portions have spacious streets and large old houses, the grandest of which change hands for a million pounds. But there are plenty of much cheaper terraced houses as well, and modern flats towards Grantchester and Barton. It's a very nice place to live, and the parts with terraced houses are handy to the shops. You'll almost certainly want a car for that stocking-up trip to the supermarket, or else you can use taxis.

A PLACE TO LIVE

Castle

Convenient for: university, city centre.

An interesting mix of Victorian terraces and modern flats at the city end, interspersed with shops, offices and a considerable press of traffic. Further out, the detached houses along the Madingley and Huntingdon Roads go for substantial sums, while the Histon Road is home to garages and tyre repair shops. It's a lively place, an easy walk downhill into the city centre for those living just across the river.

King's Hedges / Arbury

Convenient for: Science and Business Parks

Plenty of cheap accommodation, much of it built after the Second World War as the city expanded north towards the ring road. It has good transport to the centre and easy access to the motorway. The area originally housed many university service workers, but now has a much more mixed population ranging from professors to plumbers and students. The area's reputation for deprivation (in fact, limited to a few obviously run-down pockets) has been exaggerated because of the relative prosperity of the rest of Cambridge. Pleasant housing stock, if without the 'character' of older neighbourhoods.

Chesterton

Convenient for: local shops

The Chesterton Road is always extremely busy, full of shops and traffic in equal measure. But the side streets are quiet and residential, home to some of the nation's finest minds. This is where academics live in great profusion, strolling gently down to the river and cycling to work across Midsummer Common. Chesterton itself is an unsightly blend of old and new, 18th-century village houses next to spanking new office blocks. The accommodation is reasonable en route to the Science and Business Parks.

Kite

Convenient for: university, shopping, city centre, Kelsey Kerridge sports hall

Along with parts of Petersfield and Mill Road, one of Cambridge's oldest residential areas, predominantly 19th-century. A few big old terraces and lots of tiny little houses that used to be workmen's cottages before they were gentrified. Parking is difficult, accommodation often cramped –

the smallest houses have only five or six rooms altogether – but the area is highly sought after because it's so close to the action. You'll be lucky to find anything here.

Petersfield

Convenient for: university, shopping, city centre, Kelsey Kerridge sports hall, railway station

A mix of 19th- and 20th- century development, much of it substantial. The area is bordered by some lively roads with useful shops and plenty going on. It's a longish walk into the city centre, but homes close to the railway station are always in demand and will never lose their value.

DEBBIE LLOYD – CAMBRIDGE PUBLICAN

I grew up in a small town in America. I needn't go into the details of the one-room schoolhouse! I was very privileged to grow up where I knew all sorts of people. Cambridge is at heart a small town too. It's unique in the diversity of people living so close together. In a neighbourhood like this [around Gwydir Street off Mill Road] you get students, passing foreigners, people who have lived here since the day they were born and those who commute to London.

Photo by Neal E Robbins

Cambridge people can be pretty insular when they don't know you. It can take a long time to be accepted. When you finally begin to feel accepted, you suddenly find you know everybody!

But pubs are one of the places where anyone can meet and find like-minded souls. That's what's special about pubs – and I mean real pubs and not the trendy drinking palaces on the high street. The greatest pleasure I get is introducing people, initiating a spark of human communication. Whatever their backgrounds, whatever their education, whatever their income, there is a common humanity. To me that is what pubs are all about. A pub is a microcosm – and a good Cambridge pub still is.

Debbie Lloyd runs the Cambridge Blue on Gwydir Street with her husband, Chris. For the previous 22 years the couple ran the Free Press on Prospect Row.

A PLACE TO LIVE

Abbey

Convenient for: airport, Cambridge United football ground, out-of-town shopping malls

A dull area, dominated by the commercial activities along the Newmarket and Barnwell Roads. There are rows of semi-detached houses stretching away into the distance, but it's a bit of suburban anywhere. You'll definitely need a car to get about.

Romsey

Convenient for: railway station, Coldham's Lane shopping, Sainsbury's supermarket

Romsey is bisected by Mill Road, one of the main exit routes from Cambridge. Plenty of modest shops and small Victorian terraced houses. Accommodation tends to be cheaper this side of the railway line, partly because the streets are narrow and parking is cramped, but it's a cheerful place, much liked by people who live here.

Coleridge

Convenient for: railway station, Addenbrooke's Hospital

Heavily residential, a mix of semi-detached properties and more substantial detached houses around Hills Road, some of which go for a million pounds or more. You need a car for the shops, but the area is very popular, particularly with families, rail commuters and Addenbrooke's workers.

Newtown

Convenient for: city centre, private schools, railway station and Addenbrooke's Hospital

Very upmarket, especially if you manage to find an Edwardian semi along Lensfield Road, or one of the large town houses in the streets just north of the Botanic Garden. South of the Garden, you hit leafy suburbia almost at once. There are a few flats, but most people live in substantial detached houses with garages, built within the last 50 years. A big house in Chaucer Road could set you back well over a million, but at least you'd get a tennis court for your money. The area is popular with well-off families, because all Cambridge's private schools are within walking distance, but there are no shops at all. You either bike into Cambridge for your shopping or else drive to the supermarket at Trumpington, just along the road.

VILLAGE SUBURBS

These were villages in their own right before the suburbs swallowed them up. They're not part of Cambridge proper, but very popular all the same, with a mix of mostly modern housing to suit all tastes.

Trumpington

The village used to have a mill, where Chaucer set The Reeve's Tale, but is dominated now by the supermarket and petrol stations along the main road. The road is always clogged during the rush hour, so local inhabitants often bike into Cambridge instead. It's a convenient place to live, particularly with the new supermarket, which gets plenty of custom from the city itself, as well as the outlying villages.

Cherry Hinton

With the Hall, church and High Street, you can see how Cherry Hinton used to be a village in its own right, quite separate from Cambridge. Now though, it's little more than a dormitory suburb, with modern development on the outskirts. There's a good supermarket just down the road, en route to Fulbourn.

NEW DEVELOPMENTS

Once out of Cambridge, you'll notice that the buildings come to a sudden stop and there are nothing but fields beyond. This is the Green Belt, a legally protected stretch of land where no development is allowed. Scientists would like to build laboratories on it, developers would like to build homes, you yourself wouldn't mind an acre to erect a ranch-style hacienda with double garage and leylandii. But the city has to breathe, so you can't have the land and that is why house prices around Cambridge are so high.

That said though, certain areas have been earmarked for controlled development - purpose-built dormitory villages intended to soak up the overspill of population in the region. One of these is Cambourne, a whole community designed from scratch, where everything is spanking new and built with the 21st century in mind. It's nine miles west of Cambridge, on the way to St Neots.

Another is Bar Hill, which was just a muddy farm until the developers fell on it in the 1970s. It's home now to thousands, with their own supermarket, shopping mall and motorway access to Cambridge. The advantage of such developments is that they're purpose-built with modern needs in mind. The disadvantage is that they're a bit bland, with no old buildings or narrow streets to give any real sense of place.

A PLACE TO LIVE

Plans have also been mooted for developments at the MoD barracks at Waterbeach, four miles east of Cambridge. It would create 13,000 homes and 16,500 jobs by 2006 and involve a train line running from the village direct to Addenbrooke's Hospital. Another scheme involves the ex-Army base at Oakington.

VILLAGES AROUND CAMBRIDGE

If you don't fancy an artificial development, you can always live in one of the many real villages around Cambridge. These are a thousand years old, although they don't look it, varying in size from a few hundred people to four or five thousand. There is usually a medieval church in the middle, with an old vicarage next door and sometimes also a big manor house nearby. The oldest buildings – 17th or 18th century – are usually in the centre, clustered around the church. Twentieth century housing tends to be further out, often ugly new developments slapped down in the middle of a field without much regard for their surroundings.

The villages began as agricultural communities, but are now mostly dormitories for the nearest town. The larger ones usually have a school, pub, health centre, communal hall and selection of shops, although these are increasingly under threat from out-of-town supermarkets. No village is completely self-contained, so you'll need a car to get about. Buses do exist, but they are few and far between and never seem to go where you want them to.

If you do decide to live in a village, then biggest is probably best, because of the amenities. Places such as Histon and Cottenham to the north of Cambridge, and Great Shelford, Sawston, Linton and Melbourn to the south, are well worth checking out. They all have critical mass, which means that the smaller shops are dying more slowly than elsewhere. Housing is relatively expensive though, because of the villages' popularity.

On the other hand, some of the larger villages are so

Photo by Charlie Gray

No 9 Brookside, a seven-bedroom house at the top of the market

SOUTH CAMBRIDGESHIRE PARISHES WITHIN 10 MILES OF CAMBRIDGE

PARISH NAME	POP EST 1999	PRIMARY SCH	SECONDARY SCH	NEAR RAIL STA	MILES FROM CAMBRIDGE CTR
Arrington	380				9
Babraham	270	✔		✔	7.5
Balsham	1,630	✔			10
Bar Hill	4,460	✔			5
Barrington	1,020	✔		✔	7
Bartlow	120				12
Barton	830	✔			3
Bourn	1,050	✔			7.5
Boxworth	220				7
Caldecote	630	✔			6
Caxton	420				8.5
Comberton	2,340	✔	✔		4.5
Conington	150				9
Coton	740	✔			2.5
Cottenham	5,120	✔	✔		4
Croydon	190				10
Dry Drayton	580	✔			4.5
Duxford	1,820	✔		✔	8
Elsworth	620	✔			8.5
Eltisley	410				11
Fen Ditton	740	✔			2
Fen Drayton	840	✔			9
Fowlmere	1,180	✔		✔	8
Foxton	1,110	✔		✔	7
Fulbourn	4,670	✔			5
Girton	3740	✔			3
Grantchester	540			✔	2
Great Abington	870	✔		✔	8.5
Great Eversden	220	✔			6
Great Shelford	3,990	✔			3
Great Wilbraham	650	✔		✔	5.5
Hardwick	2,550	✔			4.5
Harlton	280			✔	5.5
Harston	1,670	✔		✔	5
Haslingfield	1,520	✔		✔	5
Hauxton	710	✔		✔	4
Hildersham	240				9
Hinxton	340			✔	9
Histon	4,400	✔✔	✔		2.5
Horningsea	320			✔	3
Horseheath	480				12
Ickleton	670			✔	10
Impington	3,890	(see	Histon)		2
Kingston	240				6.5
Knapwell	110				7.5
Landbeach	870			✔	3
Little Abington	520			✔	8
Little Eversden	550				5.5

continues on page 45

A PLACE TO LIVE

strung out that the inhabitants have to get in a car anyway to go to the shops. If you do have to use a car, you might just as well live in a cheaper village nearby, albeit with fewer amenities. Grantchester (though not cheap) is popular, because of Rupert Brooke and its proximity to Cambridge. So are Comberton, Barrington, Whittlesford, Duxford, Stapleford and Great Abington to the south of Cambridge, and Bottisham, Swaffham, Waterbeach, Milton, Impington and Girton to the north. But there are plenty of other villages as well. People live in them perfectly happily, even if they sometimes appear to be marooned in the middle of nowhere!

NEARBY TOWNS

If all else fails, you can always commute to Cambridge from another town. You'll need a car of course, and somewhere to park when you arrive. A few hardy souls take their bikes on the train, or else brave the long walk from Cambridge station to the city centre (*See pages 83 & 87 for more on cycles*). No solution is ideal, but lots of people do commute from nearby towns. It's definitely an option.

The towns are all market towns, protected by ancient charters that go back seven or eight hundred years. They all have a reasonable complement of amenities – schools, libraries, sports halls, health centres etc, everything you're likely to need. They're nice places to live, but check out the commuting before you commit yourself. If you have teenagers, remember also that their social life is bound to revolve around Cambridge. Harassed parents routinely sell up and move nearer to the university city, rather than drive long distances at 2 a.m., with a sullen daughter in the back saying she could easily have stayed the night at Dave's and why won't you let her?

RELOCATION AGENTS

CAMBRIDGE HOUSEHUNT, Cambridge House, 16 St Peter's Street, Duxford, Cambridge CB2 4RP, (01223 839771), www.camb.househunt@dial.pipex.com

COUNTY HOMESEARCH, 26 Greenshields Road, Bedford, MK40 3TT, (01284 354592), www.county-homesearch.co.uk or www.wefindproperty.com

FIRST SITE PROPERTY SERVICES, 17 Norfolk Street, Cambridge CB1 2LD, 01223 508020, www.firstsite.co.uk

RELOCATION EAST ANGLIA, 68B Catharine Street, Cambridge CB1 3AR, (01223 515492), www.relocation-east-anglia.co.uk

RELOCATION SUPPORT GROUP, 88 De Freville Avenue, Cambridge CB4 1HU, (01628 631111) www.relocationsupport.co.uk

Ely

16 miles N of Cambridge.

A very agreeable spot, formerly an island in the Fens – hence the eponymous eels. The town is dominated by the magnificent cathedral, begun by the Normans 900 years ago. Lots of old houses, but also new accommodation. The town itself is dull, sleepy and a little remote, but it's also quiet, dignified and highly civilised – a very decent place to live.

Newmarket

13 miles E of Cambridge

Blessed with miles of springy heathland, Newmarket has been the centre of British horse-racing for more than 300 years. There are often private planes flying in as the owners arrive and the jockeys commute to work. The town itself is dominated by the Jockey Club, the sport's ruling body, which has an imposing headquarters in the High Street. Apart from a few quaint streets though, the rest of Newmarket is a bit nondescript. It has several new housing estates on the outskirts and some large nightclubs full of teenagers and US servicemen from the nearby Air Force bases.

SOUTH CAMBRIDGESHIRE PARISHES (CONTINUED)					
PARISH NAME	POP EST 1999	PRIMARY SCH	SECONDARY SCH	NEAR RAIL STA	MILES FROM CAMBRIDGE CTR
Little Shelford	830	(see Gt Shelford)		✔	4.5
Little Wilbraham	360				5
Lolworth	120				6
Longstanton	1,170				5.5
Longstowe	200				9
Madingley	230				3.5
Melbourn	4,530	✔✔	✔		10
Meldreth	1,650	✔		✔	9
Milton	4,320	✔		✔	2
Newton	390			✔	5.5
Oakington & Westwick	1,380	✔			4
Orwell	1,080			✔	7
Over	2,780	✔			8.5
Pampisford	340			✔	8
Rampton	430				6
Sawston	7,370	✔✔✔	✔	✔	7
Shepreth	790			✔	8
Stapleford	1,720	✔			5
Stow-cum-Quy	450			✔	4
Swavesey	2,420	✔	✔		8
Teversham	2,660	✔			3
Thriplow	780	✔		✔	8
Toft	540				6
Waterbeach	5,010	✔		✔	4.5
Whaddon	530			✔	9
Whittlesford	1,590	✔		✔	7
Willingham	3,510	✔			8
Wimpole	220				7.5

A PLACE TO LIVE

Saffron Walden

13 miles SE of Cambridge

The town dates back to the Iron Age, but didn't get going until the Middle Ages, when dye from the surrounding saffron fields brought great prosperity. Much of the lavish building from those days still survives in the medieval streets around the market square. The town continues to be highly prosperous, partly because City workers live here, commuting to London from nearby Audley End. Houses are accordingly pricey, but the whole place is atmospheric and full of charm, particularly in the ancient centre. It's very popular with those who can afford it.

Royston

14 miles SW of Cambridge

Functional is the best way to describe Royston. It's a perfectly decent place to live, with plenty of everything, but rather dull. The High Street is not picturesque. The buildings are bland and could be anywhere. Royston lacks the charm of other local towns, perhaps because it is in Hertfordshire and not part of East Anglia at all. But it's a useful dormitory town, because London is less than three quarters of an hour away on the fast train.

Huntingdon

16 miles NW of Cambridge

Oliver Cromwell grew up in Huntingdon, but the town doesn't have the character you might expect. It is linked to Godmanchester, another ancient town, by a beautiful 14th-century bridge across the river Ouse. The effect ought to be picturesque, but is ruined by the starkly modern motorway bridge that has been built right beside it. The rest of Huntingdon is similarly crass – a nice old town in the centre, utterly destroyed by the industrial estates and modern developments around the edge. Huntingdon has been run down in recent years, but the Cambridge effect is gradually sweeping northwards and bringing regeneration to the area. A house bought here might well increase in value if the regeneration continues.

BUYING A PROPERTY

Your first port of call is obviously an estate agent (there's a list at the end of this chapter). Most have websites displaying a selection of properties to browse through. You should also read the Cambridge Evening News *(see 'Key Contacts' back page)*, which publishes a property supplement every Thursday with hundreds of places to buy or rent. It's important to read the paper because there's no central register of properties for sale in England. Estate agents will only tell you about their own properties, not anyone else's. The Cambridge Evening News, with a host of competing ads, is the nearest you can get to an overall view of the market.

PAT ELBOURN – MELDRETH HOUSEWIFE

Cambridgeshire is a very good, neighbourly sort of place, and certainly the smaller villages tend to be very close-knit communities. There's a good spirit in our area, Meldreth, with lots of things going on to help people out around the place, such as mobile warden schemes, car schemes, self-help groups and village associations, to name but a few. There's a very

Photo by Neal E. Robbins

caring attitude here, and community care in general is really very good in the country-side, which makes the whole place feel welcoming both to people who live here on a permanent basis and to those who may just be staying for short periods.

Of course, being within such easy reach of London, as well as being on the border of Essex, Bedfordshire and Hertfordshire, there are quite a number of commuters who work in the towns, but live in small villages. Living in small villages or towns means that they're normally incorporated into daily life quickly! Inevitably some people do find the countryside a little intimidating if they are used to city life and its bright lights – I guess it's to do with the silence of the countryside in comparison with the city.

Things have changed in some ways in the village. A long while ago, when I was first married and came down to live in this area 43 years ago from the outskirts of Dundee, I can remember talking to an old villager. He was explaining how so and so had moved far away from the village years ago. When I enquired where he'd moved to, I was told, much to my surprise, that the man in question was now living in Melbourn, which is a mere mile away, in fact – from Meldreth! Of course, now there's much more interchange between the two villages, and all the other villages and towns, for that matter!

Pat Elbourn and her husband are fifth generation fruit growers in Meldreth, near Royston. Their farm and shop has sold apples, plums, pears and goodies since 1968.

For the same reason, it's important also to register with several different agents, rather than just one or two. If you don't like anything they show you on the web, you can always tap in your own requirements - number of bedrooms, bathrooms etc - and tell them where you want to live and how much you're prepared to pay. They'll get back to you as soon as they've stopped laughing.

Indeed there seems no end to the sellers' market in Cambridge, although prices must surely reach their ceiling soon. Houses used to be put up for sale after the Easter weekend, when they are at their most attractive. That is still true in the villages, but now the season begins earlier in Cambridge and prime areas, even in January and February. Houses used to remain on the market until October, and still do in the villages, but now the Cambridge market is active through November, even after the academic year begins. It may still be true that you are likely to find a bargain in the autumn, when anybody who still hasn't sold their property might be prepared to drop the price a bit. But a lot of stuff is taken off the market then, to wait for the next year, so you'll have to seek it out from the agents.

As elsewhere, it helps to have cash or a mortgage arranged independently of the sale of another property if you can, because UK property transactions are frequently bedevilled by a chain - I can't buy yours until I've sold mine, and that depends on my buyer selling his. But if you can put the money down straight away, you are more likely to get what you want. When the market is slow, you

AVERAGE HOUSE PRICES
CAMBRIDGE NEIGHBOURHOODS – OCT 2000

DETACHED*	SEMI-DETACHED	LRG TERRACE	SMALL TERRACE
Central			
£170,000	£154,800	£119,500	£119,100
West Chesterton			
£175,000	£127,900	£113,200	£109,000
East Chesterton			
£147,500	£113,600	£100,700	£90,400
East			
£137,500	£113,500	£107,700	£98,400
South & West			
£166,700	£130,800	£115,500	£107,000
Cherry Hinton			
£144,900	£114,000	£107,000	£95,700
All areas			
£156,900	£125,800	£110,600	£103,300

(N.B. This survey, based on a sampling of about 110 properties over a two-month period by the Cambridge Building Society, excludes properties selling for over £210,000, which tend to distort the picture. *Detached housing based on limited sampling.)

might also negotiate a few percent off the price, but this would be unusual during a strong Cambridge market.

RENTING OR HOUSE SHARING

This is easier than buying, but competition is still fierce. Many places to rent go as soon as they are advertised. If you're with either of the universities, you can register with their accommodation services (see below), which will supply a list of places, usually for a minimum stay of six months. Otherwise though, it's a question of reading the Cambridge Evening News, or else going through a private lettings agency (see box, page 51). The agencies charge at least £100 and demand bank references, but it may well be worth it if they can find you somewhere to stay.

House shares are usually for younger people, available through the university accommodation services or college noticeboards such as the one at Cambridge University's University Centre on Mill Lane (www.unicen.cam.ac.uk, 01223 337766). For others, it's the Cambridge Evening News again, or else the little ads in newsagents' windows.

If you're really stuck, you can apply to Cambridge City Council's housing office (Hobson House, 4 St Andrew's Street, Cambridge CB2 1BS, 01223 457976 / 975, www.cambridge.gov.uk), which has a duty to provide accommodation for people who can't find it for themselves. The accommodation won't be too wonderful, unless

---

AVERAGE HOUSE/FLAT PRICES
CAMBRIDGE CITY AND REGIONAL TOWNS

Apart from flats or maisonettes, most properties have at least three bedrooms. A detached house stands in its own grounds, while semi-detached houses are built in twos and share a roof and party wall. Terraced houses are in a row, with a party wall either side. These figures are for the second quarter of 2000.

DETACHED	SEMI-DETACHED	TERRACED	FLATS-MAISONETTES
Cambridge			
£192,201	£132,222	£110,622	£84,556
Ely			
£118,734	£70,483	£68,591	£47,281
Newmarket			
£160,580	£82,417	£74,649	£54,883
Saffron Walden			
£227,899	£136,476	£109,593	£80,598
Royston			
£228,931	£104,692	£80,797	£57,616
Huntingdon			
£142,426	£83,379	£54,864	£33,825

(N.B. Prices vary widely according to neighbourhood.)

you're over 55. Older people qualify for sheltered housing, which is usually much nicer.

COMING FROM FAR AWAY

But if this all sounds a bit daunting, and you're too far away to do it in person, you can easily get a relocation agency to do the legwork for you. They're unlikely to produce a dream home, but they can certainly find you a place to stay until you're sorted out. They'll provide a list of suitable properties for sale or rent, make the viewing arrangements and pick you up from the hotel or airport if you want them to. They'll also negotiate on your behalf and help with removal, storage, child care etc.

The service can cost as little as £300 for a day's help looking at flats to up to £3000 or more for the VIP package

Average monthly rent November 2000

CC = Cambridge city   N = Newmarket
CC(O)=Outer Cambridge city   SC = South Cambridgeshire

	CC	CC(O)	N	SC
Self-contained studio flat				
	£389	-	£400	£363
Converted flat				
1-bed	£470	£425	£235	£365
2-bed	£580	£475	£359	£466
Purpose built flat				
1-bed	£475	£393	£400	£388
2-bed	£576	£513	£424	£431
3-bed	£891	£460	£450	£482
Terraced house				
1-bed	£476	£474	£235	£420
2-bed	£598	£544	£391	£462
3-bed	££679	£581	£425	£524
4-bed	£986	-	-	£950
Semi-detached house				
1-bed	£511	£425	-	£403
2-bed	£584	£543	£350	£460
3-bed	£691	£593	£567	£516
4-bed	£969	-	£795	£700
Detached house				
1-bed	£483	£282	-	£509
3-bed	£746	£696	£551	£613
4-bed	£983	£890	£850	£817

(N.B. Cambridge rents vary greatly depending on neighbourhood. Hills Road, Long Road, the Centre and other small pockets are considerably higher than the average. The chart reflects the bulk of property, including the many less costly rentals in places like the end of Mill Road, the estates and on the northern edge of the city.)

to buy a house, arrange schooling for children and more. It's a snip, if it saves that much in hotel bills and time lost from work.

● **what kind of house or flat?**

There are thatched cottages in every village, but most housing stock is mid-19th to late 20th-century. Estate agents routinely describe anything built before 1914 as Victorian, Edwardian or 'a period house with character'. Anything after 1950 is modern (it may even have a garage!). Modern houses are more convenient, but the agents are right for once when they say older ones have more character. Older houses are closer to the action too, whereas modern ones tend to be on large estates on the outskirts, rather than in the centre.

Much of central Cambridge is terraced (row houses without garages) for city living. Detached houses stand in their own grounds and tend to be in the suburbs or the out-

---

LETTING AGENTS

Ambassador Property Management, 54 Cherry Hinton Road, Cambridge CB1 7AA, 01223 727277, www.ambassador-property.co.uk

The Cambridge Property Practice, Orwell House, Cowley Road, Cambridge CB4 0PP, 01223 519619, www.cambridge-lettings.co.uk

Camflats Property Management, 22A Elmhurst, Brooklands Avenue, Cambidge CB2 2DQ, 01223 350800, www.camflats.co.uk

Derek Catlin Property Management, 32 Newnham Road, Cambridge CB3 9EY, 01223 328253, see Cambridge Evening News website

Crofton Property Management, 98A Mill Road, Cambridge CB1 2BD, 01223 301355, www.cpmltd.com

Eurolet, 69A Regent Street, Cambridge CB2 1AB, 01223 462007, www.eurolet.co.uk

First Site Property Services, 17 Norfolk Street, Cambridge CB1 2LD, 01223 508020, www.firstsite.co.uk

Good Properties, Barnwell House, Barnwell Drive, Cambridge CB5 8UU, 01223 500050, www.goodproperties.co.uk

Homewise, 28 Hills Road, Cambridge CB2 1LA, 01223 362111, see Cambridge Evening News website

King Street Housing Society, 89 King Street, Cambridge CB1 1LD, 01223 312294, no website

Rees & Associates, First Floor Office, 25 Hills Road, Cambridge CB2 1NW, 01223 575114, www.reesassociates.co.uk

St Andrew's Bureau, 20 St Andrew's Street, Cambridge CB2 3AX, 01223 352170, www.sab.co.uk

Spires International, 185 East Road, Cambridge CB1 1BG, 01223 300903, www.spires.co.uk

THE ESTATE AGENTS – IN THEIR OWN WORDS
(* ALSO LETTING AGENTS)

Anglia Residential*, Anglia House, 102 Cherry Hinton Road, Cambridge CB1 7AJ, 01223 413000, www.angliaresidential.co.uk - larger city and country properties

Bidwells*, Stone Cross, Trumpington High Street, Cambridge CB2 2SU, 01223 841842, www.bidwells.co.uk - properties above £200,000

Bradford & Bingley Januarys, 60 Regent Street, Cambridge CB2 1DP, 01223 363291, www.bb-ea.co.uk - any property £70,000 to £500,000

Willam H Brown, 65 Regent Street, Cambridge CB2 1AB, 01223 358285, www.wheretolive.co.uk - mostly properties around Cherry Hinton and out into the villages

Bush and Co*, 169 Mill Road, Cambridge CB1 3AN, 01223 246262, www.bushandco.co.uk - mostly Cambridge, but any property within 20 miles

Carter Jonas*, 6-8 Hills Road, Cambridge CB2 1NH, 01223 368771, www.carterjonas.co.uk - upper end of the market, usually above £250,000

Catlings*, 100-102 Regent Street, Cambridge CB2 1DP, 01223 525252, www.catlings.co.uk - any property within 50 miles, but concentrates on Cambridge

Cheffins*, 49/53 Regent Street, Cambridge CB2 1AF, 01223 443300, www.cheffins.co.uk - mostly larger properties

Connell, 70 Regent Street, Cambridge CB2 1DP, 01223 366377, www.connells.co.uk - any property, city or country

Estate Direct, Suite 29, 511 Coldham's Lane, Cambridge CB1 3JS, 01223 507722, www.estatedirect.co.uk - properties within 60 miles of Cambridge, £40,000 to £1,000,000

FPDSavills*, 24 Hills Road, Cambridge CB2 1JW, 01223 347000, www.fpdsavills.co.uk - properties above £150,000, 35 mile radius of Cambridge

Haart*, 22 Regent Street, Cambridge CB2 1BB, 01223 365931, www.haart.co.uk - 12 mile radius of Cambridge, any property up to £300,000

Hockeys, 81 Regent Street, Cambridge CB2 1AW, 01223 356054, www.hockeys.co.uk - mostly city properties, but some country as well

Pocock and Shaw, 55 Regent Street, Cambridge CB2 1AB, 01223 322552, www.pocock.co.uk - city and country properties up to £400,000

Redmayne Arnold & Harris*, Dukes Court, 54-64 Newmarket Road, Cambridge CB5 8DZ, 01223 323130, www.rah.co.uk - general agents, large properties and small

Rooke Wood and Miller, 47 Regent Street, Cambridge CB2 1AB, 01223 301616, www.RWandM.co.uk - smaller properties up to £450,000, 15 mile radius of Cambridge

lying villages. Semi-detached houses – two identical homes sharing a roof and a dividing wall – are often on 1930s estates in the outer suburbs. Purpose-built flats (as opposed to converted ones) are usually modern and usually in Cambridge. But everything is a jumble, so there are exceptions to the rule all over the place.

● **University accommodation services**

The University of Cambridge has an office for members of and visitors to the University. It has details on private-rented and University-owned accommodation. Anglia Polytechnic's service is for students. Both are also sources of lodgers / tenants for anyone who has a property to rent.

University of Cambridge Accommodation Service is at 18 Silver Street / 12 Mill Lane, Cambridge CB3 9EL, 01223 353518: www.admin.cam.uk/offices/accommodation or by e-mail to: accommodation_service@admin.cam.ac.uk

The Anglia Polytechnic University Residence and Accommodation office is at Room 15, Ruskin Building, East Road, Cambridge CB1 1PT, 01223 363271 (extension 2517), www.anglia.ac.uk

ADDITIONAL INFORMATION

● **useful books:**

How to buy and sell your home, by Keith Carlton, Prentice Hall, 1999.

Selling your home, by Susan Heal, HarperCollins, 1997.

Tenant's survival guide, by L Henderson, RHale, 1999.

● **useful websites:**

www.cambridge-estateagents.co.uk
www.propertyfinder.co.uk
www.propertymarket.co.uk/cambridgeshire.htm
www.wheretolive.co.uk – guide to estate agents, property prices, houses for sale etc
www.primelocation.com – similar to above, but national
www.upmystreet.co.uk – enter postcode for property

THE ESTATE AGENTS (CONTINUED)

Spicer McColl, 64 Regent Street, Cambridge CB2 1DP, 01223 351351, www.spicer.co.uk - general agents, many branches across East Anglia

Tucker*, 85 Regent Street, Cambridge CB2 1AW, 01223 508508, www.tucker-partnership.co.uk - mostly south of Cambridge, but some city properties

Tylers, 94 Regent Street, Cambridge CB2 1DP, 01223 302600, www.tylers.co.uk - smaller properties up to £300,000, 20 mile radius of Cambridge

Your Move, 54 Regent Street, Cambridge CB2 1DP, 01223 355476, www.your-move.co.uk - mid-range properties, Cambridge and villages

A PLACE TO LIVE

SPEAKING OF CAMBRIDGE...

Two words which have found common currency in the English-speaking world have their origins in Cambridge. 'Tawdry' comes from the days of Stourbridge Fair to describe some of the cheap baubles on sale. The fair began on St Audrey's Eve, hence 'tawdry'. 'Constitutional', in the sense of a walk, is also attributed to Cambridge and is thought to stem from the advice given by tutors to students of taking a daily three-mile walk to inspect the town boundary stone, while discussing their studies. They were told they would get better degrees as a result of their improved health, or constitution.

prices, school league tables etc in the area

www.royalmail.co.uk/paf/.gov.uk - You don't know the postcode? Enter the street name here.

www.roundyourway.co.uk - about towns and villages

www2.homecheck.co.uk - Check here for dangers of flood, subsidence, radiation etc

www.adhoc.co.uk - information on property, jobs, restaurants etc in Cambridge

www.cam.ac.uk/AreaInfoRes.html or

www.thisbritain.com/cambridgeshire - guide to phone numbers, shops, facilities etc

www.Ukonline.co.uk - guide to house prices, schools, transport etc. Give your change of address to all Government departments in one easy move

www.tagish.co.uk/tagish/links/localgov.htm - links to parish council (village) websites etc

www.camcnty.gov.uk/sub/resrchgp/houseprice99.htm - dull statistics about Cambridgeshire

● **bed and breakfast accommodation:**

A full list of guest houses is available from the Cambridge Tourist Office *(See 'Key Contacts', back page).*

CHAPTER 3
HOUSEHOLD SERVICES

HOUSEHOLD SERVICES

When you have a home, you've got to make it function. How often will my rubbish be collected? Where do I go to recycle? How do I find out about the various gas, electricity and telephone companies? How do I pay council tax? What's the best way to get repairs done? What news media do I need? This chapter aims to give you the information you need to get organised.

SECURITY / FIRE SAFETY

The usual advice on keeping your home safe – remembering to lock the door etc – all applies. The 16.2 per 1,000 household burglary rate in southern Cambridgeshire in early 2000 was not especially high compared to other regions, but precaution is advised. For a refresher on how to protect your home, read the free Home Office leaflets available from the local police station. To get them, call 'community safety' at one of the non-emergency numbers below. Under certain circumstances, a nice fireman will come out to assess a residence for fire safety as well.

THE TAX MAN COMETH

Whether you rent or own your home, nearly everyone must pay council tax, which goes to city and county government and to the police authority to pay for public services. The tax is imposed on all homes (including flats) and how much you pay depends on the valuation of the property and your situation. There are many exceptions (which we outline below). The exceptions and clauses can make the tax a source of some perplexity, especially to people who have not previously experienced an 'occupant' tax.

How council tax works

Find out what the council tax will be *before* you rent or buy as this tax is an ongoing cost of property ownership or rental. Council tax can be included in the cost of rented accommodation. Unless it is included – and the tenant is responsible for finding out – the occupant has to pay it. One person at each property, either resident or owner, is

Cover picture: a recycling bin near Victoria Road in Cambridge.

responsible for paying Council Tax. That person must be someone over 18 whose main home is the property.

The tax bill for an accommodation is determined by the property valuation. Each house or flat is slotted into one of eight tax bands set by a Valuation Office (see box above). Band 'A' is the lowest – for houses or flats worth up to £40,000 – and 'H' the highest – for houses or flats valued at over £320,000. To find out what band a specific property is in (and the rate the occupant pays) is normally straightforward: call the local council. Typically, the information is readily available – councils are eager to collect this tax and put few obstacles in the way. These are the numbers to call:

Cambridge City	01223 457754
South Cambs	01223 443000
East Cambridgeshire (Ely/Newmarket)	01353 665555
Newmarket/Forest Heath (Suffolk)	01638 719000
Huntingdon/district	01480 388388
Saffron Walden Uttlesford (Essex)	01799 510510
Royston/North Herts	01462 474501

HOUSEHOLD SRVS

Rates start at £500 to £530 a year and go up to around £1,520 to £1,600. Cambridge City tends to be at the higher end. The offices listed above can help you arrange payment. This can be made in ten monthly instalments which start in April and finish in January. Most people start out making the payment by cheque through the post and then get tired of the bother and switch to direct debit. You can also pay at any post office with a plastic swipe card, at the council office on St Andrew's Street or the area housing offices.

Various situations qualify for discounts and not everyone needs to pay. See the box below for the exceptions.

COUNCIL TAX EXEMPTIONS & DISCOUNTS

DISCOUNTS: The tax is based on two adults living in a household. If you live alone at your property, and it is your main home, the bill will be reduced by 25%. If a dwelling is no one's main home, the bill will be reduced by 50%. This applies to empty properties and second homes.

Certain people are not included when counting the number of adult residents. (You will need to supply documentary proof of your status):

- full-time students, student nurses, apprentices, youth training trainees
- patients resident in hospital
- people who are being looked after in care homes
- people who are severely mentally impaired
- people staying in some hostels or night shelters
- 18- and 19- year olds who are at, or have just left school
- careworkers working for low pay, usually for charities
- people caring for someone with a disability who is not a spouse, partner or child under 18 years of age
- members of visiting forces and certain international institutions
- members of religious communities (monks and nuns)
- people in prison (except those detained for non payment of Council Tax or a fine).

Council tax exemptions and reductions may also apply for certain kinds of property, for people with disabilities, where an annexe or similiar self-contained property is occupied by an elderly or disabled relative of the residents living in the rest of it and for people living on a low income.

If your circumstances change – such as when a person moves in, a student finishes a course of study, you move or carry out home improvements – you must notify the authority without delay as this could affect your tax payment.

You can appeal if you believe your tax bill does not reflect your situation, but making an appeal does not allow you to withhold payment of your Council Tax. An adjustment will be made if your appeal succeeds.

TELEPHONE LINES

Anyone who wants to initiate or change service, add a line or find a better deal, faces a bewildering array of choices. We won't promise to sort them all out here, especially all the secondary providers accessible for better deals on calling charges or for internet services. What we can do is shed a bit of light on a particularly local choice: BT or ntl.

British Telecom and ntl are the only choices you have for the basic telephone line that comes into your home. British Telecom is a traditional 'copper wire' telephone company, whereas ntl sells its services via cable along with cable TV. The cost of hooking up will depend on whether a line has already been brought to the residence, how much you use the phone and what kind of services you want. Price packages are designed to appeal to different kinds of users – ranging from the elderly who call out infrequently to those who call abroad and use the internet all the time.

Prices change, but here are the choices as of early 2001:

● BT in a nutshell

BT will turn on an existing hookup for free, but to install a new line costs £49.50 to £99. The basic ongoing cost is the line rental, which begins at £9.99 a month and ranges up to £19.99 a month (billed monthly or quarterly), depending on the services and discounts included. Some packages include a limited amount of call time or reduced rates on certain categories of calls, charged at a per second/minute rate.

To contact BT call 150 on a BT line or 0800 800 150 from a non-BT line.

● ntl in a nutshell

Initial line installation costs £25 and monthly rental costs £9.99 for one or £11.99 for two lines (on the same cable). For £11.99 you can also get one line and digital TV. There are fewer option packages, but call tariffs tend to be simpler, typically 3p per minute on weekdays, 2p from 6-8pm and 1p per minute on weekends. The international call rates are competitive. Students in student accommodation can get special monthly line rental rates of £5.50 to £7.50 with services like voicemail for the higher amount.

For general information call 150 on an ntl line or 0800 052 2000 on other lines. To inquire about the student discount, call 0500 501122.

VOTING AND REGISTERING TO VOTE

Anyone of British, Irish, Commonwealth or European Union nationality who is resident for at least six months may vote and must, by law, register to vote. You can register in the autumn, when a registration form is distributed, or voluntarily at any time with the council. The Cambridge City number is 01223 457048. For other areas, call the main council number.

● which one to choose?

On the face of things, ntl is cheaper, but BT offers more options and generally quicker line installation. Billing from BT is quarterly or monthly. You can almost always get a BT line but ntl is not available in certain locations.

GAS & ELECTRICITY SUPPLIERS

Apart from the minority who get gas out of a bottle or burn coal, most people have to choose a gas and electric supplier when moving into a new home. Before deregulation things were simple. You had no choice and took what you got. Today, with over 20 natural gas and electricity suppliers, you face what seems like a bewildering choice. But it gets a lot easier with the chart provided by the energy regulator, Ofgem, showing the prices and savings with each supplier.

To report a gas emergency or gas leak call 0800 111 999

Once you have the Ofgem comparisons (freecall 0800 887777 or visit the website at www.ofgem.gov.uk to get them), the process of choosing is fairly simple. Find your old gas and electricity bills for the past year (or those from the previous resident) and add up how much you have used and how much you have spent. Then use the price charts to calculate how much you will save by choosing one or another supplier. Savings can be considerable. So it's worth reviewing once in a while and certainly looking again rather than just taking up where the previous occupant left off.

If you have a complaint about a gas or electricity supplier, contact the Gas Consumers Council on 0645 06 07 08.

● installing gas appliances

Gas appliances must be installed properly to be safe and only CORGI-registered installers are properly trained to install them. When a gas line or appliance needs attention in your home, make sure the engineer is registered with CORGI, the national watchdog for gas safety. CORGI engineers carry an ID card. To check its validity, call 01256 372200.

WATER COMPANIES - CONTACT INFO

Contact information is below:

Cambridge Water Plc

(41 Rustat Road, Cambridge CB1 3QS):

General enquiries/emergency:	01223 403000
Billing, pricing and moving house:	01223 403125
Meter installation:	01223 430120
Website:	www.cambridge-water.co.uk

Anglian Water Service Ltd/AWG

(PO Box 46, Spalding, Lincolnshire PE11 1DB):

General enquiries:	0845 7145145
Billing and meter installation:	0800 919155
Website: www. awg.com	

WATER, WATER, WATER

Water comes from only a few sources. Cambridge city is supplied by Cambridge Water. Anglian Water handles all sewerage in Cambridge and water and sewerage in areas around the city. Bills come twice yearly and are based on the ratable value of the property *(see section on council tax page 56)* unless you have had a water meter installed, in which case you pay by actual usage.

Whether moving into a new residence or just tidying up your utilities, determine whether you would be better off with a meter. According to whether the residence has a dishwasher, etc, a typical family of four on a meter pays an average £325 - £375 a year, two adults pay £214 - £241 and a single person £150 - £195. The water companies can send you a chart to use in measuring actual water use and Anglian Water's website, www.awg.com, has a water-use calculator. As a rule of thumb, if your costs exceed the numbers given above, you should consider a meter. Anglian Water says bills on average drop by £100 a year with a meter. Water meter installation is free.

If you move into a metered property, you must pay by the meter. If you install a meter, you have a year to change your mind and revert to payment by property valuation. After the period, if you have not reverted, you must continue to pay by meter. You are only allowed to use a sprinkler or unattended hosepipe if you are on metered water supply. (This is rigorously enforced so if you do have a large garden it's worth going on a meter).

FIX-IT, REPAIR AND UPKEEP

We wish we could make the minefield of household services easy. We can't. But when choosing a plumber, carpet cleaner or chimney sweep, whether plucked from the telephone directory, advertising or on recommendation, the following steps are always well advised:

- Find out how long the firm or individual has been in business and enquire about qualifications.

HOUSEHOLD SRVS

- Ask for references from previous customers and contact them.
- Trade association membership may or may not be meaningful. Some regulate members. Others just *have* members – i.e. any Tom, Dick or Harry can join. Contact the organisation to find out what they do.
- Determine call-out charges before you arrange for a visit.
- Contact *three* sources for a service or product and ask each for a full estimate, in writing if possible or, better, a quote, on a job before making a selection. Specify in writing that you should be informed of any additional costs in advance.
- Read and understand the fine print. Don't let anyone rush you.
- Keep a copy of anything you sign.
- Only pay for complete work after you have thoroughly inspected the results.
- Make sure you get a detailed bill with the name and address of the supplier on it.

In addition, get advice from the independent consumer organisation *Which* and its array of publications. For information, call 0800 252100 or go to: www.which.net

REFUSE COLLECTION

This section begins with Cambridge City and telephone contacts for the other areas are on page 68.

Cambridge City refuse collection

Once a week on a weekday, a refuse truck pulls up to your house. To make sure you get your refuse picked up you have to know:

1) the day and time of the pickup
2) how to set out refuse.

Enlightenment in the eternal mysteries of scheduling and more is found by calling the city on 01223 458282. Here's what the gurus of refuse in city government will tell you:

● **pickup schedules**

Refuse collection varies by street and neighbourhood. The refuse should be set out by 7am, though the actual time of collection may be later. Pickup days change over the bank (public) holidays. You'll normally get a leaflet notifying you of the change.

● **black 'wheelie bins'**

Most people now have a black 'wheelie bin', which is, surprise, surprise, a black bin on wheels. Most residences will already have one. If not, you (or the landlord) has to buy one. You have a choice between a 240 litre bin (a bit bigger than an oil drum) or a 140 litre bin (a baby oil drum) but you will have to pay for it. Order them from the city at the number above. You pay £22.50 - £25 for showroom-fresh or

£12.50 - £15 for 'pre-owned models'.

When you have a bin, label it with your house number or address (and a funny face to give the bin man a smile). If the bin gets lost or stolen, this makes recovery easier.

● **things not left in the bin - pickups**

Anything for collection that is not inside your bin will not be collected but by calling 01223 458282 you can schedule a cleansing department pickup for things like sofas, bagged garden waste or cookers at a per item cost of £19 for one item and up to £36 for ten. They won't accept pianos, building materials, motor parts, liquid paint or hazardous waste. It may be cheaper – if you have transport – to take it to the refuse and recycling centre yourself (details page 66). The exception is domestic fridges and freezers, which the coun-

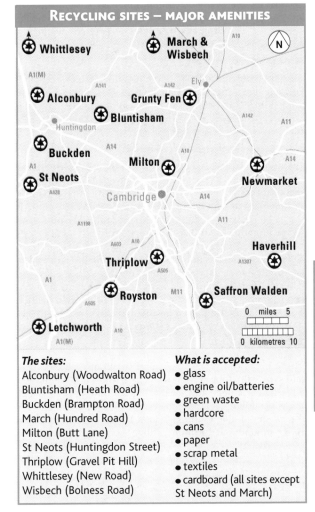

RECYCLING SITES — MAJOR AMENITIES

The sites:
Alconbury (Woodwalton Road)
Bluntisham (Heath Road)
Buckden (Brampton Road)
March (Hundred Road)
Milton (Butt Lane)
St Neots (Huntingdon Street)
Thriplow (Gravel Pit Hill)
Whittlesey (New Road)
Wisbech (Bolness Road)

What is accepted:
● glass
● engine oil/batteries
● green waste
● hardcore
● cans
● paper
● scrap metal
● textiles
● cardboard (all sites except St Neots and March)

HOUSEHOLD SRVS

cil will collect for recycling, free-of-charge (so they can dispose of the CFCs safely).

● green 'wheelie bins'

GREEN BIN-ABLES:
Grass
hedge clippings
egg shells
old fruit
tea bags
coffee filters
vegetables and peelings
stale bread
bark/untreated wood
flowers
weeds

Standard rubbish bins are black, but, in Cambridge 11,000 households (about a quarter) are on a 'green bin' scheme. If you live in an area covered by this scheme, which aims to promote recycling and reduction of waste, then you will be supplied with two bins, one black and one green. Collections alternate – one week the Council will collect your black bin with non-compostable household waste, like plastics. The next week you should leave out your 'green' bin into which you can place compostable materials such as hedge clippings, tea bags, vegetable peelings – and don't forget the egg shells.

● paper recycling

To have your old newspapers and other paper recycled, sort and stack them in plastic bags in a visible spot outside your home. They will be removed on one of the days that your regular refuse is removed but on a fortnightly schedule.

● cotton nappies for babies

Disposable nappies account for 5% of the total waste entering landfill sites every year and for every pound spent on disposables the tax payer (that's you!) pays 10p to dispose of them. If that isn't enough to persuade you, then perhaps the £10 yearly rebate from the Cambridgeshire City Council might! The rebate is arranged through Cambridge's nappy laundering service: Cotton Botties (0800 915 4195). This service is friendly, good value, reliable and takes account of your baby's individual needs as they grow. You can sell them back your old nappy covers as your baby outgrows them, thus making your next set of covers cheaper. You will pay a refundable deposit on taking out the service.
See 'cotton nappy services' page 185 for further details.

RECYCLING

These items can be recycled: glass (beer and wine bottles, jam jars with tops removed), cans (drink-cans, aluminum and steel – empty and clean), paper (newspapers, magazines, catalogues, telephone directories), cardboard, textiles (clean, dry, usable clothes), books, foil, corks, batteries, old tools, engine oil, furniture, fridges, certain plastics, and

---

DON'T KNOW THE POSTCODE?

www.royalmail.co.uk/paf/.gov.uk
Enter the street name here to find out.

CAMBRIDGE CITY RECYCLING SITES

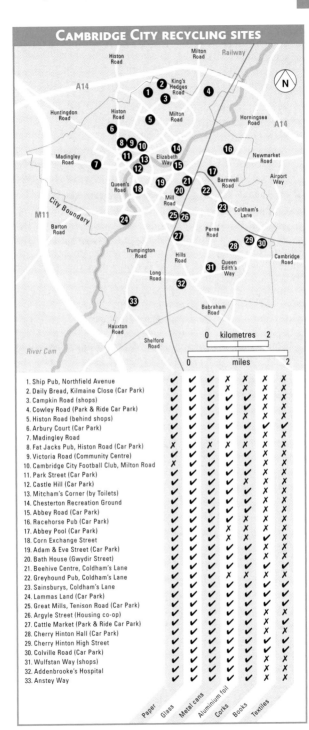

	Paper	Glass	Metal cans	Aluminium foil	Corks	Books	Textiles
1. Ship Pub, Northfield Avenue	✓	✓	✓	✗	✗	✗	✗
2. Daily Bread, Kilmaine Close (Car Park)	✓	✓	✓	✓	✗	✗	✗
3. Campkin Road (shops)	✓	✓	✓	✓	✗	✗	✗
4. Cowley Road (Park & Ride Car Park)	✓	✓	✓	✓	✗	✗	✗
5. Histon Road (behind shops)	✓	✓	✓	✓	✗	✗	✗
6. Arbury Court (Car Park)	✓	✓	✓	✓	✓	✓	✓
7. Madingley Road	✓	✓	✓	✓	✓	✓	✓
8. Fat Jacks Pub, Histon Road (Car Park)	✗	✓	✗	✗	✗	✓	✗
9. Victoria Road (Community Centre)	✓	✓	✓	✓	✓	✗	✗
10. Cambridge City Football Club, Milton Road	✗	✓	✓	✓	✗	✓	✗
11. Park Street (Car Park)	✓	✓	✓	✓	✓	✓	✗
12. Castle Hill (Car Park)	✓	✓	✓	✓	✗	✓	✗
13. Mitcham's Corner (by Toilets)	✓	✓	✓	✓	✓	✓	✗
14. Chesterton Recreation Ground	✓	✓	✓	✓	✓	✓	✗
15. Abbey Road (Car Park)	✓	✓	✓	✓	✓	✓	✗
16. Racehorse Pub (Car Park)	✓	✓	✓	✓	✗	✓	✗
17. Abbey Pool (Car Park)	✓	✓	✓	✗	✗	✓	✗
18. Corn Exchange Street	✓	✓	✓	✗	✗	✓	✗
19. Adam & Eve Street (Car Park)	✓	✓	✓	✓	✓	✓	✗
20. Bath House (Gwydir Street)	✓	✓	✓	✓	✓	✓	✓
21. Beehive Centre, Coldham's Lane	✓	✓	✓	✓	✓	✓	✓
22. Greyhound Pub, Coldham's Lane	✓	✓	✓	✗	✗	✓	✓
23. Sainsburys, Coldham's Lane	✓	✓	✓	✓	✓	✓	✓
24. Lammas Land (Car Park)	✓	✓	✓	✓	✓	✓	✓
25. Great Mills, Tenison Road (Car Park)	✓	✓	✓	✓	✗	✓	✓
26. Argyle Street (Housing co-op)	✓	✓	✓	✓	✓	✗	✗
27. Cattle Market (Park & Ride Car Park)	✓	✓	✓	✓	✓	✓	✓
28. Cherry Hinton Hall (Car Park)	✓	✓	✓	✓	✓	✓	✓
29. Cherry Hinton High Street	✓	✓	✓	✓	✓	✗	✓
30. Colville Road (Car Park)	✓	✓	✓	✓	✓	✓	✓
31. Wulfstan Way (shops)	✓	✓	✓	✓	✓	✗	✗
32. Addenbrooke's Hospital	✓	✓	✓	✓	✓	✗	✗
33. Anstey Way							

HOUSEHOLD SRVS

other electrical goods.

Check the chart to see where you can bring each type of recycling.

For information on recycling:

Cambridge City	01223 457896
Cambridgeshire County	01223 717100
East Cambridgeshire	01353 665555
Huntingdon District	01480 388368
South Cambridgeshire District	01223 443192
Newmarket/Suffolk	01638 719000
Royston/North Herts	01462 474330
Saffron Walden/Essex	01799 510510

Disposal of big or dangerous things

If you don't get the council to take things away, you can do it yourself. Bring big things and dangerous items to the local recycling centre (see text and map page 63). The Milton Household Waste Recycling Centre, Butts Lane, off the A10 at Milton and also at Thriplow (off the A505) are the closest to Cambridge City. Opening hours:

Mon-Fri	9am-8pm May-September
	9am-4pm Oct-April
Sat-Sun	9am-6pm May-September
	9am-4pm Oct-April

Contact the manager at 01223 860674, Milton, or 01223 839001, Thriplow, for more information.

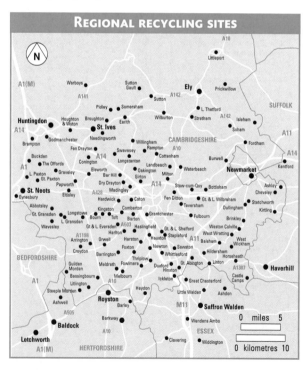

REGIONAL RECYCLING SITES

REGIONAL RECYCLING SITES — INDEX

● alternatives to amenity site disposal

Bicycles/furniture. Take them to Milton or call Emmaus (a charitable organisation which gives homeless people a place to live in exchange for the work they do) at Landbeach. They will collect your old bikes and furniture to recondition and resell (01223 863657).

Hazardous waste. This can be taken to the household waste site at Milton or telephone the Cambs County Council Cleansing department 01223 458292 who offer an advice and collection service to Cambridge residents.

Tools. Many can be refurbished and sent to the Third World - take to the City Council.

Call the Environmental Health (01223 457882) with any questions, complaints and comments.

Refuse pickup outside Cambridge

Services for other areas are similar, but for variations and options on collection of bulky items etc. phone the numbers listed below:

South Cambridgeshire	01223 235468
Newmarket / Suffolk (Forest Heath District)	01638 719000
Royston / North Hertfordshire	01462 474330
Saffron Walden / Essex (Uttlesford District Council)	01799 510510
Huntingdonshire	01480 388388
Ely (East Cambridgeshire)	01353 863864

NEWS MEDIA BAZAAR

Information being one of the key things one needs to plug into these days, we give below a review of the major local media sources, beginning with the newsagent and covering printed and electronic media.

Newsagents

The corner newsagent is your first stop for newspapers and magazines, and typically the local newsagent can arrange delivery to your door. With magazines in particular, however, be aware that you typically pay full price for publications ordered through a newsagent. You may get discounts by ordering directly from the publisher.

Print media

● The Cambridge Evening News

The main purveyor of local news fodder, and sometimes surprisingly underwhelming front page scoops, is the *Cambridge Evening News*. Owned by the Iliffe family and run actively by Lord Iliffe himself, it is part of a group including chains in Hertfordshire, Essex and Staffordshire. The Cambridge office puts out free papers in Ely, Haverhill, Huntingdon, Newmarket, Royston, St Ives, Saffron Walden and Cambridge (where it has two: *The Cambridge Weekly News* and *The Town Crier*) and the six-day-a-week

Cambridge Evening News. The free papers – for most people the main local news medium – are chock-a-block with ads plus recycled news from the Evening News. They reach 168,000 households. The Evening News sells about 41,000 copies a day at 33p a copy (£1.98 a week if you subscribe). It carries useful local information, ads and a strong business section. Its website, www.cambridge-news.co.uk, has back issues, what's on information and nice links to other Cambridge sites.

Photo by Neal E. Robbins

Birthday wishes for Cambridge

Available from newsagents and streetsellers or by delivery or, for a premium, by post. Call 01223 434434. (See also 'Key Contacts,' back page'.)

● subscription magazines

Cambridgeshire Journal, an eye-catching monthly 'coffee-table' magazine, with sister titles for Norfolk, Suffolk and Essex. Owned by Acorn Magazines Ltd, the journal is an advertising-heavy regional clone of the national country magazines, but lighter and more folksy in its focus on picturesque countryside, cooking, restaurants and lovely interiors. It sells for £1.95 a copy or £19.99 for 12 issues.

Available at newsagents and supermarkets or by subscription: 01284 701190.

● free magazines

Adhoc: The City. This weekly glossy is left in shops and dropped through letter boxes. Contains 'what's on' listings, reviews, property ads, job listings and general advertising. Designed to promote its wide-ranging and very commercial www.adhoc.co.uk events and lifestyle website, the magazine gives a young, media-mesmerized market more of the same. *Available at free distribution points in the city centre (01223 568960).*

Cambridgeshire Pride. This free monthly is similar to The Journal, but more folksy. It has been in continuous publication since 1982, making it one of the oldest magazines in the area. Available by subscription *(01733 242312).*

Art East. A 10-times-a-year free arts, threatre and events listing magazine with lots of ads and listings. Distributed in theatres and galleries around East Anglia *(01379 644200).*

Sticks. This free 'what's on' monthly tabloid circulates in Cambridgeshire, Herts, Suffolk and Essex, with some local and much shared content (01462 486810).

Business Weekly is a free tabloid newspaper mailed to

many local businesses. It carries company news and press releases (01223 264664).

Local/regional radio

This is a list of the main local outlets. Many more spill over from surrounding areas along with national stations.

BBC Radio Cambridgeshire (95.7FM in north Cambridgeshire, 96FM in the south, and 1026AM in Cambridge). On the air since 1981, the station offers news and current affairs of Cambridgeshire-wide interest, with lots of call-in programmes and talk about local issues. No advertising at all (01223 259696). Website:
www.bbc.co.uk/england/radiocambridgeshire

VibeFM (105.6FM Cambridge/106.4FM Bury St Edmunds). Has the biggest broadcast 'footprint' of all the area stations, covering a region spanning Norwich, Colchester, Peterborough and Lowestoft with 'dance format' music, news and advertising. It claims 300,000 listeners a week. Launched in 1997, it's owned by the Daily Mail group (01284 718800).

Q103FM, Histon, Cambridge. Broadcasts within a 25-mile radius of Cambridge and Newmarket. The station favours recent pop music, traffic, sport, contests, advertising and local news. Launched in 1989 and revamped in 1994, it's part of the 43-station strong-GWR Radio Services Ltd. (01223 235255).

Eagle 107.9FM, Sturton Street, Cambridge. Formerly Red Radio and before that community radio, the station was launched in mid-2000, offering 'Cambridge and the very immediate area' a commercial programme of music, chat, local traffic news, sport and weather along with advertising and contests. Part of the 300-station UKRD group Ltd. (01223 722300).

Local/regional TV

Anglia TV is the regional franchise of ITV. The Norwich-based studio broadcasts weekday regional news for East Anglia at 6pm along with various other regional and nationally viewed programmes. (01603 615151).

BBC Look East/local programming. Seen on BBC1, Look East comes on at weekdays at 6.30pm with news for East Anglia, along with bulletins at breakfast, lunch and at weekends. Broadcasting from Norwich and Cambridge, it also puts out *Matter of Fact*, a half-hour documentary at 7.30pm on Thursdays and *East at Westminster*, a political programme, on Sundays at 1 pm on BBC2. Look East works closely with BBC radio local stations. (01603 619331).

Red TV is a cable television channel with studios on Sturton Street, Cambridge. It offers local programming, typically with a youthful angle, and local news competitions. Owned by local media man, Peter Dawe. (01233 722722), www.redtv.co.uk

CHAPTER 4
TRANSPORT

Photo by Jennie Wilson

Cambridge has excellent links to London and north to the Midlands, but rapid growth in and around the city has caused traffic congestion. The traffic problem is serious – but not as bad as sometimes portrayed. Measures such as the Park and Ride system, traffic controls and other restrictions channel the flows and act as release valves. A lot more needs to be done to sort things out, but planners are hard at work looking for answers.

Proposals under study include upgrading part of the most heavily congested feeder road, the A14, into a motorway, re-laying an old railway line between Huntingdon and Cambridge and opening new stations north of Cambridge along the route. To ease the pressure from car-borne commuters, construction of new housing on Cambridge's surrounding Green Belt or a new town very near the city have been mooted, along with building a new train station north of the city at Chesterton sidings, and one to the south of Cambridge to boost access to Addenbrooke's Hospital and London.

For the foreseeable future, congestion will continue, but with a little knowledge of how things work, and perhaps a willingness to consider using a variety of transportation – bicycle, bus and train – most people find the situation quite liveable.

GETTING AROUND IN CAMBRIDGE

This section covers Cambridge city and its immediate environs.

Cambridge on foot

Cambridge city is relatively small – about three miles from edge to edge at most points. So no place in the city is more than 30-40 minutes from the centre by foot for a good walker. In the centre, walking is definitely the easiest way to get about. In fact the foot is king (after a fashion) between 10am and 4pm Monday to Saturday, when vehicles are banned from the historic centre and bicycles can only be used on St John's and Trinity streets.

Bicycles in the city

Cambridge is known as 'Cycle City' because it is so easy to get around on a bike. The land is mainly flat, many cycle lanes are provided and, especially in the warmer months, getting out and about is a delightful experience. Year-round, cyclists commute to the train station and to work from all over, children pedal down to the shops, and students, who are generally not allowed to have cars, rush to class – not always punctually – at around 9 or 10 am. Bikes are an important part of what makes living in Cambridge special.

Cover picture: Boats on the River Cam.

● bicycle safety

Cycling involves a risk – the cyclist casualty rate per head in Cambridgeshire is more than twice the average for Great Britain, with most of the accidents in the 12-19 age range in Cambridge City – but this is only because twice as many people ride pedal cycles. In fact, mile for mile, cycling in Cambridge is as safe as anywhere. Most people consider cycling a reasonable, not unduly risky proposition when compared to road use risks faced by pedestrians and cars.

The risk goes down immensely if cyclists ride defensively, anticipating car movements on the road and taking precautions – like watching out for parked cars in case a door swings open. They should wear helmets, use night lights and make sure hand signals are clear, allowing time for drivers to react. When sharing pavement cycle paths, they should travel at sensible speeds. Observing restrictions, such as day-time bicycle riding prohibitions in the historic centre is appreciated by pedestrians.

● bicycle parking

Bicycle parking in Cambridge is a casual affair, as is evidenced by the ever-present shop window requests NOT to leave bicycles there. Cycle parking is provided (in Green Street, Guildhall Street, King's Parade, Lion Yard, Market Hill, Pea's Hill, St Edward's Passage, St Mary's Passage, Sidney Street and Trinity Street) but often overflows onto walls,

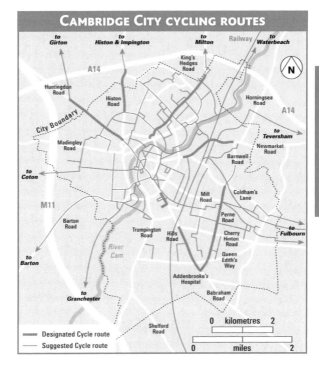

CAMBRIDGE CITY CYCLING ROUTES

Designated Cycle route
Suggested Cycle route

TRANSPORT

street lamps and trees. Wherever you leave your wheels, make sure they are not in somebody's way. Lock bikes up, even if you leave them for a short time, with a good strong cable or D-lock. Cambridge is a paradise for bicycle thieves. If you plan to leave a bike out overnight, make sure all removable parts are locked (for example removalable wheels and saddles) because most thefts occur overnight.

Getting around by taxi

Taxis are a convenient and, if used with discretion, affordable way to get around the city. Many people get along without a car by using a mix of transport including taxis, buses, bicycles and, if they drive, a rental car now and again. 24-hour taxi ranks (see also the inside front cover map) operate at the train station and, handy to shoppers, at:

- the intersection of Petty Cury and St Andrew's Street
- the bus station on Parker Street.

Most times of the day, you can order a taxi by phone and it will arrive in 10-15 minutes. On bad weather days, Friday and Saturday nights, hailing a cab on the street is a long shot. But you can generally order a taxi by phone. It may take longer at these peak times – but generally not more than 45 minutes. The companies are pretty good about letting you know how long it will take to get the car to you.

● private cabs and hackney carriages

There are hackney carriages – with a yellow 'taxi' sign on top – or private hire vehicles, which have the company name on the door, but no sign on top. Hackney Carriage prices are determined by the Council and you can hail them on the street, pick one up from a taxi rank or pre-book. You must pre-book a private hire vehicle to be insured against accident. Private hire companies set their own prices, but most use the hackney fare rates in the city.

● what it costs

Taxi fares must be displayed in the vehicle, with three price

PRIVATE HIRE TAXI COMPANIES			
CAMBRIDGE		**HUNTINGDON**	
A1 Taxis	01223 525555	M.A.	01480 435030
Cabco	01223 312444	Hunts	01480 455576
Camtax	01223 313131	ABC	01480 374673
Panther	01223 715715	Steve's	01480 413222
Regency	01223 311388	**ROYSTON**	
ELY		Meltax	01763 244444
A.K	01353 661010	Butlers	01763 247774
Alan's	01353 665050	**NEWMARKET**	
Fencabs	01353 669966	Style	01638 669966
J & R	01353 666377		0500 667890
SAFFRON WALDEN		Newtax	01638 561561
Five Star	01799 522445	Anglia	01638 668877
Crocus	01799 525511		

structures:7am-7pm, after 7pm, Sundays and bank holidays, each a step up in price, and the Christmas period the dearest. Fares range from £3.50 for a ride from the city centre to the Grafton Centre, £4 to the train station, and £4 to Addenbrooke's Hospital. Small charges are added for additional passengers, luggage and telephone bookings.

Getting around by private car

Cambridge is not a particularly car-friendly city, but it gets better if you avoid rush hour (8-9.30am and 4.30-6.30pm) and heavily used intersections. Particularly bad areas are those anywhere south of the city centre, such as Lensfield Road, where at peak times it can take half an hour to move just a couple of hundred metres!

The many bicyclists are another feature of driving particular to Cambridge. Cyclists and cycle lanes need plenty of room. Drivers should generally assume cyclists all ride around completely oblivious of the tons of metal and glass bearing down on them at speed. (Some are. Others know all too well of the danger that cars present.) Be especially careful when making left turns, as some cyclists will shoot past when you are about to make a turn.

Street parking

Street parking in the city centre is divided between residential and short-term public parking. Watch out for single and double yellow lines and keep an eye out for small rectangular signs indicating any form of prohibition. Parking

TRANSPORT

SANDRA DAWSON – CAMBRIDGE ACADEMIC

The compactness of Cambridge is really striking, and something you particularly notice after having moved here from London where you have to go long distances on the underground, bus or car. I really do like to take advantage of this by cycling everywhere - no matter what the weather! - since everything is so close at hand. To be able to travel virtually anywhere here by bicycle in ten minutes is really quite extraordinary, and in addition there are so many beautiful views and buildings in and around the city that cycling is a real pleasure.

Photo by Perry Hastings, courtesy of University of Cambridge

Personally, I especially love bicycling or walking down that narrow, old road that goes down to Trinity Hall bridge – Trinity Lane and Garret Hostel Lane. It is my favourite spot in this marvellously compact city and I think it is a very special place – I love the beautiful old bricks down either side of the street between Trinity and Trinity Hall. And I adore lingering there, on the bridge, for a while, because, whatever the season, the river always looks so lovely, so peaceful, and then I like to carry on my journey along the Backs. It is an absolutely marvellous view from there as you look down towards Clare Bridge, the other bridges, past the riverbank trees, and through the mist of the early morning or late evening. Having said that though, I also love the meadows between the Mill and Newnham, particularly when the buttercups are in flower. Again, the river always looks just wonderful there.

Those are my special places in Cambridge, but they can't compare with the very special gardens at Sidney Sussex College, which are beautiful, and, of course, the Judge Institute, which is an amazing building both to look at and to work in.

Professor Sandra Dawson has lived in Cambridge for five years and was previously at Imperial College, London, for 26 years. She is Master of Sidney Sussex College and Director of the Judge Institute of Management Studies (the University of Cambridge's business school).

penalties can be severe – £30 is typical. A limited number of 'pay and display' (typically 2-hour) areas are dotted about. A list of roads where pay and display parking (including prices) is available can be found at:

www.cambridge.gov.uk/profserv/pndlist.htm

City buses

It's worth learning which routes serve your neighbourhood. Even if you don't ride the buses regularly, they are handy for getting around on occasion. Cambridge bus station, where the bus information office is located (at the opening to Bradwell's Court) is the starting and ending point of most local services, in particular for Stagecoach Cambus.

● city bus prices and discounts

Typical prices include a single ticket to Addenbrooke's at £1 and from the train station or the Grafton Centre to the city centre at 80p. If you use the bus regularly in the city or to immediate outlying villages then buying a 'Megarider' pass for unlimited use is worthwhile. It costs £2.30/day, £6.50/week, £26/month, £75/three months and £275/year, and includes travel to Bar Hill, Dry Drayton, Comberton, Fulbourn, Trumpington, Histon, Impington, Oakington and Milton.

These are the main routes and frequencies:

2 (7.30am-6pm, 1/2 hourly) Oakington - City Centre - Rail Station - Mill Road - Cherry Hinton

3 City-Rail Link (6.30am-11pm, every 10 mins) Fison Road - City Centre - Rail Station

4/5/5A (6am-11pm every 10 mins) Arbury-City Centre-Rail Station-Addenbrooke's Hospital; then 4 (7am-6pm, every half hour) Sawston; 5 (6am-11pm, every half hour) Cherry Hinton-Fulbourn; 5A (7am-6pm, every half hour) Cherry Hinton-Newmarket Park and Ride

6 (7am-6pm, 1/2 hourly) CRC King's Hedges - Buchan Street - City Centre - Coldhams Lane - Teversham

7 (7am-6pm, 20 mins) Cowley Road - Chesterton - City Centre

8 (7am-6pm, 20 mins) Fen Estate - Chesterton - City Centre - Mill Road - Addenbrooke's Hospital

31 (8.30am-6pm, 1/2 hourly) Cambridge - Addenbrooke's Hospital

TRANSPORT

LOCAL BUS SERVICE IN NEARBY TOWNS

Ely : Stagecoach Cambus (see page 81) operates a town service (22) in Ely, which runs hourly between 9am and 3pm.

Saffron Walden: Viceroy of Essex, 12 Bridge Street, Saffron Walden operates a town service (34), which runs seven times daily between 8.30am and 6pm. (01799 508010) website:

www.uttlesford.gov.uk/saffire/travel/viceroy.html

Huntingdon: Huntingdon and District (see page 83) operates two local services, the 571 running from 7.30am - 5pm, and the 572 from 7am-6.30pm - both are 1/2 hourly.

● free city centre shuttle

A shopper's free city centre shuttle service (which normally runs on natural gas) operates every 15 minutes from Monday to Saturday and circles round the historic centre and central shopping area.

● night shuttle

For the night owl, two services operate hourly between midnight and 3 am on Friday and Saturday nights, charging a flat fare of £1. The N1 runs between Trumpington, Cherry Hinton, Newmarket Road and the city centre, and N2 runs from the city centre to Milton Road, Arbury and Chesterton.

Cambridge city for the disabled

Apart from vehicle transport (see below, under 'Getting into Cambridge', page 83) the disabled have assistance through *Shopmobility*, which provides wheelchairs and scooters to about 100 users a week. Very occasionally scooters can run out, though wheelchairs are normally always there. The scheme – free, though any donations are appreciated – is available between 10am and 4pm and collections from a city centre bus stop can be arranged as well as an escort service. It is not a pre-requisite to be a certified disabled person and staff will explain how to use the equipment.

Shopmobility is available in the Lion Yard car park level 5 (01223 457452) and in the Grafton Centre on level 4 (01223 461858) – both lines have 24-hour answering machines for messages. A similar scheme runs in Peterborough in the Queensgate Shopping Centre on level 11. The scheme here runs from 10am to 5pm (01733 313133). Shopmobility is also available in Bury St Edmunds (01284 757175), King's Lynn (01553 770310) and Norwich (01603 766430). There are also plans to set the scheme up in Ely, Newmarket and Royston.

● Parking for the disabled

Disabled parking spaces are available on the following streets in Cambridge (number of spaces in brackets): City Road (2), Guildhall Street (2), Jesus Lane (6), Napier Street (2), Regent Street (2), Round Church Street (3), Fair Street (2), Hobson Street (6), King's Parade (7), Peas Hill (4) and St Andrew's Street (6).

GETTING INTO CAMBRIDGE

Cambridge is a busy place. An estimated 30,000 car trips into Cambridge take place on an average weekday. Mix that with the medieval street layout of the city centre and thousands who come in by bus, train or bicycle, including 3.5 million tourists each year, and you've got a lot of people moving about a relatively small area. Most come from an area within about 15 miles, the Cambridge 'catchment' as it's sometimes called. The congestion focuses on the access routes, feeder roads and the main thoroughfares.

Access routes by car

Congestion along the main access routes into the city can be a problem throughout the day, but particularly at peak times – 8 - 9.30am and 4.30 - 6.30pm – and congestion spills over into surrounding parts of East Anglia. The principal access routes are:

- the M11, the motorway running north from London and passing near to Cambridge
- the A14, a dual carriageway running from Huntingdon, passing to the north of Cambridge and onto Newmarket, Bury St Edmunds, Ipswich and Felixstowe
- the A11, the main route from Cambridge to Norwich and the coast
- the A10, running north from Cambridge to King's Lynn via Ely.

The A14 is the worst problem, as traffic from Huntingdon, St Ives and the surrounding villages has no other option but to use this route, along with hordes of heavy freight vehicles going to and from ports such as Felixstowe and Harwich. Clogging spills over into the Cambridge entry routes.

● planning entry into the city

When driving to Cambridge at peak times, plan entry points into the centre in advance. Recommended are:

- *from the south or west*: drive all the way up the M11

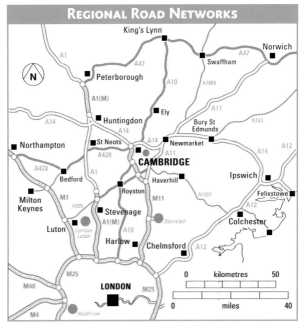

REGIONAL ROAD NETWORKS

TRANSPORT

and enter via the A1303 (Madingley Road) exit 13

- *from the north-west on the A14*, use the A1307 (Huntingdon Road) exit 14
- *from the north on the A10*, use the A1309 (Milton Road)
- *from the east on the A14*, go around to the A1309 (Milton Road)

See also the regional map under the back cover.

Forward planning on parking (see below) is also well advised.

City car parks

Expect to pay a good amount to park in the centre at Lion Yard or Park Street or at Grafton Centre East and West. Queen Anne Terrace Car Park is a bit cheaper. Charges decline after 8.30pm (after 6.30pm at the Grafton Centre car parks).

● getting to the car parks

Lion Yard Car Park (capacity 970). Best for the shops in the very city centre and market square. Can be reached via Silver Street or Trumpington Street.

Park Street Car Park (capacity 450) The next best option for the historic centre. Approach from Jesus Lane.

Grafton Centre Car Parks. Best for the Grafton Centre and just 10 minutes walk from the city centre. Reach Grafton Centre *East* (capacity 870) via East Road, *West* (capacity 280) via Newmarket Road or Maid's Causeway.

Queen Anne Terrace Car Park (capacity 630) in Gonville Place (off Park Terrace and opposite Parker's Piece). Ten minutes walk from the city centre and Grafton Centre.

Park and Ride

Cambridge is served by four main Park and Ride sites, and a fifth is to be added in the Trumpington area in late 2001. The system, set up in 1996, carries 4,600 people a week, successfully reducing City Centre congestion, cutting pollution and, as a part of the integrated transport strategy, giving shoppers and commuters an attractive way to get in.

Parking is free. A single or return bus ticket to the city centre costs £1.20, and up to two children under the age of 16 (per fare-paying adult) can travel free. There is no waiting to drive into the spaces (unlike the city centre car parks where often long lines of cars queue). The shuttle buses – with traffic light control ensuring the trip goes quickly – drop you right in the centre every 10-12 minutes between 7am and 7pm. After 7pm buses run on a 20 minute cycle.

Getting in by bus

With over 20 bus companies serving Cambridge, choosing a bus route and determining times can be a challenge. Start with the County Council's Passenger Information Line (01223 717740) or Traveline (0870 6082608) or contact the bus company for routes and timetables. See below and page 77 for contact and ticket- purchase information.

If speed is essential, then taking the bus for anything longer than a journey of about five miles, depending on the destination, will usually be slower than a car or train journey. For anywhere beyond 10 miles of Cambridge, expect indirect service, with stops in villages or towns en route. But the bus is generally inexpensive and in certain cases – for example between Huntingdon and Cambridge – a lot faster and cheaper than other options.

A list follows of the main local operators and services, with times of operation of the outbound services, the frequency during the main part of the day, and the range of prices for a single ticket on each route shown in brackets.

● **Stagecoach Cambus**

Typical single journey prices to or from Cambridge range from £1.60 to Waterbeach and £1.50 to Willingham to £4 to Bury St Edmunds, £3 to Ely and £5 to King's Lynn. Return tickets usually cost double with a 20-50p discount. Regular users' 'Goldrider' tickets for unlimited travel on all routes cost £13/week, £52/month, £150 for three months and £550 for a year. Stagecoach is the biggest local operator.

Offices: 100 Cowley Road, Cambridge, CB4 0DN (01223 423578, fax 01223 420065, e-mail: contact@stagecoach-cambus.co.uk, website: www.stagecoach-cambus.co.uk).

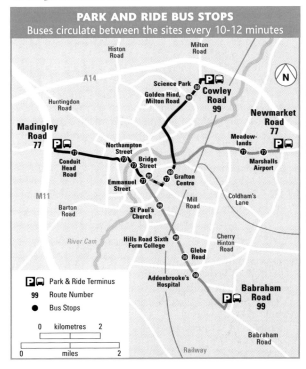

PARK AND RIDE BUS STOPS
Buses circulate between the sites every 10-12 minutes

TRANSPORT

Main routes (single fares):

9 (7am-7pm, 1/2 hourly, 60p-£1.60) Cambridge - Milton - Landbeach - Waterbeach

9A (7am-2.30pm, 3 times daily £1.60 - £3) Ely - Waterbeach - Cambridge

14 (7am-10.30pm, hourly, £1) Cambourne - Cambridge

44 (6am-1.30pm, hourly, 60p-£2.40) Haverhill - Balsham- Fulbourn- Cherry Hinton Road - Cambridge

102 & 103 (7am-11pm, 1/2 hourly, 90p-£2.70) Saffron Walden- Stapleford - Great Shelford - Cambridge

104 (6.30am-11pm, 1/2 hourly, 80p-£1.70) Cottenham - Rampton- Impington - Histon - Cambridge

111 (6am-10.30pm, hourly, 90p-£2.50) Newmarket - Burwell- Bottisham - Cambridge

112 (7am-7pm, hourly, £1.70) Duxford - Cambridge

113 & 136 (7am-12midnight, 1/2 hourly, £2.40-£2.70) Kedington- Haverhill - Cambridge

118 & 119 (7am-7.30pm, hourly, £1-£2.90) Gamlingay - Longstowe- Comberton - Cambridge

146 & X46 & 147 (7am-5.30pm, hourly, £1.20-£2.80) Guilden Morden - Royston - Barrington - Cambridge

155-159 (6am-5pm, 1/2 hourly, 80p-£1.90) St Ives - Willingham- Bar Hill - Cambridge

X8 (6am-7pm, hourly, £1-£3.55) Wisbech - March - Chatteris - Ely- Cambridge

X9 (7am-11.30pm, hourly, £1-£5) King's Lynn - Downham Market- Littleport - Ely - Cambridge

X10 (7am-12.30am, every 2 hours, £1-£3) RAF Lakenheath- Newmarket - Cambridge

X11 (7am-10.30pm, every 2 hours, £1-£4) Bury St Edmunds- Newmarket - Cambridge

X12 (6am-11.30pm, hourly, £1-£3) Ely - Soham - Studlands- Newmarket - Cambridge

X10, X11 and X12 jointly provide buses every half hour to and from Newmarket. On Sundays a very restricted service is operated on all routes and only the Cambridge city urban services (see page 77, above) offer a good range.

● Go Whippet

Typical prices Huntingdon to Cambridge, £2.15 and from St Ives £1.60.

Offices: Cambridge Road, Fenstanton, Cambridgeshire, PE28 9JB (tel 01480 463792, website: www.go-whippet.co.uk).

Service 1 (6.30am-5pm, every 1-2 hours, £1-£1.60) St Ives- Papworth - Hardwick - Cambridge

Service 1A & 5 (6.30am-6pm, every 20 mins, 80p-£2.15) Huntingdon- St Ives - Bar Hill - Cambridge

Service 2 (8.30am-5.30pm, 4 times daily, 60p-£1.20) Cambridge- Hardwick - Caldecote - Cambridge

Service 8 (7.30am-1.30pm, 5 times daily, 70p-£1.65) Papworth- Elsworth - Coton - Cambridge

Service 175 & 177 (9am-3pm, 5 times a day, £1-£3.50) Biggleswade- Wimpole - Cambridge

● Huntingdon and District

Operates one service to Cambridge, which links Huntingdon, St Ives and surrounding villages. This is the best company for travel from the towns on the route below – service is provided every 20 minutes throughout the day.

Offices: The Travel Shop, Huntingdon Bus Station, Mill Common, Huntingdon, Cambridgeshire, PE29 3PH (01480 453159, e-mail: Info@huntsbus.fsbusiness.co.uk, website: www.huntingdonanddistrict-buses.co.uk).

553 & 554 & 555 (6am-11pm, every 20 mins, £1-£2.25) Huntingdon- Oxmoor - St Ives - Fenstanton - Cambridge.

By bicycle

If you live in a village near Cambridge, then hopping on your bike provides a scenic, healthy option. Travelling door-to-door can save time too. Anywhere within a 10-mile radius of the centre is probably well under an hour's ride away as Cambridge and the Fens are one of the flattest areas of the country. You certainly won't feel isolated. Lots of people ride into the city every day, some using Park and Ride in the same way as car users. Cycle parking is provided at all of the sites. *See the bicycle route map, page 73.*

By train

Ely is particularly well served, with both WAGN and Central train services. Royston and Saffron Walden, on the WAGN line, also get frequent service. To travel in from Bury St Edmunds or Newmarket on Anglia Trains is fast though very infrequent – and you've got to be a complete masochist to take the train from Huntingdon to Cambridge, a distance of 16 miles takes nearly 2 hours! (But the bus service between these points is excellent – see above.)

Transport for the disabled

The disabled (and their carers) are entitled to free bus passes and special parking rights and permits, all of which are available from the local council. They have these options:

TRANSPORT

REGIONAL TRAIN JOURNEY TIMES AND COSTS (RETURN TICKET) TO CAMBRIDGE		
JOURNEY TIME	FREQUENCY	COST (PEAK / OFF-PEAK)
Ely		
15 - 25 mins	20 - 50 mins	£4.20/£5.70
Royston		
15 - 25 mins	15 - 20 mins	£3.70/£3.90
Audley End (Saffron Walden)		
15 - 25 mins	20 - 30 mins	£4/£4.30
Newmarket		
25 mins	1 hr - 1 3/4 hrs	£4/£5.10
Bury St Edmunds		
45 - 55 mins	1 1/2 hr	£7.50/£9.10

A Taxicard scheme is run by the city council for the benefit of elderly and disabled people who are residents of Cambridge city and are unable to use public transport. Up to 100 subsidised trips can be made each year. For details of eligibility contact the City Council representative (01223 457316).

Dial-a-Ride (01223 506335–Cambridge or 01733 394545–Peterborough) is a friendly, charity-run service for those who have difficulty using public transport in Cambridge, surrounding areas, Peterborough and the Fens. A 'ride' can be booked anytime from Monday to Friday, between 9am and 5pm. Call a day ahead to book. The minibus and a smaller vehicle are also available for hire in the evenings and at weekends. All the vehicles are accessible with a wheelchair and fares for the service are £1.80 for a single and £2.80 for a return journey (plus a one-off, £5 registration fee). The service allows carers or relatives to travel with disabled users.

Fenland Association for Community Transport (FACT) (01354 661234) runs a fleet of minibuses for hire by members in the Fenland area. The association also runs a weekly dial-a-bus service (similar to above) in Chatteris, Whittlesey and Wisbech.

TO AND FROM LONDON AND BEYOND

● **London by car – if you dare**

Normally, getting to London by train is comparatively easier than by car. With the train disruptions of late (more on this below) this may temporarily be less true. Even so, it is generally not advisable to go into London by car. Although you might think the journey from Cambridge is simple (straight down the motorway) and as quick as the train (about 1 hour), once you arrive in London you could find yourself either spending an age finding parking on the street or spending a small fortune to park in a multi-storey car park (2 hours can cost £6–£10, while 24 hours is £25–£35). For car park locations in London contact National Car Parks (0870 6067050, website www.ncp.co.uk). To park on the street is nearly impossible on any day other than Sunday or after working hours in the week, and to attempt to travel across London in a car is also wholly inadvisable. If you work or are travelling to the very centre or anywhere south, far west or east in the capital then it will definitely be quicker and easier to commute by train (and underground). Car commuting could be a good idea if your workplace is somewhere in north London or can be accessed only a few junctions east or west from the M11 interchange with the M25, or if you live in an area with bad train links to London (see below). But otherwise, keep the car at home except for the exceptional late or odd journey.

Car to points in East Anglia

Towns easily reachable in 30-60 minutes are Huntingdon, Ely, Newmarket, Haverhill, Saffron Walden, Royston and St Neots. A bit further afield, but still about an hour are Peterborough, Bedford, Stevenage and Bury St Edmunds, whereas King's Lynn, Milton Keynes, Northampton, Luton, Chelmsford, Colchester, Norwich and Ipswich take longer, either as a matter of distance or because routes to these towns tend to be along single carriageway roads where you can easily get stuck behind tractors or lorries.

Easy to reach cities and towns within two hours include Coventry, Leicester and Great Yarmouth. Oxford and Stratford-upon-Avon are no further from Cambridge, but you'll find the drive very hard-going, with journey times generally well over two hours.

Exercise extra caution on the area's rural roads. Traffic density is one and a half times that of the country as a whole and the casualty rate per head of population is 16% higher than the national average.

TRAVEL BY TRAIN

Travelling by train is generally convenient, but concerns about safety across the entire UK network have led to speed restrictions, construction delays and disruptions. The problems were expected to be resolved by mid 2001. But the train remains the popular option. Cambridge is fortunate in its good rail links, especially to London. For travel from Cambridge to other points, typically one travels to London King's Cross, and from there to one of the main London stations to your destination. A (generally) slower alternative when travelling north is to take a train to Peterborough where long-distance GNER trains stop on routes to Leeds, York, Newcastle, Edinburgh, Glasgow and beyond.

Train information

Your best point of contact for information is the National Rail Enquiries (see inset below). You will be able to request information on the best route/company to use for your journey.

TRANSPORT

PRINCIPAL REGIONAL TRAIN COMPANIES

WAGN Railway, Station Road, Cambridge, CB1 2JW (08457 445522 reservations: 0800 566566, e-mail: email@wagnrail.co.uk, website: www.wagn.co.uk).

Central Trains, PO Box 4323, Birmingham, B2 4JB (0121 6541200, reservations: 0870 000 6060, website: www.centraltrains.co.uk).

Anglia Railways, Ipswich Station, Burrell Road, Ipswich, IP2 8AL (01473 693333, reservations: 01603 764776/ 01473 693469, website: www.angliarailways.co.uk).

GNER runs trains north from Peterborough. Station Road, York, YO1 6HT (08457 225333, e-mail: customercare@gner.co.uk, website: www.gner.co.uk).

● online ticket booking and information

The Trainline (0870 0101128, www.thetrainline.com) is an internet service that can be used for booking train tickets and checking prices from and to almost any station in the UK.

The best source for all rail information, local & national, is National Rail Enquiries (08457 484950) website: www.nationalrail.co.uk).

Also, Railtrack has a great timetable checker on its website for any UK train route (Railtrack House, Euston Square, London, NW1 2EE (020 75578000 fax 020 7557 9000, www.railtrack.co.uk).

Commuting by train

Commuters to London from Cambridge, Ely, Royston, Saffron Walden (via Audley End station) and Huntingdon have good access and frequency – Newmarket and Bury St Edmunds much less. Normally, train journeys are swift, comfortable and reliable. Occasionally, bad weather, rail construction (especially at weekends) and other incidents can cause delays. Even so, commuting to London by train is quite a reasonable proposition and many people do so.

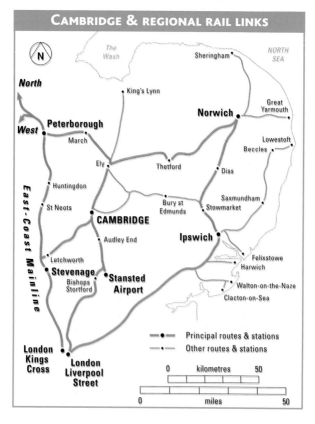

CAMBRIDGE & REGIONAL RAIL LINKS

See Chapter 11, 'Employment', page 221, for more on commuting.

London travel time, frequency & costs

Take the 'Cambridge Cruiser' service non-stop to King's Cross in 45 minutes. It departs every half-hour between 5.30am and 7pm and every hour after 7pm. There are also hourly services that stop at most stations on the route, taking just over an hour. Up to four services (including those to Liverpool Street, see below) leave every hour at peak times and two or three every hour in the evenings.

A return Cambridge-to-London ticket costs £28.70 at peak times (Mon-Fri before 9.30am) or £14.60 off-peak (weekends and Mon-Fri after 9.30am) with an extra 70p-£1.30 for unlimited travel on the underground included. Children under 16 travel for half the price of an adult ticket. Students, young persons (aged 16-25) and senior citizens over 60 may purchase a discount railcard.

● trains to Liverpool Street

If you get on the train to London Liverpool Street the journey takes a little longer (70-90 mins) as the train stops at stations on the way.

● early, late and weekend train service

All the services are operated by WAGN (see above) and on Monday-Friday operate between 4am and 11pm to Liverpool Street, and between 5.30am to 11.30pm to King's Cross. At the weekend there is one 'Cambridge Cruiser' service every hour, one train stopping at stations to King's Cross hourly and one stopping at stations to Liverpool Street once an hour. Weekend trains to King's Cross leave between 6.30am and 11pm, while to Liverpool Street they run from 7.30am to 11pm.

TRAIN TIMES, COST TO LONDON (RETURN)			
Travel time	Frequency	Cost peak/off	Chng
Cambridge			
45mins -1 1/4hrs	15-30 mins	£14.60-£28.70	No
Ely			
1 1/2 hrs-1 3/4 hrs	20-50 mins	£17.90/£29.40	No
Royston			
55 mins - 1 1/4 hrs	15 - 20 mins	£13.50/£24.40	No
Audley End			
1 hr	20 - 30 mins	£11.80/£21.40	No
Huntingdon			
70 - 80 mins	1/2 hr	£15.10/£29.10	No
Newmarket			
1hr 40 mins - 2 1/2 hr	1 hr - 1 3/4 hr	£14.60/£29.80	Yes
Bury St Edmunds			
2 - 21/2 hrs	1/2 hr - 1 hr	£26.40/£43.00	Yes

MONTHLY TICKET PRICES TO LONDON FROM:	
Cambridge	£290
Ely	£296
Royston	£272
Audley End (Saffron Walden)	£257
Huntingdon	£301
Newmarket	£294
Bury St Edmunds	£406

To include underground, bus and train travel in London add about £45 onto the price.

Taking a bicycle on the train

Unless you have one of those commuter bicycles that fold up into the size of a suitcase, taking a bike with you on the train is restricted. When bikes are allowed on, the cost is generally very small, about £1, sometimes even free. For local services it may be possible to turn up with your bicycle, but space on long-distance trains is often restricted and it is best to book the service in advance. Check with the company to see if you can take your bike on a particular train.

Travelling by bus

Any major city in the UK can be accessed from the bus station on Drummer Street in Cambridge either directly or via changeover points like London, Milton Keynes and Birmingham. Most long-distance trips will take longer by coach than by train, though a coach will often work out cheaper, in particular if you are travelling on a weekday before 10am when train journeys can cost up to double in price. The bus is certainly cheaper than train to get to London (£12.50 return) but the journey takes over 2 hours.

● **bus operators**

National Express, PO Box 8026, Birmingham, B5 6ED (08705 808080, website: www.gobycoach.com) runs services to all major cities in the UK. The bus to London links to all the main departures to European cities with Eurolines, 4 Cardiff Road, Luton, LU1 1PP (08705 143219, fax 01582 400694, website: www.eurolines.co.uk).

Jetlink (see page 91 'by airport bus') has services to Norwich (£12 return), Ipswich (£8.25 return) and Oxford (£14 return).

Stagecoach United Counties (01604 620077, website www.stage-coachuc.co.uk) runs its Stagecoach Express Varsity Service X5 to Bedford, Milton Keynes, Bicester and Oxford 16 times every day.

TO AND FROM THE AIRPORTS

● **Cambridge airport**

Lest it be lost in the shuffle, we begin by noting Cambridge has a small, private airport (01223 292525) on Newmarket Road. You can hire helicopters for leisure flights or business or to only one destination – Amsterdam. ScotAir (0870 6060707, website: www.scotairways.co.uk) flies three times daily (Monday to Friday) to Amsterdam.

Choosing an airport

Stansted is closest to Cambridge, less than an hour away and cheap and easy to reach. It's handy for flights to Europe. Luton is next, but a lot harder to get to. As smaller airports, they are easier to get around and less susceptible to delays. Most flights go to Europe. Most long-haul flights, as well as European routes, fly from Heathrow or Gatwick, huge, international airports, which take two or three hours to reach from Cambridge.

London Stansted. A number of important operators to European destinations, such as Lufthansa, fly from here, as well as the recognised budget operators Ryanair, Buzz and Go. (0870 0000303, www.baa.co.uk/main/airports/stansted)

London Luton. This airport has come to prominence with budget operators such as Easyjet and Monarch, who fly from here. Its principal destinations are Spain, France, Switzerland, Scotland and Northern Ireland. (01582 405100, website: www.london-luton.com)

London Heathrow. Flights from Heathrow, the second largest airport in the world, go everywhere. Being so big, and relatively further away, Heathrow is best for travel to other parts of the world. (0870 0000123, website: www.baa.co.uk/main/airports/heathrow)

London Gatwick. Gatwick offers more US destinations (23 at present) than any other airport in Europe. Charter flights and package holidays to European destinations are also very popular from Gatwick, although there are more and more scheduled flights. (01293 535353, website: www.baa.co.uk/main/airports/gatwick)

Best ways to get to & from the airports

For Heathrow or Gatwick, if you like train rides and don't mind lugging bags from train to tube, then the train is reliable and, especially off-peak, the cheapest option. It's the faster option for Gatwick. If you don't want to carry bags and like bus travel, the airport bus is direct and reasonable. For Stansted, train or, possibly, taxi/car is definitely easier and more direct, while bus or, possibly, car/taxi works well for Luton. Taxi can be easy and quick if cost is not a major consideration. Travel by car, taxi or bus to any of the airports is always subject to delays due to traffic.

● **lots of luggage or group travel**

A taxi hire or transfer service may be cheaper, more comfortable and quicker when travelling in a group or with a lot of luggage. Most local taxi companies will take you to the airport (and pick up if you call in advance) or you can check the telephone directory for the the airport transfer companies like Airport Lynx (01954 201350, website: www.airportlynx.co.uk/homepage.htm)

A single car for up to four people costs about:£30 Stansted,

£40 Luton, £65 Heathrow, £80 Gatwick. If more are travelling then a large vehicle transfer takes up to eight people and is even better value.

Heathrow

● by car

The 89-mile journey usually takes about two hours, but traffic jams bedevil the motorways so allow an extra hour on top of the normal two at peak times.

● by train

Leave two and a half hours for the trip. From Cambridge, or the other way round from the Heathrow end, catch a train to King's Cross, take the tube direct on the Piccadilly line all the way to the airport with a Travel Card (£15.30/£34.50 single or return). Alternatively take the Hammersmith & City or Circle line from King's Cross to Paddington rail station, where you can travel directly to the airport (between 5am and 11pm) via the 15-minute trip on the Heathrow Express (0845 6001515, www.heathrowexpress.co.uk), costing, all inclusive of the Cambridge leg and the tube, £27.60 single or £38.80 off peak return and £55.20 peak return.

● by airport bus

Hourly services operated by Jetlink (08705 757747, website: www.gobycoach.com) depart from Cambridge Drummer Street station and Heathrow. The 797 and the 787 service both take two hours and 25 minutes to arrive at the airport. A single ticket costs £18 and a return ticket £26. As with the car journey, the bus may be delayed if there are traffic problems on the M25, so allow an extra hour.

Gatwick

● by car

The 97-mile journey usually takes about two and a half hours. Allow at least an extra hour for possible delays, especially on the M25 motorway.

● by train

From Cambridge, or the other way round from the Gatwick end, take the train to King's Cross, where you change to the Thameslink train (0207 6206333, website: www.thameslink.co.uk) connection to the airport, costing (inclusively) £20.10 for a single and £26.20/£31.40 for a 5-day/unlimited return. It runs between 7am and 11.30pm. Alternatively, for the same cost, take the Victoria line from King's Cross to Victoria rail station and connect to the 30-minute trip Gatwick Express (08705 301530, website: www.gatwick-express.co.uk). It runs every 15 minutes between 5am and 1am, and every hour between 2am and 5am. Either route takes two hours and 35 minutes in total.

● by bus

Hourly services operated by Jetlink (see Heathrow bus above) depart from Cambridge Drummer Street and Heathrow. The 797 and the 787 service both take three hours and 25 minutes to arrive at the airport, and cost £20 for a single and £30 return. As with the car journey, the bus may be delayed if there are traffic problems on the M25, so allow at least an extra hour to arrive.

Stansted

● by car

This 30-mile journey takes just over half an hour as the route runs on the motorway almost all the way.

● by train

Direct trains operated by Central Trains (see box page 85) run from 5am to 8.30pm. The journey takes 30 minutes and costs £6.50 to £6.80 for a single and £13.60 return.

● by bus

Buses run every hour with the combination of two services operated by Jetlink (see 'airport bus' above) which depart from Cambridge Drummer Street. The 757 service takes 40 minutes and the 797 takes 45 minutes to arrive at the airport, and costs £8 for a single and £12 for a return.

Luton

● by car

The 35-mile route to the airport is mostly on small country roads and passes through the centre of a number of towns, so you should allow about an hour and a quarter to reach the airport, with an extra half hour at peak times.

● by train

There is no direct line. Go via London King's Cross and the Thameslink service (see Gatwick above). The trip takes two hours and costs (peak/off peak) £25.70/£21.70 single or £46.80/£36.60 return.

● by bus

Buses run hourly with the combination of two services operated by Jetlink (see 'airport bus' page 91) which depart from Cambridge Drummer Street station. The 767 service takes one hour and five minutes and the 787 takes 1 hour and 15 minutes to arrive at the airport, and both services cost £8 for a single and £12 for a return ticket.

RENTING WHEELS - CAR AND BICYCLE

● bicycle hire

Expect to pay between £4 and £8 for a day's hire, and you should be provided with a helmet, safety lock and night lights. The rate declines for long periods of hire and in the winter, and if you want to try cycling before deciding on which bike you wish to purchase, you can hire a bike for two weeks for £20-£25.

● car hire

Hiring a car is a relatively simple affair. It'll give you freedom to go wherever you like around the region, and you'll be able to get to all those hard-to-get-to places! You will need a valid driving licence (either British, EU or International), a secondary form of identification, a contact address in the UK, and a credit card. Normally you must be over 21 for most cars and vehicles, though some companies are stricter with minimum age requirements of over 23 or 25. If you are under these ages, you may either be refused hire or have to pay a supplement.

BICYCLE SHOPS WITH RENTALS IN CAMBRIDGE

Geoff's Bike Hire, 65 Devonshire Road (01223 365629). Gives guided cycle tours of the historic city lasting over two hours.

Ben Hayward Cycles, 69 Trumpington Street, CB2 1RJ (01223 352294 www.benhaywardcycles.uksw.com). Centrally located with an excellent stock ranging from mountain to city bikes.

Cambridge Cycles, 61 Newnham Road, CB3 9EN (01223 506036). Small and friendly. Cycle hire costs about £10 a day, £20 a week.

Mike's Bikes, 28 Mill Road (01223 312591). A large range of bicycles. Specialises in second-hand bikes and offers a group-hire discount.

A Mill Road bicycle seller.

ADDITIONAL INFORMATION

● bicycling organisations

The following organisations provide advice and further information such as detailed maps of local cycle routes.

Cambridge Cycle Friendly Employers' Scheme (01223 712455) is funded by Cambridge City Council and can help companies to implement and encourage sustainable travel alternatives for their employees.

Cambridge Cycling Campaign, PO Box 204, Cambridge, CB4 3FN (01223 504095, e-mail: camcycle@pobox.co.uk, www.ccdc.cam.ac.uk/camcycle). Collaborates with the county council to encourage safer and more convenient cycling for all.

Cyclists' Touring Club (01223 365003) and *Cambridge*

CAR HIRE IN CAMBRIDGE

Enterprise Rent-a-Car, 162 Histon Road, Cambridge, CB4 3JP (01223 368400 website: www.enterprise.com). A Corsa for a day costs £27, a week is £130, and a weekend is about £50.

National, 264 Newmarket Road, Cambridge CB5 8JL (01223 365438). Day rentals start at £31, a week is £144 and weekend £48. Rents haulage vans too

University Autos, Coldham's Lane, Cambridge CB1 3EP (01223 515151 www.cambridgecarehire.com). A local firm with special discounts for visiting scholars to the universities (ie £6 day for 3 months or more). Rates: £18 per day, £100 a week.

Value Auto Rentals, The Cattle Market, Hills Road, Cambridge, CB2 2RH (01223 412655). Used cars with manual or automatic drives are available from this dealer. Prices start at £25 per day, £40 for the weekend and £125 for a week.

Vauxhall Car and Van Rental, 137 Histon Road, Cambridge, CB4 3JD (01223 356695, fax 01223 366755, e-mail: murketts@murketts.co.uk, www.murketts.co.uk). Daily hires range from £30 to £46, weekend hires from £60 to £92 and a week is £160 to £240.

For many more listings, especially for areas around Cambridge, see the telephone directory.

TRANSPORT

The way it was: 1905 double decker loading up in Market Hill

Photo courtesy of the Cambridgeshire Collection

Cycle Club (www.cambridge-cycling-club.co.uk 01223 842917) are amateur groups for cycling enthusiasts. They organise outings and meet to discuss cycling in Cambridge and the surrounding countryside.

Cycle Training for Adults (01223 712429) is offered by the County Council's Road Safety Section.

● **organisations for the disabled**

The following groups exist to ensure awareness among the disabled of special transport facilities by providing any sort of advice or support, and to ensure that access to transport is maintained and improved.

Cambridge Disabled Access and Transport Group, 4 Plantation Road, Sawston, Cambridge, CB2 4JN (01223 562925). This group provides advice on how disabled people can gain access to regular transport facilities.

Tripscope, Alexandra House, Albany Road, Brentford, Middlesex, TW8 ONE (0208 580 7021) is a national organisation that can also provide advice and information on transport for the disabled and elderly.

● **general regional information**

Cambridgeshire Rural Transport Partnership. Promotes transport in rural areas. 23 Main Street, Littleport, Ely, Cambs. CB6 1PJ (01353 860850).

Cambridge Area Bus Users' Campaign
www.cambuc.org.uk

Environment and Transport Directorate, Cambridge County Council, Shire Hall, Castle Hill, Cambridge, CB3 OAP (01223 717740, fax 01223 717789)
e-mail: passenger.transport@camcnty.gov.uk

UK Public Transport Information (Traveline) (0870 6082608 www.pti.org.uk)

CHAPTER 5
SHOPPING

Photo by F Kember

Shopping made easy. That could be the subtitle for this chapter. Covering the main areas of daily and household needs, from food to computers, it describes the best places to get what you need. The views expressed here are based on our own experiences and, as elsewhere, our opinions are independently reached.

For ease of reference, the outlying areas (which offer less, but are nevertheless of interest) are listed by name at the end of the chapter with a brief outline of the shopping facilities they offer, while for Cambridge itself, facilities are listed under subject categories.

As a regional centre, Cambridge 'punches far above its weight' in terms of what you can get, especially in clothes, with over 100 shops alone, and books, with near 40. When locals still can't find what they need, they make a trip to London or the huge mall in Peterborough. This chapter doesn't venture that far.

What's the best way to get in and around the city? See 'Transport' page 71.

We also don't cover all the interesting nooks and crannies. That we leave to our companion volume, *Cambridge Secrets 2*. Look there for delights like pick-your-own raspberries, locally-produced honey and good value on things for the house and garden.

It also lists many of the fairs and festivals that take place in the area in its calendar and has 20 wonderfully descriptive pages of Cambridge market stalls together with maps of their location and days each stall operates.

For the places to eat and drink, consult the other companion volume, *Best Cafés, Pubs, Clubs and Restaurants in and around Cambridge 2001*, with over 220 listings, lots of vouchers for money off meals, city and regional maps and extensive and easy-to-use indexes. Both books are in book shops or available from the publisher.

CAMBRIDGE PLACES TO SHOP

Below we describe the shopping areas and afterwards we explain where to go for particular goods.

Historic Central Cambridge

As 2001 opened, there were 770 retailers in Cambridge itself, providing food, clothes, electrical goods, books, music, gifts, cars, jewellery and furniture as well as more obscure needs from Belgian chocolates to toy soldiers. The historic city centre is fascinating and attractive, and the shopping area large enough for good choice but not so large that it's overwhelming. Street artists and buskers add interest and colour, especially in the summer, when the proliferation of outdoor café tables give the centre a continental atmosphere. Don't overlook the interesting but quieter Green Street shops and the eclectic blend on King Street.

Cover picture: Fruit on sale on market square, Cambridge.

The Cambridge Market

In the market square next to Great St Mary's church Cambridge, you'll find the weekday market, open Monday to Saturday from 9.30am to 4.30pm (excluding bank holidays). Goods for sale include fresh fruits and vegetables, meats, cheeses, baked goods, flowers, clothing, hats, second-hand books, soaps, pottery and gifts. On Sunday, 10.30am to 4.30pm, the market changes to a craft and farmers' market.

For further information, you can also call 01223 457446 or check cambridgemarkets.co.uk. See also the dedicated section, page 98, below.

The Grafton Centre

The Grafton Centre, located between East Road and Newmarket Road, houses 70 retailers, including major department stores, along with places to eat. Attractive handcart stalls offer an interesting array of crafts and gifts.

The Centre is open from 9.30am to 5.30pm Mondays to Saturdays, and 11am to 5pm on Sundays, with late night shopping on Wednesdays till 7.30pm. For further information contact the Grafton Centre Management Office 01223 316201, Centre Director or the Grafton Centre Information Kiosk, open Mon-Sat 10am-5pm, Sun 11am-5pm.

● Cobble Yard shopping area

Through the Grafton Centre and out at the back (follow the signposts in the Centre) lies Cobble Yard off Napier Street which has an unusual selection of shops and a Post Office.

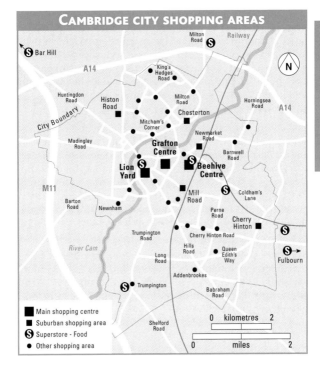

CAMBRIDGE CITY SHOPPING AREAS

SHOPPING

■ Main shopping centre
■ Suburban shopping area
Ⓢ Superstore - Food
● Other shopping area

Mill Road

Mill Road boasts the highest concentration of speciality food markets, tiny off-beat cafés, computer shops and discount bicycle sellers, among other things. It is worth exploring from one end to the other just for the sheer range and variety. The stores tend to be small and owner-run, making shopping here a lot more fun.

It's strictly NO PARKING on Mill Road. Try Gwydir Steet pay-and-display or the Queen Anne car park on Parker's Piece.

Newmarket / Coldham's Lane

The commercial stretch of Newmarket Road, from the Elizabeth Way roundabout down to the railway bridge and the spur on Coldham's Lane including the Beehive Centre (future home of Walmart/Asda), has most of the 'warehouse' superstores, ranging from carpet to kitchen discounters.

SUPERMARKETS AND FOOD

In the historic city centre, the food shopping choices are the market square, Sainsbury's and, the more specialized, Marks & Spencer. Otherwise, you have smaller chain outlets in the mini-malls and the big, super-sized supermarkets dotted around the outskirts of the city.

Food at the Cambridge Market

You can't beat the open market for fun and some of the best and cheapest fruit and veg, much of it locally grown or raised. Other foods include home-baked goods, fresh fish, meats, tea and coffee beans, cheeses and marinated olives, wholefoods and exotic vegetables. The farmers' market sells beef, pork, dairy produce and local vegetables but also commodities such as wild boar and Norfolk seafood.

Historic Centre food stores

The centre is great for variety, convenience and choice. As some foods can be heavy, it helps to buy more frequently and in smaller quantities. If you have more than you can carry, getting goods home can be a challenge, but you can stagger over to the taxi rank on St Andrew's Street or call for a taxi from Sainsbury's. The taxi cannot use Sidney Street from 10am-4pm except on Sunday, but will pick you up at the Halfords on the corner of Jesus Lane.

● Sainsbury's on Sidney Street

Sainsbury's offers a full range of goods. It has recently been expanded to include a snacks and coffee section. Sainsbury's selections tend to be looked upon as a cut above the other supermarkets, in part due to the influence of cookery guru Delia Smith.

44-46 Sidney Street (01223 366891). Open Mon-Fri 8am-9pm, Sat 7.30am-9pm, Sun 11am-5pm.

● Marks & Spencer on market square

A good M&S (high quality and classy) which offers excellent food if you like your baking potatoes washed and cling-wrapped (as opposed to rough and ready on the market a few steps away). It also does a wide range of ready meals and salads, good wines, gorgeous nibbles and chocolates. *See also, below, under 'department stores'.*

Market square. (01223 355219) Open Mon-Tue 8.30am-7pm, Wed 8.30am-8pm, Thu-Fri 8am-8pm, Sat 8am-7pm, Sun 11am-5pm.

Big supermarket shopping

● Sainsbury's in Coldham's Lane

This much larger Sainsbury's underwent major refurbishment in October 2000. It boasts a Food To Go counter, salad bar, restaurant, Adams children's wear and Early Learning Centre toys, electrical section and Homeshop, and good deli, meat, fish and bakery stalls.

Brooks Road, off Coldham's Lane, a short drive eastwards out of the city centre (01223 246183), Mon & Tues 8am-10pm, Wed-Thu 8am-11pm, Fri 8am through to Sat 10pm, Sun 10am- 4pm.

● 24-hour Tesco Bar Hill, Fulbourn & Milton

A huge 'Tesco Extra' store selling food, clothes, DIY, gardening equipment and more (and where staff get about on roller skates) is at Viking Way, Bar Hill, five miles north-west of Cambridge on the A14, while a couple of miles northeast on the same road there's a more manageable version (but

SHOPPING

without the clothes and music) at Cambridge Road in Milton. Both have pharmacies. There's also a Tesco at Yarrow Road in Fulbourn, which does home delivery around Cambridge via www.tescodirect.com. Tesco is good, reliable and practical but somehow never quite achieves the upmarket image of Sainsbury's.

Tesco, Bar Hill (01954 227400); Tesco, Milton (01223 548400); Tesco Fulbourn (01223 548300). All are open 24 hours Mon 8am through to Sat 10pm, Sun 10am-4pm.

● Waitrose

Waitrose, which opened in October 2000 on Hauxton Road, Trumpington, doesn't sell petrol but you can scan your shopping yourself if you're a Waitrose or John Lewis card holder, to save time. It also has a ready meal bar with Indian and Chinese takeaway food, organic produce and salads. You can have your shopping delivered, and for its size (220 parking spaces) the range is good.

Open: Mon-Thu 8.30am-8pm, Fri 8.30am-9pm, Sat 8.30am-7pm, Sun 10am-4pm (01223 845777) or www.waitrose.com.

● Asda/Walmart former Beehive Centre

In late 2001 at the earliest, a new 70,000 square-foot Asda food store or Walmart, which one is not clear at the time of writing, will open in what was known locally as the Beehive Centre off Coldham's Lane. Watch this space...

Ethnic supermarkets

Cho Mee 108 Mill Road (354399) sells Chinese food stuffs, noodles, Chinese cabbage and other fresh vegetables.

Balv's Superette, 158 Mill Road (01223 213182), sells Afro and Asian foodstuffs.

Oriental Stores, 37 Newnham Road (01223 314416),

Select specialist food outlets

Burwash Manor Farm. New Road, Barton (01223 264600). Farm shop, café and craft shops. See 'Home Decor' below.

The Cambridge Cheese Co, 4 All Saints Passage, Cambridge (01223 328672). Fine cheeses, olives etc.

Derby Street Stores, 26 Derby Street, Newnham (01223 354391). Continental and special treats – go in just for the smell.

J. Curtis, 45 Burleigh Street (01223 354396). Fabulous speciality breads.

Limoncello, 204 Mill Road (01223 507036). A cheerful little Italian deli.

Loch Fyne Oyster Bar, 37 Trumpington St (01223 362433). Beautiful, sumptuous displays of fish.

Waller and Son, 15 Victoria Avenue (01223 350972). Proudly old-fashioned meats and game.

W Eaden Lilley, 15/16 Sussex St (01223 365473). A food hall with tempting cheeses and savouries and a café with a wide range of quality speciality and gourmet foods.

sells Thai and Southeast Asian and Indian foods.

Nasreen Dar 18-20 Histon Road (01223 568013) sells the best selection of Indian foods along with a wide range of general items.

Al Amin at 100A-102A Mill Road (01223 567397) sells Mediterranean, Middle Eastern, Sri Lankan and Indian ingredients.

The nearest parking for these stores is on sidestreets. They are most convenient for on-foot access.

Cut-price food stores

Recommended for cut-price foods is *Aldi* on Histon Road, next to the Esso station. It sells decent everyday food with no fancy displays at bargain prices with an adequate car park and the fastest checkout in the known galaxy. There is also an *Iceland* (for frozen foods) next door and at 8-10 Fitzroy Street.

Aldi is open Mon-Wed 9am-6pm, Thu-Fri 9am-7pm, Sat 8.30am-5.30pm, Sun 10am-4pm. Customer services (0990 134 363). Iceland is on Histon Road (01223 324948) and 6 Fitzroy Street (01223 369879). All foods are GM free.

Health foods, organic & fair trade

Arjuna Wholefoods, 12 Mill Road (01223 364845), a vegetarian cooperative committed to organic foods and stocking a vast range of teas, flours, breads, jams and even organic wine and fresh organic vegetables.

Daily Bread at 3 Kilmaine Close, King's Hedges Road (01223 423177), a superb wholefood warehouse providing practical aid to the Third World and a vast range at excellent value and organic vegetables. You can park outside.

Emerald Wholefoods, a highly recommended market stall.

A *Fair Trade Shop* is located in the foyer of the Emmanuel United Reformed Church on Trumpington Street (at Little St Mary's Lane). Open on Wednesday, Thursday and Friday from 10.30am-3pm, it sells Traidcraft gifts and foods (tea, coffee, dried foods, nuts, chocolate and more) and is also a café run by the disabled. You can also buy the goods after the service on Sundays (approx. 12.15pm till 1pm).

In the city centre you'll also find *Cambridge Health Food* at 5 Bridge Street (01223 350433) (which also does delicious hot or cold takeaways) and *Holland and Barrett* at both 4 Bradwell's Court (01223 368914), and 58 Grafton Centre (01223 314544). *Culpeper* the herbalist at 25 Lion Yard (01223 367370) sells honey and spices.

DEPARTMENT STORES

In the section following this one, we detail the outlets specializing in each area. But we don't want you to overlook (as if you could) the department stores, which typically cover the gamut – house and garden, clothes and computers/electronics – and often a lot more. Here we briefly describe each one and its particular qualities.

● Robert Sayle

'Never knowingly undersold' as their slogan says, and ultra-reliable. Old fashioned service and proper advice. Clothes of all descriptions plus a huge choice of fabrics, curtain-making service, an upmarket choice of housewares and lighting, crockery, cosmetics, a large selection of toys, computers/audio among other things.

12-17 St Andrew's Street (01223 361292) closed Mondays and Sundays

● Marks & Spencer

The name for quality food (see page 99 above) and affordable, durable family wear. Where every woman buys most of her underwear and from where all men receive socks and jumpers for Christmas. Making a big push to join the fashion bandwagon.

6-11 Sidney Street and on market square (01223 355219).

● BhS

A good balance between upmarket, affordable and practical. Wide range of family clothes, accessories and an excellent lighting department.

Unit 29, Grafton Centre (01223 358126).

● Debenham's

Clothing, makeup, handbags, kitchenware, bedding – an all-encompassing store of the type now less seen.

36-40 Grafton Centre (01223 353525).

● Argos

Not a department store, but sells much of the same range at discount, if you don't mind ordering from a catalogue and waiting in line (or getting it delivered – 0870 600 2020).

A big, new store at the Cambridge Retail Park, on Newmarket Road, and one in Bradwell Court on St Andrew's Street: www.argos.co.uk .

MEDICINES AND TOILETRIES

There are numerous dispensing chemists in both city centre and surrounding areas. At Christmas/New Year some stay open on a published rota that can be obtained from GPs or the police in an emergency. Here are the big outlets:

● Boots the Chemist

The three local branches all dispense prescriptions and sell a wide range of drugs, medicines and sundries. At the city-centre branches you can drop off a prescription and call back later to collect it. Grafton Centre Boots is open late on Wednesdays.

28 Petty Cury, Mon 9am-5.30pm, Tue-Fri 8.45am-5.30pm, Sat 8.30am-6pm, Sun 11am-5pm (01223 350213); 41-42 Grafton Centre, Mon-Tue & Thu-Fri 9am-5.30pm, Wed 9am-7.30pm, Sat 9am-6pm, Sun 11am-5pm (01223 302576), and a major new megastore on Newmarket Road (01223 356305).

● pharmacy at Tesco

There is no longer an evening rota published in the press for pharmacists, except occasionally for bank holidays, so Tesco is the best bet for out-of-hours prescriptions.

The Milton branch's pharmacy (Cambridge Road Industrial Estate, 01223 548400) is open from 8am to 9pm Mon-Sat and 10am-4pm on Sundays. The Bar Hill Tesco's pharmacy (on Viking Way, 01954 227400) is open from 8am till 10pm Mon-Sat and 10am-4pm on Sundays. There is no pharmacy at the Fulbourn branch of Tesco.

See Tesco above under food for more details.

● Superdrug

Superdrug is a useful shop for general medical needs such

RECOMMENDED CONVENIENCE STORES

Alldays convenience stores, 40b Green End Road (01223 425632) and 249-251 Chesterton Road (01223 566721). Run-of-the-mill foods for when you run out.

Andrews, 24-25 Burleigh Street (01223 311709). Butcher with fish and deli.

Chester and Son, 30a Chesterton Road (01223 355556). Fruit and veg and very friendly.

Co-op stores are dotted about on Chesterton Road, Grantchester Street, Hills Road, Mill Road, Histon Road and Milton Road. Again, useful for when you just want to top up but don't expect to find sun-dried tomatoes.

Nasreen Dar 18-20 Histon Road (01223 568013). Sells the best selection of Indian foods along with a wide range of general items.

Samuel A. Smiley, 68 Trumpington Street (01223 518864). Interesting grocer's.

Thornhills, 41 Burleigh Street (01223 35701). Bakers and confectioners.

as cold remedies and the Sidney Street branch has a dispensing chemist.

Branches are at 38 Fitzroy Street (01223 352917) and 59 Sidney Street (01223 362499).

HOUSEHOLD

This section covers the main things one typically needs for a house or flat with garden or windowbox.

Kitchen goods

Elizabeth David Cookshop, 22 Fitzroy St, (01223 3321579). Has a good range of quality kitchen utensils.

Lakeland Ltd, 52 Sidney Street (01223 301418). Everything from an oyster knife to a garden table.

Spoils Kitchen Reject Shop, 4-7 Sussex Street (01223 316518). Great bargains. Also at the Grafton Centre. Not just kitchen stuff – all kinds of household accessories.

Woolworths, Sidney Street, (01223 357168). A wide range at attractive prices.

Big Household & DIY

For the do-it-yourself consumer the large chains provide more small portion, bubble-packed options, and often economical choices on the standard range of goods. Advice, and sometimes assistance, can be hard to find and quality can vary. The builder's merchants can be very competitive, often give expert advice and carry many more speciality and professional products.

● big DIY stores

B & Q, 400 Newmarket Road, (01223 323432). A vast warehouse-sized store for everyman's DIY paint, decorations, lighting, tools and garden. Open Mon-Sat 8am-8pm, 10am-4pm Sun.

Homebase, Coldham's Lane (01223 360888). Offers a particularly wide range of low-cost goods. Open Mon-Sat 8am-8pm, Fri 8am-9pm, Sun 10am-4pm.

Great Mills, Tenison Road (01223 362000). A bit smaller, but with a similar array to B & Q. Open Mon-Sat 8am-8pm, Sun 10.30am-4.30pm.

● builder's merchants, DIY speciality

Mackay's, 85 East Road (01223 517000), sells a good range of power and hand tools along with ironmongery, speciality paints, ladders and garden goods. Park round the back. Open Mon-Fri 8am-5.15pm, Sat 8am-5pm, Sun 10am-4pm.

Ridgeons, a local builders' merchants with a consumer side, has sites at Cromwell Road and at Nuffield Road (both 01223 466000). The former in particular offers a wide choice, speciality items unavailable in chain stores, and excellent quality. Open Mon-Fri 7.30am-5pm, Sat 8am-4pm.

● Small stores

Bishop's DIY, Cambridge Road, Histon (01223 570555), has most of what you usually need and is small and friendly. Open Mon-Sat 8.30am-5.30pm.

Cutlacks, 264 Mill Road (01223 246418). For DIY and household goods. Enormously helpful.

Garden

Apart from the places listed below, the Cambridge University Gardening services sell off quality spare plants at good prices twice yearly in mid-May, end September. Call 01223 357059 for information.

● big local outlets

Ansell's Garden Centre, High Street, Horningsea (01223 860320). Largish, varied gardening centre with conservatories, aquatics, furniture, gift shop etc.

Scotsdale Garden Centre, 120 Cambridge Road, Great Shelford (01223 842777). Huge, imposing, impersonal and sometimes overpriced centre, but it does stock just about everything. There's often a little display of tents through the hedge in the adjoining field that's also worth looking at.

● big and medium outlets in the area

Frost's at Willington Garden Centre, Sandy Road, Willington, near Bedford (01234 838777). Well worth going a few extra miles, but you need half a day to look round. An award-winning and extremely large centre with a huge range, lots of water features (more tasteful than many) and a café overlooking a beautiful small lake.

The Garden Centre at Saffron Walden, Thaxted Road, Saffron Walden (01799 527580). Another one with a good name, worth a visit. Coffee house, gift shop, aquatics and water features, sheds and furniture.

Photo by Dan Porter

Roxton Garden Centre, Roxton (on the A421 to Bedford) (01480 212701). Again, worth a little drive out. A pleasant medium-sized centre with prices usually a little lower than average.

Tyler's Garden Centre, Inglewood, Shepreth (01763 260412). Pots, plants, water features and café. Keen prices and a very large choice.

The Grafton Centre by night

SHOPPING

● small and speciality outlets

Coton Orchard, Cambridge Road, Coton (01954 210234). Makes a pleasant trip. Good large café, homemade apple juice and large gift section.

Madingley Mulch, St Neot's Road, Coton, Cambridge (01954 212144). Not a garden centre but a supplier of a fascinating range of mulches, composts, soils, sands and gravels all with names and descriptions that sound appetising enough to eat. Delivered to your door in vast bags - get your fiver back when you return the bag.

Oakington Garden Centre, Dry Drayton Road, Oakington (01223 234818). Small and friendly. Plants, shrubs, houseplants.

Sanders, 40 Hobson Street (01223 350091). The only garden specialist in the city centre. Useful if you're in town and desperate for something, otherwise go to one of the larger suppliers as Sanders is quite small. No credit cards.

Home decor & furniture

● department store options

Robert Sayles (see details under department stores, above) offers a full home decor service, with all accessories and some furniture.

Habitat, 9-17 Fitzroy Street (01223 323644). A branch of the London chain with everything from fabrics to furniture. Has its own minimalist style.

MFI, 266 Newmarket Road (01223 360522), a massive superstore with economy, self-assembly furniture.

● dedicated furniture stores

Blend of Magic Ltd, 2 Tredgold Lane, Napier Street, (01223 303202). Sells ethnic and contemporary, solid hardwood and softwood furniture bought from around the world - India, Java, Mexico and Indonesia.

Cambridge Dreams, 172 East Road (01223 300822) sells a wide range of beds and futons.

Futon Company, Regent Street, (01223 303537) quality futons and accessories.

Tohiti Interiors (King Street Furnishing), 6-16 King Street (01223 361668) and 208 Cherry Hinton Road (01223 412662). A mix of contemporary and classic choices, with an especially good choice of quality, clean contemporary lines and Scandinavian style. Assembly service.

Multiyork Furniture Ltd, 1 Milton Road (01223 313463). A chain outlet famed for sofas with made-to-measure covers.

Pine Merchant, 69a Lensfield Road (01223 314377). Has a good selection of stripped pine with polite service.

Sharp's Bedrooms Ltd, 57-61 Burleigh Street (01223 350633). Makes specialist fitted bedrooms.

Wesley Barrell, 62 Regent Street (01223 460377). A mainly traditional branch of a national chain.

Soft furnishings

At Home, 44 Newnham Road (01223 321283). Sells the unusual fabrics, wallpapers and borders. Patient staff. Couple of parking spaces in front of the shop.

Curtains, 16 Norfolk Street (01223 319191). An exchange and try-out service for quality second hand.

Curtain Workshop, Dapple Farm, Oakington Road, Girton. Loads of room to park. Ring 01223 575669 to find when the shop is open.

East, 62 Sidney Street (01223 324577). Has Anokhi soft furnishings.

Laura Ashley, 14 Trinity Street/Green Street (01223 351378), was recently refurbished. Their full range is also available through Homebase (see page 104 above) and can be ordered from their catalogue. Known for their fresh, country style cottons and pretty accessories.

Providence and *Summerhouse,* Burwash Manor Farm, New Road, Barton (01223 264600). Two lovely shops in a lovely setting selling special paints, fabrics etc.

Roseby's, 34 Fitzroy Street (01223 312170). Curtains and soft furnishings made-to-measure. Practical rather than exciting.

Soft Options, St Peter's Street (01223 311656) Luxurious quality in pretty shop. Park in adjacent streets.

● economy furnishings

QD, 62 Burleigh Street (01223 323174). One of Cambridge's all too rare bargain shops. Always worth a poke around – curtains, rugs, crockery, baskets clothes.

● rugs and other accessories

Evolution, 3 Fitzroy Street (01223 367983). Interesting and more economical accessories, throws and ornaments from around the world.

Fired Earth, 3 Bridge Street (01223 300941). Sells tiles and rugs to drool over. Can be pricey.

Nomads, 5 King's Parade (01223 324588). Has a fabulous range of kilims and Eastern artefacts.

SHOPPING

Original artworks, crafts & framing

All Saints' Garden Art and Craft Market, Trinity Street. 10am-5pm Saturday plus Fridays in June; Thursdays and Fridays in July and August; Fridays in November; Wednesdays, Thursdays and Fridays in December and summer bank holiday Mondays. All stall holders are local and they make everything they sell. City council information ring 01223 457512 or go to www.cambridge-art-craft.co.uk

Balthazar Crafts, Fisher Hall, Guildhall Place (01223 247370). Selection by East Anglian artists, hats, devore scarves, prints, handmade cards. Gold and silver jewellery can be commissioned. Repairs and cleaning. Open 9.30am to 5pm every Saturday, some weekdays in December.

Broughton House Gallery, 98 King Street (01223 314960). Regular exhibitions of British and International contemporary art. Open Tue-Sat 10.30am-5.30pm.

Cambridge Contemporary Art, 6 Trinity Street, (01223 324222). An exciting collection of paintings, prints, sculpture and crafts. Framing service.

Conservation Gallery, 6 Hills Road (01223 211311). Wide selection. Paintings, jewellery, bags and wall hangings.

Julia Heffer, 2 Sussex Street (01223 367699). Selection of contemporary jewellery, studio glass, ceramics, leather bags, furniture and textiles.

Lawson Gallery, 7/8 King's Parade (01223 313970). Antique prints and maps, modern art posters, postcards.

Primavera, 10 King's Parade (01223 357708). Leading British contemporary ceramics, wood, glass, craftwork, metalwork, painting, sculpture, furniture and jewellery.

St Barnabas Press, Open-access Printmaking Studio and Gallery, The Belfast Yard, Coldham's Lane (01223 576221). See the artists at work and view their works.

Sebastian Pearson, 3 Pembroke Street (01223 365454) Watercolours and oil paintings.

Suisho Gallery, 11 Norfolk Street (01223 575065). Work of artists from the UK, USA, Japan, Peru, Spain and China.

(See also 'Exhibitions and Galleries', page 169)

CLOTHES & FOOTWEAR

Cambridge has over 100 clothing shops. The Grafton Centre, with over 25 big-name outlets, houses the wide-ranging department stores: *BhS* (01223 358126), with nicely designed practical wear, and *Debenham's* (01223 304163) which stocks other retailers' and designer lines.

The historic centre has a number of the big names too, along with most of the fashion and independent shops and the all-important clothing staple of the English home, *Marks & Spencer* (01223 355219), with clothes for the entire family, on market square and 6-11 Sidney Street.

High street and brand name stores

● **women's wear**

Dorothy Perkins, Grafton Centre (01223 323674) and Petty Cury (01223 316684), has practical, bearably priced, young to middle-aged fashion including maternity wear.

Evans, for women size 16 and above, is at the Grafton Centre (01223 461503) and at Lion Yard (01223 369274).

French Connection, Rose Crescent. Also sells men's wear (01223 311966).

The Gap, market square, also men's and children's wear in Gap Kids next door (01223 352154).

Hobbs, Trinity Street (01223 361704).

Jaeger, Trinity Street, also for men (01223 361745).

Jeffrey Rogers, Lion Yard (01223 311448).

Jigsaw, Market Street (01223 312955).

Karen Millen, Market Street (01223 304502).

Laura Ashley, (01223 351378), Trinity Street/Green Street, clothes and home furnishings.

Monsoon, Sidney Street (01223 353226) and its sales store on Rose Crescent (01223 361507) do women's and children's wear.

Next, with slightly upmarket practical fashionable men's, women's and children's wear, is at the Grafton Centre (01223 462282) and at Petty Cury (01223 369396).

Phase 8, Trinity Street (01223 316412).

Principles, Grafton Centre, (01223 313187). Sells classy women's and men's wear including smart work and party gear, suits and lingerie.

Richards, Grafton Centre, (01223 362439). Smart, practical women's wear plus dressier clothes.

River Island, Petty Cury (01223 369280).

Viyella, on Trinity Street (01223 354055).

● men's wear

Austin Reed, on Sidney Street, sells smart men's suits, coats and casual wear (01223 356982).

Burton Men's Wear, Grafton Centre (01223 313933). A long-established all-encompassing men's wear shop.

Ciro Citterio, (01223 355979) in Petty Cury.

French Connection see above.

Gap, see above.

Jaeger, see above.

Jigsaw, see above.

Next, see women's above.

Principles, see above.

The Suit Company, in Petty Cury (01223 356347). Sells men's suits and formal wear.

Topman, Market Hill (01223 316405).

Designer, fashion and independents

Many of the smaller, independent designers have chosen to set themselves apart, on the quieter side streets and lanes.

● women's clothing

Baska Design, 18 Magdalene Street (01223 353800). Silky scarves and special hats and accessories, from formal to slightly weird.

Blu Max, 2 and 18 King Street (01223 352668). Designer jeanswear, (eg Moschino, Versace, D & G, Iceberg, Valentino) smart/casual, for men and women.

Bowns, 25 Magdalene St (01223 302000). Vivienne Westwood, John Rocha, Boyd, Paul & Joe, Ozbek and more.

Catfish 5 Green Street (01223 368088), (first floor, above *Dogfish*, for men 01223 368008). Upmarket designer streetwear, including Diesel. Chiefly mid-20s clientele.

Christiane Roberts, 2 Bene't Street (01223 361752). Range of designer labels.

East, 62 Sidney Street (01223 324577). Clothes and accessories in colourful natural fabrics, designed to be very individual. See also under 'Soft Furnishings'.

Giulio, 20-32 King Street (01223 316100). Designer retail – Jill Sander, Paul Smith, Prada, Voyage, Burberry, Gucci, Earl Jeans, Joomi Joolz, Custo Barcelona and accessories. See also under men's below.

Gun Hill Clothing, 17 King's Parade (01223 350449). Women's and men's casual clothing: Mulberry, Jackpot, Whitestuff among others.

Hero, 3 Green Street (01223 328740). Special, feminine designer clothes, unusual cuts and fabrics. Different.

Jane/Brides at Jane, 17&19 Sussex Street (01223 314455). Cream of British, Irish and continental designers. Huge variety in literally every size, and they can kit you out from hat to shoes. One-to-one personal service for weddings, formal to informal. Qualified fitters on the premises.

Javelin, 17 Green Street, (01223 327320). Casual and smart wear – Peter Werth, French Connection, Gas, Quicksilver, O'Neill, Lipsy, Firetrap etcetera.

Pachamama, Green Street (01223 367768). Colourful knits made in Equador and Nepal and accessories.

Sahara, 3 St Mary's Passage (01223 366277). Describes its range as 'designs for alternative, free-spirited individuals, comfortable and elegant'.

Troon Ltd, 16 King's Parade (01223 360274). All ages, all sizes, all budgets, but goes right up to top designers - Betty Jackson, Jasper Conran, Adolpho Dominguez and more.

● **men's clothing**

Antony, Trinity Street, (01223 360592). Hugo Boss, Canali, Eton shirts.

Arthur Shepherd, Trinity Street (01223 353962). Quality country clothing, eg Barbour.

Blu Max, see above.

Dogfish, see Catfish above.

Fellow's, 5 Bene't Street (01223 301001). Wide-ranging designer wear for anyone from 16 to 65. Smart suits to casual T-shirts and jumpers. Accessories - shoes, cufflinks etc.

Giulio, 20-32 King Street (01223 316100). Designer retail – Prada, Maharishi, Jill Sander, Giorgio Armani, Hugo Boss, Paul Smith, DKNY, Burberry and more, plus accessories.

Gun Hill Clothing, see above.

Javelin, see above.

Reeves, 62-64 King Street (01223 322301). Casual, designer wear – Lacoste, Thomas Burberry, Firetrap and more.

Maternity & children's

There are a number of outlets in the city centre which offer a good and reasonable range of maternity wear:

SHOPPING

● maternity

Dorothy Perkins, see women's wear.

Robert Sayle, see listing under department stores above.

Mothercare, 26 Grafton Centre   01223 460325). Specialises in all requirements from conception to reception.

● children's clothing

Baby Care, 34 Burleigh Street (01223 355296). Baby clothes and goods.

Gap Kids, 2 Market Hill (01223 324101) and *Gymboree*, 23 Market Street (01223 353527) Trendy children's wear.

The Gap, see women's wear.

Monsoon, see women's wear.

Mothercare, 26 Grafton Centre, (01223 460325) and *Adams* 30 Grafton Centre (01223 462720). Babies' and children's wear.

Next, see men's and women's wear.

QD and *QS*, (see below) are good for cheap familywear.

Sunrise, 8 Burleigh Street (01223 350661) and *Tammy Girl*, 65 St Andrew's Street (01223 353771) Young fashion.

Young Things, 59 Grafton Centre (01223 312236). Babies' and children's wear.

Miscellaneous & economy

● suit hire, college ties, gowns etc

Below are the fine, longstanding Cambridge/University establishments from the old school – just going in makes you feel part of Cambridge's history. Suit hire and college ties, gowns etc.

A.E.Clothier, 13 King's Parade (01223 354339).

Ede and Ravenscroft, 71 Trumpington Street (01223 350048).

Ryder and Amies, 22 King's Parade (01223 350371).

For low budget clothes shopping you can't do any better than Burleigh Street – it has no less than seven charity shops, as well as *QD* (see under Home Decor, above), and there's also *QS* just round the corner on Fitzroy Street (01223 314131). Further charity shops can be found at 30, 42 and 110 Regent Street and 21 Magdalene Street.

The market is another good source of bargains, with a wonderful ethnic stall. *Dixie Jane* has a bargain table with £1 items, but the rest of the items are more. *See also Royston and Saffron Walden, below.*

● T-shirts

Talking Ts, 37 Bridge Street, will print your design on a quality T-shirt and sells a huge range of their own designs.

Sports & outdoors

● Grafton Centre sports/sports wear

Allsports (01223 460789). Carries skateboards, general

sports wear, trainers, shoes and some accessories.

Gilesports (01223 462257). Has clothing and equipment for sports – rugby, tennis, football, running etc.

● **historic centre sports/sports wear**

First Sport, Lion Yard (01223 356855). Has ranges of sports footwear and fashion clothing for men and women. Also, hockey, tennis, snooker and swimwear.

Grays Sports, 36 Sidney Street (01223 362428). Traditional sports shop specialising in hockey, tennis and cricket. Also has a big range of running and swimwear.

Hobbs, 38 Trinity Street (01223 358449). Rugby gear, sports equipment. Small and very friendly.

JJB Sports, 1-5 Bradwell's Court (01223 351330). Tracksuits, swimwear, shorts, good range of sports clothing and accessories. Not too much in the way of sports equipment – emphasis is on clothing.

Team Spirit, 2 Emmanuel Street (01223 313135). Specialists in football – replica shirts, shirt printing for Premier League and also Formula One racing gear.

● **camping, hiking, outdoors and travel**

Army and Navy stores, 29 Hobson Street (01223 502645) and 39a St Andrew's Street (01223 576564). Sells armed forces surplus goods.

Blacks, 38 Regent Street (01223 314335). Useful city centre outdoor clothing and camping outlet.

Milletts, 26 St Andrew's Street (01223 352169). Again, usefully placed. Thermals, fleeces, outdoor gear, camping.

Open Air, 11 Green Street (01223 324666) and a boots shop at no. 29 Green Street. Specialises in lightweight camping and trekking. Probably the largest outdoor clothing range in Cambridge. Quality stuff.

Rohan, Trinity Street (01223 356729). Well-designed travel clothes for the sophisticated traveler.

Simpers, 17 Mercers Row (01223 351729). A brilliant range. Outdoor clothing warehouse. Barbour, Driza-bone, Berghaus. Camping equipment also.

YHA Services Ltd, 6 Bridge Street (01223 353956). Down the stairs – outdoor clothes, camping equipment – they've usually got what you want. Friendly too.

Footwear

Many of the clothes stores listed in the Clothes section, above, supply shoes to complement their ranges.

● **department stores**

Robert Sayle has a good shoe department with high quality names for outdoor, casual and special occasions if you have the energy to walk upstairs.

Marks and Spencer stocks a good range of practical and comfortable shoes which usually manage to be fashionable without being outlandish and sensible without being

SHOPPING

fuddy-duddy.

BhS Same as for Marks and Spencer.

Debenham's with higher priced designer and special occasion shoes as well as the more practical kind.

● **high street and brand name stores**

Barratt's, Grafton Centre (01223 323676). Practical fashion and school, low to middle price range.

Clark's, Grafton Centre (01223 314374 also at Petty Cury, 01223 368486). Quality comfort shoes.

Dolcis, Lion Yard (01223 300293). Trendy girl's and women's.

Dorothy Perkins, Grafton Centre (01223 323674). Small range of women's fashion shoes among the clothes.

Ravel, Petty Cury (01223 302982). Pricier range designer shoes.

Stead and Simpson, Grafton Centre, (01223 369584). Similar to Barratt's.

● **small and independent retailers**

A. Jones and Sons, 5 St Andrew's Street (01223 354983). High quality shoe shop.

Amanda Green, 16 St John's Street (01223 300677). Decorative, special, feminine, classy and non-budget.

Blu Max, 18 King Street (01223 500710). *See under women's and men's wear, above.*

Jonathan James, 61 Burleigh Street (01223 354989). Budget shoes, chiefly for young things and family.

K Shoes, 9 Bradwell's Court (01223 356270). The comedienne Victoria Wood says you know when you're getting older when you pass a K shoe shop and think, 'Mmm, they look comfy.' It's true, and they are.

Smiths, 127 Milton Road (01223 356842). Excellent for kids with unusual sizes. Attention paid to fitting properly.

Sundaes/Eccolet, 37 Green Street (01223 361536). Beautifully made handmade shoes and Ecco, for when comfort, but not cost, is paramount.

Raw, 7 Peas Hill (01223 302306). Hefty, aggressive-looking shoes for those for whom street cred is a must-have.

BOOKS AND MUSIC

With nearly 40 booksellers and stationers in Cambridge, you can usually find or at least order just about anything. This list has been hand-picked for good service and interest.

● **mainstream booksellers**

Borders the big American bookshop opens in 2001 on Market Street, next to the WHSmith. It is renowned as a leader in mixing media with cafés.

Browne's, 56 Mill Road (01223 350968). Friendly shop with a good selection of popular titles.

Cambridge University Press Bookshop, 1 Trinity Street,

(01223 333333). Sells the press's vast range of books, mainly academic, but including many popular and even some children's titles.

Heffers, 28b Grafton Centre (01223 568573) and 20 Trinity Street (01223 568568). Reliable and reputable bookstores, now a part of the Blackwells chain, but homegrown. Trinity Street also stocks academic, art and architecture, antique books and large scale maps. Children's Heffers is at 29-30 Trinity Street (01223 568551).

Waterstone's, 6-7 Bridge Street (01223 300123) and 22 Sidney Street (01223 351668). Two large general stores, one a few doors further down from the other. Both have pleasant cafés upstairs, plus plenty of interesting events and-signings.

● remainders and bargain books

Booksale, 14-16 Bradwell's Court (01223 361529). Budget books and stationery which often includes some remarkable bargains - worth a root round any time you're passing.

CB1 Internet Cafe, 32 Mill Road (01223 576306) and *CB2 Internet Bistro*, 5-7 Norfolk Street (01223 508503). Eat, drink and browse through thousands of second-hand books.

Galloway & Porter, 30 Sidney Street (01223 367876). Large bargain bookshop containing some real finds, new and secondhand, and glossy 'coffee table' books.

Oxfam, 28 Sidney Street (01223 313373). Surprisingly big selection of second-hand books.

● antiquarian & speciality

Monthly antiquarian book sale takes place at Fisher Hall, on the second Tuesday of the month (01245 361609).

Amana Books Ltd, 1 All Saints' Passage (01223 366033). Bibles, Christian books and the writing of Watchman Nee.

The Haunted Bookshop 9 St Edward's Passage (01223 312913). Second-hand books, collectable children's books and ephemera.

G. David, 16 St Edward's Passage (01223 354619). Cut-price new books, antiquarian, with expertise and atmosphere. Must not be missed by any with true book addiction.

Music / media and instruments

● big national outlets

The big national chains all have outlets, including *Virgin Megastore*, 28 Grafton Centre (01223 360333); HMV, 12-15 Lion Yard (01223 319090), and the smaller, *Virgin*, 4 Bridge Street (01223 363221). All assail you with loud music and cater more for the populer/younger market, especialy the teen buyer.

● local popular music sellers

But if you want a bit more individuality, try:

Andy's, 29-33 Fitzroy Street (01223 361038). Comprehensive, well-chosen selection of records, tapes or CDs.

Garon Records, 70 King Street (01223 362086). Books and music.

Jays, 50 Burleigh Street (01223 368089). Specialises in Indie, HipHop, R & B, dance and Vinyl.

Parrot, 93 King Street (01223 312552). Stocks a popular selection.

Rhythm Syndicate, 5 Cobble Yard (01223 323264). Specialises in records.

Streetwise Music, 76 King Street (01223 300496). Music and posters for younger age range.

● speciality/classical music sellers

Brian Jordan, 10 Green Street (01223 322368). Musical scores and books.

Heffers Sound, 19 Trinity Street (01223 568562). The first choice for classical and other music but try also *MDC Classic Music*, 8 Rose Crescent (01223 506526) and *Wesley Owen*, 88 Regent Street (01223 352727), which has books too.

● musical instruments

Miller's Music Centre, 12 Sussex Street (01223 354452).

The biggest local provider of musical instruments, especially pianos, (including electronic keyboards) with a good selection of sheet music.

Mark's, 27 King Street (01223 462002). Music store.

Further out but invaluable to the musician are:

The Music Gallery/Cambridge Pianoforte Centre, 12 King's Hedges Road (01223 424999). Pianos and string specialists, but covers all musical requirements and does international music and accessories by mail order.

Woodwind and Reed, Russell Street (01223 500442). Woodwind and brass, sheet music, accessories and repairs. Closed Mondays. Both the above have small parking areas.

TOYS, GAMES & GIFTS

Robert Sayle (see listing above), and *Woolworths,* 13-15 Sidney Street (01223 357168) stock a good range of toys. Robert Sayle has pre-school, boys' and girls' sections, plus sections for soft toys, board games, large outdoor toys and electronic toys. Woolworth's has five sections; games and puzzles; pre-school, boys'; girls' and educational.

● **children's toys**

Toymaster Kingdom, 15 Burleigh Street (01223 350386). Toys and cycles.

Early Learning Centres, 30a Grafton Centre (01223 314565) and 31 Lion Yard (01223 314413). Good quality educational toys and equipment for young infants.

Rocking Horse, Burwash Manor Barns, New Road, Barton (01223 264674). 'A real old-fashioned toy shop.' Traditional toys, nearly new and nursery equipment.

● **games, puzzles and tricks**

Games Workshop, Ltd, 8 Bridge Street, (01223 313350). Table-top war games and toy soldiers.

Games and Puzzles, 6-7 Green Street (01223 355188). Wide selection of both.

Lingard's, 7 Rose Crescent (01223 363257). Traditional and parlour games, jigsaws and brainteaser puzzles.

Magic Joke Shop, 29 Bridge Street (01223 353003). Just what it says, though we couldn't find any plastic ants.

Toy Soldier, 16 Magdalene Street (01223 367372). Toy soldiers, accessories and second-hand fantasy figures.

● **speciality toy and gift shops**

Balloon the Gift Shop, 14 Fair Street (01223 312609). Handmade rag dolls, dolls' houses and wooden toys.

The English Teddy Bear Company, 1 King's Parade (01223 300908). Every kind of bear.

The Disney Store, 4-5 Petty Cury (01223 313258). Disney merchandise galore.

The Nature Reserve, 64 Grafton Centre (01223 363400). Fascinating shop carrying anything to do with wildlife, from games and jigsaws to cuddlies and educational.

SHOPPING

COMPUTERS, APPLIANCES, & OFFICE SUPPLIES

The only department store in Cambridge to offer a full range is *Robert Sayle*, (see above) in the misleadingly named Audio Department. Here you can find TVs, videos, hi-fi and personal audio equipment, computers, printers, telephones and answering machines, with the added benefit of reliability and good advice.

Computers, software etcetera

Many people tend to find computers, software and related equipment cheaper by mail order. Suppliers include: *Dabsdirect* 0800 138 5125; *Global Direct* 0870 729 7929; *MacWarehouse* 0800 131 332; *Multiple Zones* 0800 393 696; or *MacLine* 0800 389 8528). But if you want to see what you're getting or need advice, local retailers can often be a big help.

● big national outlets

PC World, 330 Newmarket Road, Unit 5 (01223 353153). Opened in 2000, offering its huge range of goods, but you can also get quite a lot at *Staples* and *Office World*, listed under 'office supplies' below.

● local, speciality & economy outlets

Cambridge Computer Centre, 21 Signet Court, Swann's Road (01223 576516). PCs ready-made or built to your specification. Multimedia, home, office.

Computer Resale, Mill Road, second-hand PC computers (01223 305007).

Cantab Millenium (01223 500247) and *Computer Stop* (01223 506300) on Mill Road sell PC drives, boards etc for those building their own.

Evesham, 5 Glisson Road (01223 322883). PC specialist with good service.

Tiny Computers Ltd, 1 Emmanuel Street (01223 355222). Small shop. Ironically, Britain's largest PC manufacturer.

World of Computers, Cambridge Road, Milton 01223 724500. Service for home and business, PCs built for you. Sales, service and support.

● computer software and games

Games Ltd, 10-11 Lion Yard (01223 366944). Games consoles, PC accessories, software, DVDs.

Electronics Boutique, 3 Petty Cury (01223 303262). computer games, consoles and DVD.

Photo by Findlay Kember

City centre shopper

Electronics, appliances & phones

Andrew McCulloch, 20 Norfolk St, 11 Nuffield Road and 44 Arbury Court (free call 0500 600873). A local seller with a full range of appliances. Friendly and helpful.

● national outlets in the centre

Dixon's, Lion Yard (01223 359111). General electrical.

Virgin Megastore, 28a Grafton Centre (01223 360333). Electronic entertainment.

● national mall outlets

Powerhouse, Beehive Centre, Coldham's Lane, (01223 311117) or 24 hour online shopping at www.powerhouse-online.co.uk. Electronics/home appliance superstore.

Comet, Newmarket Road, order direct on 0845 6007002 or visit their website at comet.co.uk. Focuses more on white goods.

Currys, Cambridge Retail Park, Newmarket Road, (01223 327108). A brand new superstore with a wide range of electronics, including computers, but with a focus on white goods. Open Mon-Fri 9am-8pm, Sat 9am-6pm, Sun 10.30am-4.30pm.

● TV, radio, electrical rentals

Granada, 6 Lion Yard (01223 350118). TV Rental and home technology.

Radio Rentals, Grafton Centre (01223 300052). TV rental.

● electrical specialists

Tandy, 27 Fitzroy Street (01223 353244). General electrical.

Hughes Electrical, 43 Grafton Centre. (01223 460750). TV and Audio.

Maplin, 46-48 St Andrew's Street (01223 369758). General and speciality electronics and parts.

● telephones

These shops seem to pop up like mushrooms overnight. There are several phone shops within a few metres of one another on Market Street alone, plus a *BT shop* at 1 Lion Yard (01223 304114) and *The Link* at 19 Grafton Centre (01223 361822) and 36 Petty Cury (01223 360099).

Office supplies

Office World, Newmarket Road (01223 393395). A big chain outlet. Sells a broad range of office supplies, some office machines. Reasonable prices.

Staples, 121 Chesterton Road (01223 303232). A good range of PCs, printers, office machines, telephones and software, along with a warehouse full of paper, pencils, envelopes, furniture and even tea and coffee for the office cupboard. Handy parking on the roof. Good service.

Rymans, 53 Sidney Street (01223 312095). Small, a bit costlier, but handy to the centre.

SHOPPING AROUND CAMBRIDGE
Ely and north of the city

Ely, 18 miles north of Cambridge, is a pleasant place to visit and shop with its striking Cathedral. Around the Cathedral area are some interesting shops of the craft/book variety, and a few bargain shops such as *Wilko* (off the Market Place) and *Thing-Me-Bobs* (Market Street) can be found nearby. *Iceland*, *Waitrose* (Brays Lane) and *Tesco* (on Angel Drove) provide for bodily needs but there are also several good butchers and a farm produce shop (also on Market Street) along with a *Farmers' Market* on the first Saturday of each month. Ely's weekly market is on Thursdays and there is a craft market each Saturday.

Other shopping attractions include *The Maltings* (crafts, Christmas market and books as well as concert and restaurant facilities), *Waterside Antiques*, a three-floor Aladdin's cave of an antique warehouse by the river (reputedly haunted) and a few 'country' shops including a rare specialist shooting goods shop on West End.

Huntingdon and west

Oliver Cromwell's old stamping ground has a few interesting extras. The industrial estate houses a large *Tesco* and *Dunelm*, an outlet for pottery and linen seconds. In the town centre are a large *Sainsbury's* and *Waitrose*, and there is an *open air market* on Wednesdays and Saturdays in market square. For the crafty minded there's *Centre Crafts* dealing in such things as wools, embroidery and cake icing equipment, plus a *Singer Sewing Centre*, both on High Street, as is a useful cut-price book shop.

At the end of the High Street nearest the Old Bridge is *The Old Curiosity Shop*, for those who like to poke around – bygones, old music and knitting patterns abound. On the ring road is *Elphick's*, which stocks top-class furniture.

In nearby Godmanchester you will find a further bookshop and a curio shop on Post Street, and two good women's clothes shops, *Patricia's* and *Jackson's*, by the Chinese bridge.

St Ives

Its river views make St Ives another pleasant place, and it has a good range of the expected outlets (*Boots*, *Woolworths*, *Superdrug* etc) and supermarkets (*Waitrose*, *Rainbow Co-op*, *Budgen*) but also some less predictable places such as a *mobile fish stall* (sited next to Boots) and a specialist *fishing tackle shop* (opposite the Post Office), two butchers and a bakery and a good bookshop. Clothes range from charity shops through *Mackay's*, *New Look* and the *Edinburgh Wool Shop* to designer wear.

The regular market is on Mondays, apart from bank holidays, when it is replaced by a large market with a variety of goods. A smaller vegetable market is held on Fridays.

There is a small department store, *Bryant's*, on Bridge

Street, and the Free Church in the market place is worth a visit for decent coffee as is *Traidcraft* – fairly traded hand-made goods such as cards, ethnic clothing and candles.

Cromwell Furniture Barn, with a vast range of suites, fabrics and pine, is at 1-2 New Road.

St Neots

Another historic market town, St Neots has a varied selection of shops, high street multiples and supermarkets. *Waitrose* and *Somerfield* are in the town, a larger *Tesco* on the edge. There is also *Lidl*, a German outlet for budget food. Nationally known retailers occupy prominent sites in the market square and High Street, along with established local firms such as *Brittain's the Furnishers* (58-62 High Street) and *Barrett's Department Store* (market square) both of which have served St Neots for around a century.

The *traditional market* is held every Thursday in market square. For toys and clothes, try *Westgate*. The book-shop (1-5 New Street, but you can also get in via Barrett's) has a good reputation and offers a special order service, bargain books, maps, stationery and CD Roms as well as a wide range of books of all kinds.

Newmarket and east

As Newmarket is famous as a centre for horse breeding and racing, many of its shops are, unsurprisingly, oriented to riding and country pursuits. *Gibson's Saddlery* is one of several shops for all riding equipment; try also *Golding's* for countrywear and *Busy Bee* cobblers for riding boots and repairs. The charity shops tend to have good quality clothes, but if second-hand isn't your thing you might prefer *Wardrobe*, which stocks labels such as In-Wear, or *Jane and Judith Fisher*, specialising in clothes for older women.

An establishment bearing the name *That Little Shop* offers an intriguing range of gifts, and *Tindall's* is excellent for books and art/craft supplies. *Moons* toy shop is recommended for its huge range ('they stock everything') and its friendly staff. There is also a *Tesco* on Fordham Road, a small *M&S*, *Boots* and a *Waitrose* on High Street.

Peterborough

Forty miles up the A1, Peterborough is another historic city, with a spacious precinct fronting its cathedral. Cathedral Square has a regular pitch of handcraft stalls and there is also a covered market (closed Sundays and Mondays), a street market Tuesday, Wednesday, Friday and Saturday with a food hall and 150 stalls in Northminster. Five multi-storey and seven surface car parks are within reach of the main shopping areas, which offer all the big retail names and some independent boutiques and specialists. The *Queensgate Centre* (right next to bus/railway stations, website: www.queensgate-shopping.co.uk) has 80 of the best known high street stores (including 20 designer

SHOPPING

clothes shops) in covered malls and can provide wheel-chairs and scooters on free loan (01733 313133). Shopping until 8pm on Thursdays. There are two other such centres, the *Rivergate* (open every day) and the Hereward Cross.

Peterborough boasts the largest *Tesco* in the UK, which is at the retail park in the Southern Township.

Royston and south

Royston, south-west of Cambridge on the A10, has an underground cave among its tourist attractions. Two miles east of the town, you can find *Bury Lane Nursery and Deli* which, as well as plants, provides good coffee and wonderful cheeses. On Old North Road on the outskirts of the town is a *Tesco*, while a smaller *Somerfield* is on Baldock Street in the centre. Baldock Street is also home to *The Cave Shop*, an unusual blend of items such as aromatic oils and interesting books, and *The Shop On The Corner*, which has all kinds of gifts including the weird.

Market days in Royston are on Wednesdays and Saturdays and include a popular W.I. stall, and *Market One*, next to the church, operates seven days a week. On the High Street *Howorth's* shoe shop stocks Hotter shoes (the most comfortable on earth) and the *Stationery Cupboard* has high-quality office goods. For classy china and glass there's *Fantasia* on Kneesworth Road, while those into partying should go to *Beautiful Balloons* on Market Hill.

Quality clothing for women is found at *Marcelle* (High Street), *Cream* (John Street) and *Romany* (Angel Pavement). Brilliant discount clothing is sold at *Clothing World*, Orchard Road, a huge outlet for slightly imperfect M&S and similar.

Saffron Walden

This picturesque and ancient market town will be attractive to the compulsive potterer, having lots of small shops. There are larger shops too, such as the department store *Eaden Lilley* at 6 Market Place (behind which, incidentally, is an interesting shop selling beads, ribbons and other such gewgaws) and *Weaver's*, specialising in Moorcroft and Lalique ware. In general Saffron Walden is to be recommended for antiques and presents.

The excellent market, which is run on Tuesdays and Saturdays, has a fascinating mix of plants, clothes, old tools, antiques, picture framing, a wonderful jumper stall and very good veg. *Tesco* is situated on Radwinter Road and *Waitrose* in Hill Street. Designer clothes and shoes (not seconds) at discount prices can be found at *Labels for Less*, Emson Close, and *Leather for Less*, 7 Market Row.

ADDITIONAL INFORMATION

Yellow Pages (0800 671444) and *Thomson's Directory* (01252 555555) usually arrive free, or visit www.yell.com or www.thomweb.co.uk. If you need a copy, call.

CHAPTER 6
HEALTH CARE

Welcome to Addenbrooke's

↑ Accident and Emergency
↑ Main Entrance
← Medical Admissions Unit
Out-patients Car Park →
↑ Out-patient Department
← Patient and Visitor Parking →
Blood Donor Centre on this site →

This chapter first deals with the typical health consumer, covering practical basics ranging from the National Health Service, private and alternative medicine to dentists, pharmacies, opticians, counselling and myriad support services. It then covers health services like support groups and alternative medical care, such as acupuncture and reflexology. These and many other alternative treatments are strong in the Cambridge area.

For more on health for mothers see Chapter 9, 'Families & Children', page 181.

CAMBRIDGE AREA HEALTH

The National Institute of Epidemiology report in the late 1990s found people in Cambridge live longer than anywhere else in England. By gender, the men of Cambridge lead in longevity nationwide, while women came in third, just behind Bromley and Dorset. More widely, Cambridgeshire as a whole is quite healthy, with both sexes living one or two years more than the national average. Why? The scientists will cite general affluence contributing to good physical and mental health, but there's more to it. Cambridge has the sort of strong community that fosters good health, with the opportunity to be active, involved and have a good social life.

Of course, this area has its health problems as well. Compared to other areas, there are more instances of cancers and circulatory diseases, 35% more traffic deaths and a 25% higher death rate among the elderly due to falls. In addition, the health of the area varies widely with ethnicity and other factors. The poor and vulnerable groups like the elderly, children and those with mental illness rely heavily on medical services.

Population growth will put pressure on health services. In south Cambridgeshire the population is forecast to soar by 25% in the next 20 years (four times the national rate). In order to keep pace with demand, authorities will be hard pressed to lay on additional hospital services fast enough.

NHS MEDICAL CARE

The National Health Service provides everything from hospital care and community health services to a new 24-hour phone-in advice service (see page 126 below). Except for certain short-term visitors from outside the European Union (more on eligibility below) everyone is entitled to free health care with nominal charges for things like prescriptions. Typically, NHS care is as good or better than you'll get in other advanced countries.

The Cambridge area is especially well provided for, having two of the world's leading hospitals – Addenbrooke's, the University of Cambridge's main teaching hospital, and

Cover picture: Sign outside Addenbrook's Hospital, Cambridge.

Papworth, a world-renowned heart centre – combined with many other smaller specialised hospitals, surgeries and specialist treatment centres.

NHS waiting lists

The main downside of the NHS is its waiting lists. While routine care, emergency care and most services are typically readily available, the combination of medical/technological advances, finite resources, a booming population and the rising expectations of patients has stretched the NHS, sometimes to breaking point. The demand to see specialists and for specialised treatments has resulted in waiting times of weeks, months or well over a year, with times depending on the urgency of need and availability. For the vast majority, this is mainly an inconvenience, but, exceptionally, care does come late.

● waiting times in Cambridgeshire

Waiting times vary according to the procedure or operation, but here are a few examples from the Cambridgeshire lists in 2000. Time to see a consultant for someone in need of:

- heart bypass surgery was three to five weeks, and then another five to 11 months to get treatment.
- cataract removal required 12 to 28 weeks to see a consultant and then six to 13 months for treatment.
- hip replacement takes up to 29 weeks to see a consultant and up to 17 months for treatment.

HEALTH CARE

Around East Anglia, waiting times are on the long side, in a few cases hitting the 18-month government limit.

To find out the waiting list times contact the Waiting List Helpline: 0208 983 1133. If you face a long waiting time for a hospital procedure it is worth ringing the helpline to find out if other hospitals locally have shorter waiting lists.

Waiting lists are the main reason for growth of a parallel private medical system, where patients pay for private treatment and wait less. The specialists working in the smaller, but still extensive, private systems are often NHS doctors, the same ones that a patient sees on the NHS.

ROUTINE NHS MEDICAL CARE

If you are ill or just need routine care, see an NHS General Practitioner, or GP at the local surgery or health centre.

...for visitors

If you are staying in the area for less than a few months and need to see a doctor during that time, you can visit any local surgery and register as a temporary patient. If you are a foreign visitor from a European Union country you will not need to pay; however, if you are from a country outside the EU then there is a charge which is made at the discretion of the doctor (charges vary but are usually somewhere in the region of £15 for a consultation and £30 for a home visit). If hospitalization is required, the NHS typically charges at a fixed rate per day, regardless of the medical treatment, a fee that is normally paid by the patient's insurance. Uninsured visitors will be asked to pay this amount themselves.

...for residents / long-term visitors

If, however, you are planning to move to the area for a longer period, you will need to register with a local doctor as a regular patient. Any person who is legally resident is entitled to free medical care. To register, you should take along your medical card, which has your NHS number on it. If you don't have a medical card, you will be asked to apply for one by filling in a form detailing your name, address and date of birth (You normally don't need any documents to prove your identity).

NHS DIRECT - HELP BY PHONE

NHS Direct is a national telephone service staffed by qualified nurses, giving confidential health care advice and information 24 hours a day, 365 days a year on:
- What to do if you are feeling ill
- Health concerns for you and your family
- Local health services
- Self help and support organisations

To contact NHS Direct, telephone 0845 46 47 or go to www.nhsdirect.nhs.uk.

To find the local GP's office, contact your primary care group or trust or health authority (see box below). Alternatively, consult the telephone directory (under 'Doctors (Medical Practitioners)'), ask for the information at the nearest Town Hall or just ask a neighbour.

Once registered, you can usually choose to see any of the doctors taking more patients. If the doctor you choose is unable to take new patients, the staff will provide the names of the alternatives. You may even want to interview a few or ask for recommendations from friends before making a choice. You can always change later and see whichever GP at the practice you feel comfortable with.

● **GP hours and home visits**

The majority of practices have between one and four doctors working together. They see patients from Monday to

---

WHO RUNS WHAT – THE ORGANISATIONS

● *Health authorities* analyse the types of health care residents in the area are likely to need during the year and, with its *Primary Care Groups* (PCGs) and *Primary Care Trusts* (PCTs), arrange, with *NHS Trusts* and other providers, such as GPs, dentists, opticians, pharmacists, nursing homes, private clinics and hospitals, for these to be available. The emphasis is on providing care for people in their homes and community clinics and local surgeries wherever possible, and requiring them to attend hospital only when it is appropriate. The needs of the population are assessed on the basis of the mix of men, women, children and older people who live in an area and on the strength of historical patterns of service, as well as taking into account any local factors that may influence these decisions. The local *health authorities* are:

Cambridgeshire, Huntingdon (01480 398500)
　　　www.cambs-ha.nhs.uk.
Suffolk, Ipswich (01473 323323)
　　　www.suffolkhealthauthority.nhs.uk
East & North Hertfordshire, Welwyn Garden City (01707 390855)　www.enhertshealth.nhs.uk
North Essex, Witham, Essex　(01376 302100)
　　　www.ne-ha.nthames.nhs.uk

● *Primary Care Groups* (or trusts) run the doctors' surgeries and manage care in the community. Contact them for information about specific doctors, dentists, pharmacists, opticians and chiropodists in a particular areas. The Primary Care Groups are:

Cambridge City (01223 885723)
East Cambridgeshire (01353 654200)
Huntingdonshire (01480 308222)
South Cambridgeshire (01223 885700)
North Herts, Hitchin (01462 431003)
North Essex (01621 875336)

HEALTH CARE

Friday, but hours vary from practice to practice. At some, you pre-book an appointment to see your doctor and at others you just go to the surgery and wait your turn. If you need to see a doctor outside of surgery hours, ring your normal surgery number and an answerphone message will tell you what to do and who to ring.

Doctors will make home visits if the patient cannot get to the surgery. If you need a home visit, contact your local surgery to arrange it.

● **what GPs / health centres offer**

Doctors' practices vary dramatically in size and in what services they have to offer. All GPs do routine exams and give advice and prescriptions for medical care. Some surgeries will carry out minor surgery on in-grown toenails, cysts and warts. Many practices offer comprehensive health checks and run regular screening programmes for asthma, diabetes, heart disease, hypertension and so on. Some offer services like counselling, physiotherapy, acupuncture, speech therapy, chiropody and support services to help smokers give up nicotine. Each practice also has a midwife and health visitors who look after the needs of women throughout their pregnancy and during their first few months as a new mum.

Seeing a specialist

You cannot go directly to a specialist or consultant through the NHS. To see specialists, who typically work at the hospitals, your GP must give you a referral and schedule a visit for you. Depending on the demand for a particular speciality and on the urgency of your need, you are likely to be asked to wait your turn. The waiting times can vary from a week or two to much longer, but in most cases the time period is not unreasonable. If you find that the period is too long, and can afford it, you are free to jump the queue and see the specialist privately below. We explain how to see doctors privately below.

Routine care at the universities

Neither Cambridge nor Anglia Polytechnic University has special links with doctors' surgeries, although APU has a GP's surgery on the Cambridge campus and in-house optical services and Cambridge University has a dental service (see below). Students and staff are advised to register with a local health centre of their choice when arriving.

PRESCRIPTIONS & PHARMACISTS

If you have been given a prescription for medication by your doctor you will usually need to go to a pharmacist to collect it. Most people have to pay for their prescriptions (currently £6) but there is quite a list of people who are exempt from payments, including under 16s, under 19s in full-time education, over 60s, people on income support, patients with certain medical conditions and so on. For a comprehensive list of exemptions, ask your local pharmacist or look on the back of a prescription.

If you are feeling under the weather but don't feel that it warrants a trip to see your doctor, pharmacists are also well qualified to give advice on medication for ailments like common coughs, colds and stomach upsets.

For more information on pharmacists see Chapter 5, 'Shopping', page 103.

DENTAL CARE

NHS dentists who are still taking new patients on the NHS are becoming a rare commodity in this area. If you fail to find what you want through the telephone directory under 'Dental Surgeons' or through your local Town Hall, the health authority's dental helplines (see below) lists dental offices with places – but you may have to travel.

What dental care costs

You pay for NHS and private dentists. Both offer the same sorts of treatment with a similar quality, but with a marked difference in cost. Private treatment typically costs twice as much as the NHS treatment and sometimes five times as much. Many dentists have both private and NHS patients on their books. Once you've found a practice that is taking new patients, all you need to do to register is to ring up and book an appointment. If you urgently need to see a dentist out-of-hours you should call your local dental surgery to find out what to do. If you are not yet registered with a local dentist, you should ring the appropriate health authority number on page 127 or consider going to a dentist privately.

● **University of Cambridge dental care**

Students, staff and their spouses and children can use the University Dental Service. It is necessary to register. For information call the clinic at 01223 332860.

HEALTH CARE

DENTAL HELPLINES

To get up-to-date information on available NHS dentists call the health authority dental helpline:

Cambridgeshire	01223 415126
Suffolk	01473 323323
	ask for 'contractor services'
East & North Hertfordshire	01707 376826
	ask for X 2111
North Essex	01376 302218

Alternatively, contact NHS Direct on 0845 46 47.

OPTICIANS

Finding a local optician is usually quite simple. There are lots on the high streets and definitely no waiting lists. Dispensing opticians are the professionals that fit and set up your spectacles. Ophthalmic opticians are those who carry out eye examinations. All you need to do to register with an ophthalmic optician is to ring and make an appointment.

Most opticians offer a total eye examination including sight testing and, if necessary, diabetic and glaucoma screening for both NHS and private patients. People over 60 years of age are entitled to free eye care, as are over 40-year-olds who have glaucoma in the family. In addition, people receiving state benefits or those suffering with diabetes are given free eye care. Most other people have to pay for their treatment. Sight tests cost in the region of £15.50.

● APU optical service

Staff, students and the public can use the optical services provided through the optical courses run at APU, including a free eye test done by third-year eye students with supervision (01223 363271 for information). If you have an eye test done, you can buy frames there for 30% less than high street prices.

HOSPITALS AND EMERGENCIES

There are different types of hospitals. Those that have an Accident & Emergency department are called acute hospitals; community hospitals deal predominantly with the elderly and mentally ill, and then there are private hospitals where patients pay for quick access to health services. To confuse the issue, each hospital can provide any combination of acute, community and private services, although not all do.

In a real emergency...

To call an ambulance, contact the police or fire brigade, all you need to do is call 999, which can be dialled toll-free, anywhere in the country, but should only be used in a very serious or life-threatening situation. East Anglian Ambulance NHS Trust looks after all the emergencies (999 blue light ambulance) and non-emergencies (taking patients to clinics for appointments) in Cambridgeshire, Norfolk and Suffolk.

Alternatively, if you have an emergency but don't think that the situation is immediately life-threatening, consult your GP or there are Accident and Emergency (A & E) Departments in some hospitals (including Addenbrooke's, Hinchingbrooke and West Suffolk, see below) which you can walk into and get treatment. These A & E departments can get very busy and, although your situation will be assessed on arrival, there can be long delays in getting treatment if your 'emergency' isn't as life-threatening as the other people attending at that time.

Unless admitted through Accident and Emergency, you must have a doctor's referral to get treatment at a hospital. Below, we describe the area's main hospitals and what they offer.

Addenbrooke's Hospital

Addenbrooke's, formally 'Addenbrooke's NHS Trust,' on the southern edge of Cambridge, is an acute hospital offering NHS and some private treatment. It is classed as a leading international centre for biomedical research and medical education. A national and regional centre for cancer services and organ transplants, it is also rated highly in news media surveys for confidence in its doctors and high staffing levels.

The hospital is vast (and can seem a little overwhelming at first). It has over 1,000 beds and employs some 5,000 staff. In addition to the main hospital, with its 18 operating theatres, five intensive care units and 12 clinics, the site includes The Rosie Hospital for women's services *(see page 182 'Families & Children')*.

Addenbrooke's NHS Trust, Cambridge, Hills Road, CB2 2QQ (01223 245151) www.addenbrookes.org.uk

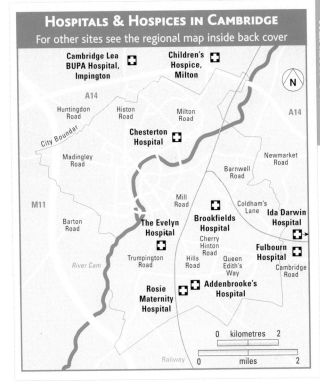

HOSPITALS & HOSPICES IN CAMBRIDGE
For other sites see the regional map inside back cover

HEALTH CARE

Papworth Hospital

Papworth Hospital is a specialist heart hospital 12 miles northwest of Cambridge in the village of Papworth Everard. Specialities offered at Papworth include heart and lung transplants, cardiology, cardiac surgery, thoracic surgery and respiratory medicine (including cystic fibrosis). Papworth Hospital gives very special care and attention to its patients and is regarded as a very friendly hospital. It has a quiet and cosy atmosphere, with a duck pond in its grounds to which patients and visitors become very attached.

Papworth Hospital, Papworth Everard, CB3 8RE, (01480 830541), www.papworth-hospital.org.uk

Hinchingbrooke Hospital

Hinchingbrooke is an acute hospital which also provides a full range of community health services in clinics in Huntingdon, St Ives, St Neots and Ramsey and also in GP surgeries, as well as a wide range of services within the hospital setting. Modern and well equipped, its specialities include: obstetrics & gynaecology, children's services including learning disabilities, adult and elderly mental health, physiotherapy, occupational therapy, chiropody and dietetics, general and elderly medicine. The Mulberry Suite at Hinchingbrooke Hospital is dedicated to private patients.

Hinchingbrooke Hospital, Huntingdon, PE18 8NT (01480 416416).

Community services

In addition to the major hospitals mentioned above, there are additional, smaller hospitals which provide services and care for patients either in their own homes, in the smaller hospitals or in a community centre setting. Again, you will need to be referred by your doctor for treatment at these hospitals. The 'community' services in south Cambridgeshire, ranging from respite care for the elderly to child development services, are provided by Lifespan Healthcare NHS Trust (01223 884043) www.lifespan.org.uk

Photo by Neal E. Robbins

That's the way to the Rosie Hospital

PRIVATE MEDICAL CARE

Many consultants and surgeons split their time working for both the NHS and privately, which means the treatment is often exactly the same, but you won't have to wait as long for it. As a general rule of thumb, private clinics/hospitals usually have a higher standard of decor than NHS facilities and can often have a 'hotel' feel about them. Private hospitals are often better equipped and have more staff on hand to look after their patients. There is usually a decent menu to choose from, unlike the notoriously grim NHS food which sometimes arrives cold and congealed! Other facilities such as televisions, washing facilities and telephone services are much more abundant in private hospitals. Visiting hours are usually more flexible.

To find out about private specialists, begin by approaching some of the private health care companies (see below). They keep lists of specialists and hospitals.

Private health care costs money. You can either dig deep into your pockets and pay for a treatment or take out a health care insurance plan that will provide private care. Typical prices for the most common treatments include the following: cataract removal £2,500; heart bypass £11,500; hip replacement £8,500; varicose vein removal £1,500. These would be free on the NHS.

Private medical insurance

Some companies give their employees free medical insurance as part of their employment package. Others offer a discount into a scheme. Private health care companies offer insurance schemes tailor-made for all sorts of needs. These are the leading private health care companies:

BUPA, Head Office, London WC1A 2BA (0207 656 2000) www.bupa.com

PPP, general enquiries, 0800 335555, www.PPPhealthcare.co.uk

HEALTH CARE

LOCAL PRIVATE HOSPITALS

These private hospitals locally provide a full range of medical services:

BUPA, Cambridge Lea Hospital, Cambridge, CB4 9EL (01223 266900).

Bury St Edmunds Nuffield Hospital, Bury St Edmunds, IP33 2AA (01284 701371).

Bury St Edmunds MRI Centre, Bury St Edmunds, IP33 2QQ (01284 724241).

Cromwell Clinic, Huntingdon, PE18 6DP (01480 411411)

For a full list of private hospitals in the UK, contact, PPP Healthcare, Tunbridge Wells, TN1 2PL (01892 512345) www.PPPhealthcare.co.uk

COUNSELLING & PSYCHOTHERAPY

Counselling and psychotherapy are more widely available on the NHS these days, but it will be down to your GP as to whether you will be referred and there might be a long waiting list. If you go privately look for psychologists who are members of the British Psychological Society, the organisation regulating chartered psychologists. There are two practitioners in Cambridge and one in St Neots. The British Confederation of Psychotherapists has a regional register of psychotherapists who specialise in counselling adults, children and adolescents. There are two practices in Cambridge specialising in psychotherapy. Costs are likely to be about £30 per session.

A few GPs will use hypnotherapy for those who have phobias and addictions. Some psychotherapists also use hypnotherapy. For private patients it is very important that they find a hypnotherapist who is an approved member of a professional group bound by a strict code, such as the National Council for Hypnotherapy or The British Hypnotherapy Association, which has a register of therapists. An appointment, approximately two hours, will cost around £50. Here are the contact details:

The British Confederation of Psychotherapists, 37 Mapesbury Road, London NW2 4HJ (0208 450 8965) www.bcp.org.uk

The British Hypnotherapy Association UK Register, 14 Crown Street, Chorley, PR7 1DX, freephone (0800 7318443).

National Council for Hypnotherapy, PO Box 5779, Burton on the Wolds, Loughborough LE12 5ZE (0800 9520545).

British Psychological Society, St Andrews House, 48 Princess Road, Leicester LE1 7DR (0116 254 9568).

Photo by Sam Tanner, courtesy of Age Concern

An Age Concern volunteer at a day care centre

Transcendental Meditation

is a simple, natural mental technique which provides a unique state of restful alertness beneficial for health and resulting in greatly increased clarity of mind, energy and creativity. Regularly used this effortless procedure for enjoying profound relaxation while the mind has access to a silent reservoir of inner intelligence allows the body's fine-tuning mechanisms to achieve an optimum level of health and balance. Accumulated stress and strain, contributing to many problems such as insomnia, headaches, high-blood-pressure and anxiety, are cleared from the system so that performance improves and life is enjoyed to the full.

TM involves no changes in life-style, attitude or beliefs and can be practised by anyone over the age of ten. All teachers are professionally trained, and offer a simple seven-step course plus follow up. An introductory talk is free, without obligation and very interesting. To book a talk on a Wednesday evening, or at another time to suit you phone Mrs Patrice Gladwin on 01223 570873.

Do look at our web sites **www.transcendental-meditation.org.uk • www.meditation-cam-org.uk**

SUPPORT GROUPS

A phenomenal number of groups serve the young and the elderly, those with disabilities and troubling medical conditions. As we cannot list them all, the focused here is on the more local outlets that otherwise could be easily overlooked.

Finding the right group

A good place to start when you are looking for specific support groups is the *Directions Plus Handbook*. The book is supplied by an affiliate of *Dial UK* called *Directions Plus* located at Orwell House, Cowley Road, Cambridge, CB4 0PP (01223 569600 and 01353 669431). It is an information service for disabled people and their carers living in Cambridgeshire and has a drop-in service at Addenbrooke's Hospital (Tues-Fri, 10am-4pm). It will support and represent clients experiencing difficulties with statutory bodies and produces a handbook each year. You can contact them for information about membership, about being a volunteer or committee member or to obtain a copy of the handbook.

The handbook is funded by the National Lottery Charities Board and lists sources of support and services for people with learning difficulties, physical disabilities or sensory impairments between the ages of 16 and 65. Information in the handbook will be produced on request in large print, audio tape or Braille. You can get the most up-to-date information in a constantly updated version of the book on www.directions-plus.org.

Local tourist offices also often provide lists of support groups *(A full list of tourist offices is on page 180)*.

Support for the disabled

Below we give you a selection of support groups particularly active in the area.

● **transport for the disabled**

Cambridge PHAB Club (Physically Disabled and Able Bodied) Hester Adrian Centre, 23 Sedgwick Street,

Cambridge (01223 240163). Provides social and physical opportunities for physically disabled and able-bodied people to meet.

Manderson Trust for the Disabled, 6 Headlands, Fenstanton (01480 460047). Facilities for disabled anglers, wheelchair friendly pathways. Disabled anglers can fish free of charge.

For more on transport for the disabled see pages 78 & 83

● **sensory impairments support**

Cambridge Talking News (01223 565401). Free, weekly postal news tape for visually impaired people or people who cannot read because of a disability.

Cambs Deaf Association, 8 Romsey Terrace, Cambridge (01223 566151). Sign language classes, social meetings, monthly church service interpreted in sign, and a monthly kids club.

Camsight, 167 Green End Road, Cambridge (01223 420033). Supports blind and the partially-sighted. Including workshops in Braille and Moon, social and recreational visits and home visits.

Isle of Ely Society for the Blind, Room 7, The Dartford Business Centre, The Old School Buildings, Dartford Road, March PE15 8AN (01353 656726). A locally registered charity caring for the needs of visually-impaired people. It provides home visits, information and advice, radio-cassette players and social activities.

Fenprobe (01353 861153). Free tape recording service for people who are blind or visually-impaired, living in Ely and the surrounding district. It provides weekly news tapes, monthly magazine tapes, special features and talking prescriptions.

● **disabled and the universities**

If you come either to work or study at the University of Cambridge a disability adviser can be reached at The Disability Resource Centre, DAMTP, Silver Street, Cambridge (01223 332301) www.cam.ac.uk/CambUniv/Disability/
Support is for prospective and existing students and staff who have a disability or chronic illness.

For support at Anglia Polytechnic University contact the Students Union on 01223 460008 and ask for the Welfare Officer. The officer will advise students on disability issues. The officer will also introduce students who need counselling to trained counsellors.

Medical conditions

Body Positive (Cambridge) (0800 612612). Local branch of a national organisation with a telephone helpline giving emotional support, practical help and information for everyone affected by HIV or AIDS. Also contact:

PAUL BAIN – CARER FOR THE HOMELESS

Cambridge may seem to have a notorious homelessness problem but it actually has a better system for dealing with it: Wintercomfort, English Church Houses, Jimmy's Night Shelter, Cambridge Cyrenians and Emmaus offer orchestrated options. The homeless are attracted to the area by its affluence and because the homelessness organisations exist.

The organisations are there in part because people here have compassion – whether they get involved in a hands-on way or by digging into their pockets. Recently a couple asked friends to give to our appeal rather than buy presents for their wedding anniversary. That means a lot to us. I am constantly amazed; Cambridge challenges your preconceptions.

At the same time, misunderstanding persists. People have always lived on the streets in Cambridge, but in the old days the courts would conveniently decide in the cold months that people who had failed to pay a fine and were found wandering around should be locked up – which was humane. It kept them from freezing to death in a doorway. Now, we have a better system but the statistics fail to reflect the real level of homelessness – undercounting is common – and the public still lacks understanding.

When I was a policeman, I would sometimes check people wandering around at 3am with a bag of newspapers. Some were university professors who were effectively 'dossers', to use the old term. People walk around thinking 'this guy's such a waste'. How can they tell what has happened in his life? That person has not always been that bag of humanity that you are walking past.

Because a person is homeless, it doesn't mean that they are bad. When I was in the police force most people I was dealing with weren't out and out bad – the majority faced circumstances that were out of their control, be it drink, drugs or whatever. The homeless are seen in the same way – as ending up on the streets because of drink and drugs – but that is rarely the case. Lives fall apart first. Drink and drugs come afterwards.

Paul Bain, a policeman for 16 years, joined Emmaus in 1992 and is now coordinator. Emmaus provides a community where the homeless live and work.

Cambridge AIDS Action, Dales brewery, Gwydir Street, Cambridge on (01223 508805).

Cambridge Cancer Help Centre, 1a Stockwell Street, Cambridge (01223 566151). Support and free complementary therapies. Home visits and free transport available.

Cambridge and District Branch of Diabetes UK (01223 841383). Meetings on the second Tuesday of every month at Addenbrooke's Board Room, 8-10pm.

Cambridge District Stroke Club (01223 842144 or 01223 870167). Meetings on the third Wednesday of every month at the Addenbrooke's Rehabilitation Unit at 7.30pm. Also the *Ely District Stroke Club* (01353 860470/01353 861297). The club meets at Bedford House, Ely.

Cambridge Tinnitus Support Group (01223 460616). Opportunities for people with tinnitus to learn more about the ailment. Bi-monthly meetings.

Continence Advice Centre (01353 652050). Telephone help-line with advice on aspects of continence.

Overeaters Anonymous (01440 7043880). A self-help group for anyone with eating disorders with meetings at Brookside, Cambridge and Oddfellows Hall in Newmarket Road.

Mental / social health support groups

● counselling for couples

Relate, 3 Brooklands Ave, Cambridge (01223 357424). Provides counselling for any relationship between partners. The charity asks for participants to pay toward the costs of the service, but only as much as they can afford.

Local drop-in centres for youth

Bridge Drug Information and Treatment Service. Drug information, counselling and treatment,154 Mill Road, Cambridge (01223 214614).

Centre 33. Free and confidential counselling for young people aged under 25, free pregnancy testing service, 33 Clarendon Street Cambridge (01223 316488).

Information Shop. Advice on almost anything for 14-25 year olds, Broad Leas Centre, St Ives (01480 386011).

Helplines for children/teens

Childline. For children and young people in distress or danger, 0800 1111

NSPCC Child Protection Helpline. For concerns about children at risk of abuse, 0800 800500

Family Planning Association. Confidential advice and information on contraception and sexual health (020 7837 4044).

Careline. Counsels children, young people and adults 0208 514 1177 (Mon-Fri 10am-4pm 7pm-10pm).

This office and its outposts also cover Huntingdon and St Neots areas. To find out what office covers other areas call the headquarters 01788 573241.

● **bereavement**

Cambridge Cruse Bereavement Care, St Luke's Church Centre, Victoria Road, Cambridge (01223 302662). A local branch of a national voluntary organisation which gives support and encouragement to bereaved people including drop-in coffee sessions and individual help for children and young people.

● **sexual abuse**

Choices, 7c Station Road, Cambridge (01223 314438/ Helpline 01223 467897). A free and confidential counselling service for those whose lives are affected by child sexual abuse and those who are experiencing the long-term consequences of being abused in childhood. A voluntary organisation and a registered charity, Choices has a comprehensive library on the effects of child sex abuse and information about other organisations and services for survivors, their partners and families. Study days, public awareness events, individual training and courses are also available.

● **general mental/social support**

Lifecraft, The Bath House, Gwydir Street, Cambridge, CB1 2LW (01223 566957) is a self-help organisation run by users and ex-users of mental health services, offering a daily social club, information service, lifeline, counselling and newsletter. They also produce a handbook which covers all areas of mental health, listing both services and support groups in the area. Called *The Mental Health Handbook*, it is mainly for people aged between 16 and 65 living in Cambridgeshire, although there are short sections on services for children and older people. It can be obtained from Lifecraft.

Cambridge Manic Depression Fellowship Self-Help Group, 6 Beechwood Avenue, Melbourn (01763 260315/e-mail: mdfcamb@lineone.net). Support for people with manic depression, their families and carers.

Cam-Mind, 100 Chesterton Road, Cambridge (01223 311320). A voluntary organisation affiliated to the national organisation Mind, running clubs and a befriending scheme for people with mental health problems.

The Cambridge Samaritans, 4 Emmanuel Road, Cambridge (01223 364455). The local line affiliated to a national organisation committed to listening to people with severe worries and stress.

National Schizophrenia Fellowship (Cambridge Group) 3 Hedgerley Close, Cambridge (01223 353566), (Ely Group) 20 Northwold, Ely (01353 661918). A voluntary group run by carers for carers of people with psychotic

HEALTH CARE

mental illness in the Cambridge area. Helpline, campaigns on mental health issues and increasing the profile of carers' issues. Group meetings, guest speakers and socials.

The Survivors of Mental Health Services in West Suffolk (01284 724456). User-run service with a weekly club in Newmarket.

● **For the University of Cambridge**

The University of Cambridge also has a counselling service at 14 Trumpington Street, Cambridge (01223 332865). One-to-one counselling or group work is free to students and staff of the university.

ALTERNATIVE HEALTH CARE

What defines alternative medicine is always a matter of debate. But those services which could be paid for by the NHS, like physiotherapy, chiropody and osteopathy, we have left out. This list focuses on other complementary medicine - homeopathy, acupuncture, aromatherapy, reflexology and a range of massage therapies. Practitioners of these alternatives have found people in the area both open to alternatives and, this being a fairly affluent place, able to afford them. You'll find most treatments available only for a fee privately, but nationally, at least (reputedly less in Cambridge) about a third of NHS doctors will refer patients to practices specialising in these kinds of treatments. Private health care plans often pay half of treatments using approved complementary medicine. As complementary medicine is not entirely regulated, it is advised to use practitioners approved by professional associations, the names of which we give below.

Centres of complementary medicine

Many practitioners work from their homes, but as we do not list individuals in this guide, we can only suggest you locate these practitioners through the usual sources – advertising, word of mouth and the telephone book. Other practitioners operate from accessible centres of complementary medicine, providing a number of therapies at one site. This has the advantage that they can often approach a need from a variety of perspectives. The Cambridge area has at least ten centres of complementary medicine. The most varied and active are in Cambridge:

Arjuna Natural Health Centre, 12a Mill Road, Cambridge, CB1 2AD (01223 566122) is based above the Arjuna Wholefood Shop. The centre offers a wide range of holistic treatments including aromatherapy, massage, herbalism, acupuncture, reflexology, counselling, iridology, reiki, homeopathy, Indian head massage, Alexander technique, hypnotherapy, psychotherapy and shiatsu.

Andreasen Centre for Holistic Health, which meets at the Friends Meeting House, Hartington Road, Cambridge (01223 321157/890220), is a registered charity at which therapists offer spiritual healing, reflexology and facial massage for a small donation.

Other area centres, all of which offer access to various specialists:

Cambridge Complementary Health Practice, 34 Rustat Road, Cambridge (01223 415117).

The Oaktree Practice, 26 Victoria Street, Cambridge (01223 319155).

Cambridge Chiropractic Clinic, 19 Hamilton Road (01223 312020).

Royston Complementary Health Centre, 31c Market Hill (01763 247440).

Parks Physiotherapy, 86 Cambridge Street, St Neots (01480 394715).

Newmarket Natural Health Centre, Rutland Chambers, High Street, Newmarket (01638 508432).

Huntingdon Complementary Health Clinic, 6 Cambridge Road, Godmanchester (01480 455221).

Ely Complementary Health Centre, 29a St Mary's Street, Ely (01353 664476).

● homeopathy

Homeopathy is one of the most popular treatments. If you want to consult a specialist in the Cambridge area, *The British Homeopathic Association* will recommend doctors – and dental and veterinary surgeons for that matter – who are members of the Faculty of Homeopathy. A first consultation will cost in the region of £45. Many homeopathic treatments are also available over the counter at chemist shops and health food stores.

British Homeopathic Association, 15 Clerkenwell Close, London, EC1R OAA; 0207 566 7800; e-mail/web: info@trusthomeopathy.org and www.trusthomeopathy.org

● acupuncture

If you want to pin down a reliable acupuncturist, (pun intended) *The British Acupuncture Council* can be contacted for information about local practitioners. All members of the British Acupuncture Council (BAcC) must observe a Code of Practice and have full medical insurance.

HEALTH CARE

ALTERNATIVE HEALTH CARE FOR CHILDREN

Many people use alternative therapies as an option for mild problems in babies because of the reduced risk of side effects. However any health problems should be checked by a GP first. The following are local outlets:

Homeopathy, Kid's Clinic, 255 Hinton Way, Great Shelford, Cambridge (01223 842075). E-mail kidsclinic@rol.co.uk Saturdays only 9.30-12.30 am. Best to call for an appointment although you can drop in. Costs: about £45 for an initial consultation.

Oakington Therapy Centre, 12 High street Oakington (01223 237459). Offers a range of alternative therapies for children and babies as well as adults.

Children's Osteopathic Clinic, 349 Hills Road, Cambridge, (01223 242828). Cranial osteopathy and paediatric osteopathy.

In Cambridge there are at least 10 acupuncturists in practice, while Ely, Newmarket and Saffron Walden can boast two and Royston and Haverhill each have one. A consultation fee costs around £35 and treatment is about £28 an hour.

The British Acupuncture Council, 63 Jeddo Road, London, W12 9HQ (020 8735 0400).

● massage

Massage is available both in complementary health establishments for the relief of pain from medical conditions, as well as at many private health clubs (see page 152) and beauty salons for the relief of stress and helping tired muscles if you have been overdoing it in the gym. Treatments cost between £20 and £30.

The people who could most benefit from massage to relieve stress, however, are usually those who find it the most difficult to get time off work to take advantage of it. If it is difficult for you to get time away from work, then *TOC, Touch of Class*, might appeal. This mobile service gives massage to office staff in their own chairs at their own tables (01353 648269 or 07879 626675). The treatments are performed through the clothes, working on the upper body to increase circulation, invigorate and relieve tension. The full routine takes 15 minutes, but can be shortened.

● aromatherapy

Approved aromatherapists are likely to be be members of the *Guild of Complementary Practitioners*, the *International Federation of Aromatherapists* and the *International Society of Professional Aromatherapists*, all of which have a code of conduct or practice. Practitioners all specialise in one area or another, including the supply of essential oils and herbal products, massage, massage specially for infants, cranio-sacral therapy, reflexology and hydrotherapy massage, and massage for muscle, back and neck pain. There are plenty to choose from, either working for themselves or out of centres.

Guild of Complementary Practitioners, Lidell House, Lidell Close, Finchampstead, Berks, RG40 4NS, (0118 973 5757) www.gcpnet.com. The guild has a referral register which is constantly updated on the website.

International Federation of Aromatherapists Chiswick High Road, London W4 1PP, (0208 742 2605 182), www.int-fed-aromatherapy.co.uk. The federation has a list of recognised practitioners.

● reflexology

About 20 reflexologists practice in the area, again working for themselves or in centres. Full members of the Association of Reflexologists will have the letters MAR after their names, are fully insured and have a code of practice and ethics which they follow. Appointments cost about £25 an hour.

Association of Reflexologists, 27 Old Gloucester Street London WC1N 3XX (0870 5673320).

CHAPTER 7
SPORT & FITNESS

Photo by Robert Parr

Cambridge is well provided with participatory sports – many of which are also spectator sports – along with a growing number and variety of fitness and health clubs. Plenty of activities cater to the interests of children, teens and the disabled. So, whatever your interest – from a gentle run on a treadmill to a rousing game of rugby – you'll find what you want.

SPORTS FOR EVERYONE

● Cambridge city

Apart from the many private groups devoted to sports, CitySport, Cambridge City Council's sports development service, holds events and classes to get people of all ages involved in sport. For information ring 01223 457534/5 or see www.citysport.org.uk

Residents of Cambridge city may get discounts on some activities with the Leisurecard and THEcard. For details see Chapter 8 'Leisure' page 156. Outlying areas are well served by the many village and community colleges.

● Finding the sport you want

This chapter deals with the major sports. If you want sports not found here try the city number given just above or: www.cambridgesport.org.uk. Another good source is the Cambridge Evening News's comprehensive Citizen's Guide (*See 'Key Contacts', back page*). These are the categories in the Cambridge Evening News list:

American football	Cycling	Rugby
Angling clubs	Dance	Running
Archery	Darts	Sailing
Athletics	Football	Shooting
Badminton clubs	Golf	Skating
Basketball clubs	Gymnastics	Squash
Billiards, snooker	Hockey	Swimming
and pool	Judo	and diving
Bowls	Kickboxing	Table Tennis
Boxing	Korfball	Target sports
Canoeing	Martial Arts	Tennis
Cricket	Motor racing	Volleyball
Croquet	Parachuting	Waterpolo

Below, sports are categorised by types (football, golf, etc) and those particularly geared to children and teenagers bear the words *CHILDREN* and *TEENS*, respectively. After individual sports come fitness clubs and information about village and community colleges.

● sports around the region

A comprehensive directory to the South Cambridgeshire village college sports centres – key locations for sports and fitness activities of all kinds – is published by the District

Cover picture: Parkside swimming pool in Cambridge

Council. The directory, including a list of sports clubs and grants for sports clubs and young people, is available in local libraries and village colleges. You can request a free copy from the Sports Development Officer at the district council at 01223 724149.

Cricket

There are numerous village teams which belong to Cambridge Cricket Association and play in the league. The three major clubs (which have a history of rivalry) are Cambridge Granta, Cambridge St Giles and Camden.

There has been a huge growth in youth cricket in the area over the last few years, and children are starting much earlier, from about eight years upwards. There's a good pyramid structure for young cricketers, with children's leagues during the school term and high quality coaching. *CHILDREN/TEENS*.

For information about the above clubs and cricket opportunities for people of all abilities in the surrounding area contact the Cambridgeshire County Cricket Development Officer, 01223 932244. For information on women's evening cricket sessions ring 01954 211580.

Football

● **for watching**

Cambridge United Football Club, Abbey Stadium, Newmarket Road 01223 566500 and Cambridge City Football Club, Milton Road (01223 357973).

● **for playing**

Cambridgeshire Football Association Ltd, 3 Signet Court, Swann's Road. There are numerous local teams including Cambridge City, Histon, Ely and Newmarket. Ring 01223 576770 to discuss your needs and Cambs F.A. will guide you to a team in your locality which suits your level.

SPORT & FITNESS

SPORTS JUST FOR CHILDREN AND TEENS

CitySport hosts Top Play Fun Days and Saturday Club, fun sessions for 4-7 year olds to build up skills such as throwing, catching, kicking and hitting a ball.

Tennis coaching for 7-9 year olds and 10-12 year olds.

Fencing for 8-13 year olds.

Mini Hockey for 8-12 year olds.

Gymnastics for girls aged 5-7 years.

Trampolining for 7-14 year olds.

Self Defence for 9-13 year olds.

Organised away-days for 9-14s include ice-skating in Hemel Hempstead, 01442 292203, skiing at Gosling Ski Centre, Welwyn, 01707 331056, and cycling in Thetford Forest, 01842 815078. (Or book to go on your own on these numbers.) Contact CitySport for information on the above.

CHILDREN/TEENS. Cambridge United Football in the Community Programme runs courses for 6-14 year olds after school, in the evenings, on Saturdays and during holidays. It also runs coaching courses for adults. Ring Dave Toombs on 01223 416238 for full details.

Golf

There are over 40 golf clubs in the area. Generally you get what you pay for – budget courses start at £10-£12 per round, while the higher quality ones cost between £25 and £40. Most clubs in the area are accepting members, as the county has got more facilities than it needs. A selection near Cambridge and in the surrounding areas follows:

Bourn Golf Club, Toft Road, Bourn (01954 718057). A mid-to-upper price range club which has the distinction of a health club, swimming pool and gym as well as its 18-hole course.

Cambridge Golf Club, Longstanton (off the A14 at Bar Hill) (01954 789388). Par 72, 18-hole course offering good value for money budget golf, probably the best in the area. Floodlit driving range, clubhouse, club hire. Membership available.

Cambridge Lakes Golf Course, Trumpington Road (01223 324242). This has a 9-hole, par-3 course with putting green and practise facilities. You can hire clubs and receive coaching, and there are discounts for juniors. Coffee shop.

Cambridge Meridian Golf Club, Comberton Road, Toft (01223 264700). 18-hole mid-to-upper range.

Ely Golf Club, Cambridge Road, Ely (01353 662751). Mid-to-upper price range 18-hole course with the usual changing facilities, bar and resaurant.

Girton Golf Club, Dodford Lane, Girton (01223 276169). 18-hole parkland course established in 1936 with club house.

Gog Magog Golf Club, Shelford (01223 247626). Viewed as a bit more upper crust, and definitely in the upper price range, this club has two 18-hole courses on chalkland, so it stays dry in the winter when others can be under water.

Hemingford Abbots Golf Course (off A14 between Huntingdon and St Ives) (01480 495000). This one operates on the pay-and-play basis and is open to non-members. It also has a bar, restaurant and discount shop.

Links Golf Club, Cambridge Road, Newmarket (01638 663000). Slightly more expensive and difficult to get into, as it's a very good all-year-round dry course on sandy subsoil. Just across from the race course, horses frequently gallop round the edge.

Rowing

Rowing is probably the sport with which Cambridge is most associated, so naturally both townspeople and students are keenly involved. There are about half a dozen town clubs which between them cater for all ages and abilities, from eight years old to just old. There are facilities for serious athletes who want to train hard or those who just want to muck about on water, but all will help you achieve your personal rowing goal, whatever it might be. Every club has a different slant, but in general the set up in Cambridge is very good.

The main clubs are the *Cantabrigian Rowing Club*, (contact Clive Dixon, 01223 721566,) the *Rob Roy* and the *City of Cambridge* (contact Paul Haines, 01223 361866).

They cater to all ages and have links with schools. *CHILDREN/TEENS.*

There is also the *Cambridge University Boat Club*, Goldie Boathouse, Kimberley Road (01223 467304), (for students), the *Cambridge 99 Rowing Club*, The Boating House, Kimberley Road (01223 367521), (a strong club but without facilities for women and children) and the *Free Press* (for the maturer rower – again contact Paul Haines). All offer training both on and off water.

Rugby

Cambridge Rugby Club on Grantchester Road is the main club for all ages, offering mini-rugby (under seven to under 10), midi-rugby (under 11 to under 12) and youth (under 21) as well as adult. You can turn up for free and try them out for three weeks before deciding to join. All the groups are eligible for county play and there are qualified coached at all levels. *CHILDREN/TEENS.* Call Martin Howes (01223 893078) for details.

There are other teams in the area: Shelford, on Trumpington Road (opposite Scotsdale's) for players over 13 contact William Hellier on 01223 872244; and Newmarket, contact Adrian Simmons on 01638 552123.

Students can contact *Cambridge University Rugby Union Football Club*, University Football Ground, Grange Road (01223 354131).

Running and Athletics

Cambridge and Coleridge Athletics Club, Wilberforce Road Athletics Track. This is really the only full athletics track in the area, including high, long and triple jump, hockey pitch, huge clubroom and catering.

Participants (minimum age 14) are assessed and put into groups of similar ability. Trained coaches are on hand to give advice. Contact Barry Wallman (10 West Field, Little Abington, Cambs CB1 6BE) on 01223 893013. *TEENS*.

Hash House Harriers, The St Radegund, 129 King Street, Cambridge (01223 311794). Non-competitive running for 'drinkers with a running problem'.

Swimming & Diving

All of the pools below have programmes for *CHILDREN/TEENS*. In addition, paddling pools dot the city parks at Cherry Hinton Hall, Coleridge Recreation Ground, Lammas Land, King's Hedges and at Abbey pool.

● seasonal outdoor pools

Jesus Green. Just short of 100m length, this traditional Lido-style pool operates seasonally from May to September. It's lovely swimming outside but be prepared for 'invigorating' water temperatures. Some people wear wet suits! (01223 302579).

● city pools

Parkside Pools, Gonville Place (01223 446100). Eight-lane 25m competition pool, diving pool, children's pool, flume rides. Full range of tuition for children and adults in swimming and diving. Swimming Club, Water Polo Club. www.cityswim.org.uk

The Abbey Pool, Whitehill Road (01223 213352 and www.cityswim.org.uk). 25m pool plus learner pool, newly refurbished gym, sauna and astroturf and children's soft play area.

King's Hedges Pool, Buchan Street, Cambridge (01223 213352, www.cityswim.org.uk). A learner pool with courses for all ages.

● sports centre pools

Village colleges including Impington, Melbourn, and Sawston have indoor pools, while Comberton and Cottenham have outdoor pools. Numbers are listed at the end of the chapter.

TIDDLYWINKS CHAMPIONS

The two major world records in tiddlywinks were both recorded in Cambridge. The highest jump (11ft 5 ins) was achieved by the Cambridge Tiddlywinks Club in 1989 and the longest jump (31ft 3 ins) by the St Andrew's Tiddlywinks Society at Queens' College in 1995. (Guinness World Records 2001).

Lawn Tennis

Cambridgeshire Lawn Tennis Association, Hills Road Sports and Tennis Centre, Purbeck Road, is the fount of all knowledge on a huge range of tennis activities in the county.

CHILDREN/TEENS. There are affiliated clubs in most villages and almost all have coaching for adults and juniors. Several have Robinson Aces, providing children of 12 and under with fun, competitive opportunities on a regular basis. For information on what is on offer nearest to you ring 01223 210111.

The main clubs in Cambridge itself are *The Cambridge Lawn Tennis Club*, Wilberforce Road (01223 560477) which offers the above amenities for children and social and competitive play for adults, and *Cocks and Hens Lawn Tennis Club*, Clerk Maxwell Road (01223 360995) which has a range of activities for all ages but no Robinson Aces.

A choice for hard courts is the *Long Road Tennis Centre*, Long Road, Cambridge (01223 507430). It has indoor and outdoor courts, with changing rooms at the college. Courts are £7.50 to £13 per hour.

Sports for the disabled

The following offer fitness classes adapted to the participant's abilities by trained instructors. Except for Parkside Pools, call the sports development service at 01223 457535 to get information. See also its newsletter for the disabled or: www.disabilitysports.org.uk

Hills Road Sports and Tennis Centre, Purbeck Road. Offers wheelchair basketball.

Meadows Community Centre, St Catherine Road. Offers disability tennis for young people.

Cherry Hinton Village Centre, disability trampolining for those with visual and sensory impairments.

Abbey Pool offers Red Cross swimming sessions on Wednesday nights.

Parkside Pools (01223 446100) offers disability swimming and informal, fun sessions during term and holidays.

See also angling, Manderson Trust, page 136; gardening, Wysing Arts page 169, and YMCA, below.

KEEP FIT & SPORTS CENTRES

If you need to slim down, tone up or just get fit there are plenty of places. The problem is choosing a venue that suits you. Provision falls into the more inexpensive tax-payer subsidised sites – those run by the local authority's amenities services and community colleges – and the pricier private clubs and health suites of major hotels and the not-for-profit outlets like the YMCA.

Not-for-profit health and fitness

Cambridge YMCA, at Queen Anne House, Gonville Place, Cambridge (01223 356998), offers everything from exercise to music to weight-training gym and has a befriending scheme for people with special needs or disabilities, including mental health problems. Equipped to cater for all medical conditions, with programmes for the disabled endorsed by Addenbrooke's Hospital. Costs range from £20 a year with a £2.50 fee per session (£10 yearly fee for students and £1.50 a session), to an all-inclusive £35 a month for unlimited use with classes.

Fitness at the universities

The fitness suite at the *Education Centre* at Fenners in Gresham Road, Cambridge, is open to staff of Cambridge University and their families. Membership costs £50 a year and there are aerobics classes and circuit sessions. Staff are also able to use the athletics track at the University's sports ground in Wilberforce Road, Cambridge, for a charge of £25 a year. Staff can book on 01223 336580.

For *Anglia Polytechnic University*, contact the physical education lecturer, student services, 01223 363271 ext 2298 for information.

Cambridge sports centres

Kelsey Kerridge Sports Hall, Queen Anne Terrace, Gonville Place, Cambridge, www.kelseykerridge.co.uk (01223 462226), is the biggest local authority leisure amenity in the area. It has machines and circuit training and aerobics classes suitable for both men and women. Eleven teachers take classes ranging from powerfit to Pilates

COMMUNITY/VILLAGE COLLEGES

For details of the classes at the village colleges telephone South Cambridgeshire District Council Leisure Services on 01223 443019 or call the colleges directly:

Bassingbourn Village College	01763 246136
Bottisham Village College	01223 811372
Burwell Village College	01638 741901
Cambridge Regional College, King's Hedges Road	01223 418200
Chesterton Community College	01223 358689
Coleridge Community College, Radegund Road	01223 712301
Comberton Village College	01223 264721
Cottenham Village College	01954 288944
Ely Community College	01353 667763
Gamlingay Village College	01767 650259
Impington Village College	01223 200401
Linton Village College	01223 891233
Manor Community Clg, Arbury Rd	01223 355745
Parkside Community College	01223 712600
Sawston Village College	01223 832217
Soham Village College	01353 722297
Swavesey Village College	01954 230366

(which promotes overall toning and flexibility). 'Step and pulse' classes can be pre-booked but all other classes are on a first come, first served basis. Prices per session range from £3.80 for the fitness suite to £4.25 for weight training. Members pay £41 a year and £2.50-£2.75 per session. Discounts for off-peak use by the unwaged.

Hills Road Sports and Tennis Centre, Purbeck Road, Cambridge (01223 500009) has a fitness suite and a sports hall for fitness classes, games like badminton and volley-ball, even for children's parties. A local authority site affiliated to Hills Road Sixth Form College, it also has indoor tennis, outdoor clay courts and facilities for cricket and squash. Until mid-2001, annual membership costs £49 per adult, £18 up to age 17, £71 for families and £5.10-£12.60/£5.90-£16.90 (member/non-members, non-peak to peak per hour-long session) for tennis courts. The fitness induction, covering blood pressure, heart rate, weight, body fat percentage, flexibility, lung capacity, aerobic ability and a lifestyle consultation, costs, £11.50 and it is £3.50-£4.60 per session.

The Abbey Sports Complex, Whitehill Road, Cambridge, (01223 213352). Has a top-of-the-range fitness suite. Monthly membership costs £32.60, or pay as you go, which is £3.85 a session. Swimming costs £2.60 a session. Ladies aqua aerobics session are held in the pool on Tuesdays, but times vary depending on the time of the year.

Cherry Hinton Village Centre, Colville Road, Cherry Hinton (01223 576412). Another local authority facility. It has a range of activities, from aerobics in the evenings, to badminton, five-a-side football, yoga and Thai boxing.

Netherhall Sports Centre, Queen Edith's Way, Cambridge (01223 712142). Offers classes, hire of the sports hall and field areas and opens its multi-gym four nights a week and at weekends for £3.50 a session. Call first to arrange a visit.

Leys Sports Complex, Trumpington Road, Cambridge (01223 508900). Part of the Leys School is open to block bookings of a week or more in the evening and on weekends. It has badminton, squash and tennis courts, weights and an all-weather surface for football and hockey.

Huntingdonshire facilities

Huntingdonshire District Council has very good leisure centres in each of the towns of the old county, that's Huntingdon itself, St Ives, and St Neots, all with regular classes, excellent fitness suites, swimming pools, sports hall and floodlit outdoor recreation areas. Community education keep-fit classes are also arranged via Huntingdonshire Regional College (01480 457939) in the evening at many schools in the area. Godmanchester Community Primary School (01480 375115) has the only Nordic pine swimming pool of its kind in the country. Aquafit classes are held there twice a week, as well as a number of other swimming activities and learn to swim and improvers classes.

For information on facilities in Huntingdonshire telephone the district council on 01480 388388.

Facilities east and north

The Dome Leisure Centre, Bury Road, Mildenhall (01638 717737) has a fitness studio where they take referrals from GPs. The facility has squash and tennis courts, trampolining and table tennis. A badminton court costs £2.25-£5.50 (off-peak/peak), use of the fitness suite £2.30-£3.30 and monthly fitness use £20.70.

Paradise Centre in Newnham Street, Ely (01353 667580) offers 16 fitness classes every week, including the rigorous body blasting and body sculpting. Its Palms health Club has technogym and resistance equipment together with fitness evaluations. Monthly direct debits cost £20 to £25 with individual sessions of about £3.

South Cambridgeshire and around

The Lord Butler Fitness and Leisure Centre, Peaslands Road, Saffron Walden (01799 522777). Facilities include a swimming pool and the Images Health Studio with dance studio for classes and gym. Adults £26, family £60 a year plus fee (£2-£5) per use or £34.50 monthly payment without per-use fees.

Melbourn Swimming Pool (01763 263313). Offers lessons and an outdoor multigame area.

Otherwise, the south of Cambridgeshire and other areas are well served by the many village and community colleges, with a huge range of day and evening classes, including sports, languages, art forms, music, cookery etc which run all year. They offer fitness classes and play host to an extensive range of sports. Most have swimming pools open to the public at certain times during the day and at weekends. *(See list of village/community colleges on page 150).*

PRIVATE FITNESS CLUBS

The commercial establishments have an impressive array of classes and facilities including air-conditioned gyms with cardiovascular and resistance equipment, aerobics studios and personalised programmes. Some of the larger establishments offer other services such as massages and beauty treatments, while a few even have creche facilities, eateries or bistros and pools.

Types of membership vary. You can pay a monthly or annual fee or pay as you go. Most will give you a fitness trial and personal programme to work to. Your goal might be to lose weight or to tone up a certain area of your body for instance. The instructors at these gyms will advise you on what you need to do to achieve your goal. The clubs will have lockers and showers and some provide towels.

Atrium. At 11,500sq ft the Atrium's high tech gym is the largest in East Anglia. It offers six full-time instructors, classes from Pilates to yoga, a daily two-hour creche, a back clinic, cardiovascular equipment and a large free weights suite suitable for muscle builders. Monthly membership ranges from £29 to £39, dependent on a £99 joining fee. Atrium also has a smaller branch in Ely with a 15m pool. For membership details contact the Cambridge branch at 64 Newmarket Road on 01223 522522, or Ely at 39 Newnham Street on 01353 668888.

The Barn, Oakington Road, Girton, Cambridge (01223 519548). The Barn has in its favour an idyllic setting on a four and a half acre site, not to mention a well-equipped air-conditioned gym, pine sauna, classes in a studio, aromatherapy steam room, beauty treatments, creche, bar and café and free car parking. A pool is planned. Monthly membership costs £35, with a £75 joining fee. The annual fee is £385, without a joining fee.

Glassworks, Thompson's Lane, Cambridge (01223 305060; e-mail: healthfitnesslife@hotmail.com). A designer's fest of a fitness club created by Terence Conran (of Habitat fame), Glassworks is smaller than some but closest to central Cambridge. The gym includes a cardio-theatre. There are classes in the studio, a spa with jacuzzi overlooking the River Cam, sauna and steam room, all with towels provided. A café and 'juice bar', complementary therapies, massage and treatments for sports injuries complete the picture. Membership fees start at £56 a month with a joining fee of £250.

Greens Health & Fitness, 213 Cromwell Road, Cambridge (01223 245200). Part of a chain of big, luxurious clubs all over the country, you choose from 47 classes in a studio with a timber sprung floor. Offers a fully equipped gym, a 25-metre pool, aroma steam room, pine sauna and personal TV and music in the cardio-room, women-only health and beauty treatments. Membership costs £55 a month, with a £250 joining fee subject to discounts.

Q.ton revolution, Cambridge Science Park off Milton Road (01223 395899; Web: www.qton.com; e-mail: enquiries@qton.com). Part of a complex featuring a business conference facility and restaurant. The facilities are small but handy to the Science Park. Offers keep fit classes including beauty therapy, personal programmes, physiotherapy, sauna, solarium, squash courts, steam room, treatment room and facilities for the disabled. Membership costs £39 a month with a £50 joining fee.

Specialist/small fitness clubs

Fitness Works, 5 Church Road, Hauxton (01223 870077, www.fitnessworks.co.uk.) One-to-one tuition from international athletes and regular fitness testing. Consultations cost about £40, while one-to-one supervised training sessions cost about £25. Clinic for all abilities, including disabled and stroke victims. No membership fee – just pay as you go.

Images Hair, Beauty, Health and Leisure, 33 High Street, Over (01954 230949). A 'ladies only' health club with gym, pool featuring a fluvo for the stronger swimmer (a force of water to swim against), Swedish massage and beauty salon and sunbed. Membership costs £350 a year.

Cambridge Squash and Fitness Club, 295 Histon Road (01223 358088). Four good squash courts, coaching for all levels, aerobics, supervised gym with personal fitness programmes. Bar, lounge and some creche facilities.

Bodywork, 11 Angel Pavement, Royston (01763 243550). Gymnasium, sauna and sunbeds. www.bodywork.uksw.com

● hotel health suites

Club Moativation, The Cambridgeshire Moathouse, Bar Hill (01954 249986/249901) and The Garden House Moathouse in Cambridge, Mill Lane, Cambridge (01223 259901).

These two complexes, part of the same hotel chain, promote motivation for a healthier lifestyle. The facilities, which include pool, gym and beauty salon, are for people staying at the hotels, but members of the local community are also actively encouraged to take out annual memberships. Membership at Bar Hill costs £30 a month off-peak, and £44 a month peak, with a joining fee of £95. The Garden House, is more central to Cambridge, but works out costlier at £53.50 a month with a joining fee of about £325, although there are discounts at various times of the year. A towel is provided.

The Edge Health and Fitness Club, Bedford Lodge Hotel, Newmarket (01638 666075). Offers a fitness studio, personal programmes and a swimming pool. Off-peak membership costs £34.50, peak is £49.50, and the joining fee is about £200, discounts at different times of the year and for joint or family membership.

Bedford Lodge Hotel Leisure Club, Bury Road, Newmarket. 01638 666075). Recently refurbished and extended, pool, gym, sauna, whirlpool and steam room. Membership (individual couple) £34.50-£61.50 to £49.50-£88.50 a month or £13.50 a day.

CHAPTER 8
LEISURE

This chapter introduces entertainment, culture and organised leisure activities, except sport, which is grouped with 'Sport and Fitness' in Chapter 7. There is such a wealth of choice, changing and developing all the time, that a comprehensive list would be impossible, but those mentioned are tried, tested and recommended, and have been selected to appeal to the widest range possible – students, singles, couples, families and seniors.

Activities are categorised under different headings (Music, Cinema etc) and those particularly geared to children and teenagers bear the words *CHILDREN* and *TEENS* respectively for easy reference. A list of recommended guidebooks and other sources are given at the end of this chapter for those wanting fuller details.

The highlights, must-sees and particularly interesting sights are marked with:

☆   worth a visit if you have time
☆☆   very good – try to see this one
☆☆☆   definitely don't miss

We give sources of information throughout the chapter, with a full listing at the end of the chapter. Note that the tourist offices in the region, given at the end of the chapter, welcome enquiries from residents as well as visitors.

GETTING STARTED

● get the discount

If you are reading this guide, you're probably here for some time and so before you spend good money, take a moment to do what smart residents do: get a 'Leisurecard' (and 'THEcard' version for children). Cambridge City Council's Leisurecard system offers discounts at several venues in the city, including punting and the swimming pools. If you are a Cambridge city resident (i.e. you pay council tax to Cambridge City Council) you are eligible for the card, which is well worth getting as it quickly covers its cost. Leisurecard B costs £6.50 a year (children 3-17 half price for their own THEcard), and Leisurecard A, which is for those receiving benefits, costs £2.50 (again, half for children).

For full details ring 01223 446121 or see the Cambridge City Council's useful website: www.cambridge.gov.uk

● bus tours

If you are new to Cambridge or have a friend visiting and want to show them the town, a good way to see Cambridge is to take the *Guide Friday* tour bus, open-topped and with a commentary. This includes some of the places listed below and you can get off the bus, look around and get back on a later bus. Tours run all year round. You can join the bus at any one of 14 stops including Cambridge Railway Station, Emmanuel Street and Madingley Park and Ride.

Call 01223 362444 for more details. Tickets £8.50 adults, £7 students or seniors, children £2.50.

● **guided walking tours**

There are also splendid walking tours of Cambridge with official *Blue Badge Guides*. These leave from the Tourist Information Centre on Wheeler Street every day, lasting two hours. On Tuesdays during July and August, there are *Drama Tours* with costumed characters who bring to life Cambridge's history. You might meet Henry VIII, Elizabeth I or Isaac Newton. Leaflets from Cambridge Tourist Information Office or the City Council. (*Contact information found on page 180 and the back page of the book.*)

CLUBS, SOCIETIES & GROUPS

Cambridge and the surrounding area has hundreds of clubs, societies and groups of every description, some of which have been meeting regularly for many decades. A full list with the updated contact information is provided in the annual Citizen's Guide, usually available for £1 from the Cambridge Central Library, or from the publisher, the Cambridge Evening News. (*See back page 'Key Contacts'*).

The listings include the following categories:

Allotments	Computer Clubs	Motoring Clubs
Gardening &	Dance	Music groups / clubs
flower clubs	Drama	Orienteering
Bridge Clubs	Flying	Outdoor Activity Clubs
Calligraphy	Gliding	Railway Clubs
Camera Clubs	Homing Societies	Self-Defence
Chess	Literary Groups	Service Clubs
Clubs for the	Model Clubs	Women's Groups
unattached	Motorcycling Clubs	Youth Groups

CAMBRIDGE MUSEUMS & SITES

● **Cambridge and County Folk Museum**

Set in the nine rooms of the 17th-century White Horse Inn, the museum displays domestic bygones such as cleaning appliances, clothes and toys. It has activities for children during the holidays. ☆ ☆ *CHILDREN*.

Open from April to September, Monday to Saturday, from 10.30am to 5pm, and on Sundays from 2pm to 5pm. From October to March Tuesday to Saturday from 10.30am to 5pm, and on Sundays from 2pm to 5pm. 2-3 Castle Street. Adults £2, children 50p. (01223 355159).

● Cambridge Museum of Technology

A working Victorian pumping station complete with coal-fired turbines. A lot of fun. ☆ *CHILDREN*

The Old Pumping Station, Cheddar's Lane, Cambridge. Entrance and parking on Riverside. Open April to October on Sundays from 2pm to 5pm and from November to March on the first Sunday of each month from 2pm to 5pm, plus special steam days. Adult admission £2 (£4 on steam days, concessions for children, OAPs, families. (01223 368650).

Major University museums & sites

● The University Botanic Garden

A refreshing and delightful 40-acre garden, famed for its trees, with plants from around the world, winter and rock gardens, tropical glass houses and a lake. ☆ ☆ ☆

The entrance is on Bateman Street and admission is free on weekdays from November 1st to February 29th (a charge of £1.50 or £1 concessions is made at weekends and the rest of the year). Open Monday to Sunday, 10am to 4pm in winter, until 5pm in spring and 6pm in summer. The greenhouses close at 3.45pm (01223 336265). Website: www.plantsci.cam.ac.uk/Botgdn/index.htm

● The Fitzwilliam Museum

Magnificent building with 27 galleries of antiquities from Ancient Egypt, Greece and Rome. Ancient coins and manuscripts. Paintings by artists including Titian, Rubens, Van Dyck, Canaletto, Hogarth, Gainsborough, Constable, Monet, Degas, Renoir Cezanne and Picasso. There is a programme of lectures and lunchtime talks. ☆ ☆ ☆

Trumpington Street. Admission free. Open from Tuesday to Saturday from 10am to 5pm and on Sunday from 2.15pm to 5pm when there are guided tours. There is no visitor parking even for people with disabilities. People in wheelchairs are advised to call in advance on 01223 332900 or 332937 so they can have help in a building which is magnificent but built in a less thoughtful age. Families are welcome but prams and push-chairs are not allowed. However, baby slings and harnesses are available and there are full baby changing facilities. www.fitzmuseum.cam.ac.uk

Other University Museums & Sites

(Some of the university museums may be closed in the holidays. See also Kettle's Yard, a University of Cambridge facility listed under Art Galleries, below.)

● The Scott Polar Research Institute

Polar life and exploration based on actual expeditions.

Lensfield Road. Admission free. Open Monday to Saturday from 2.30pm to 4pm (01223 336540) www.spri.cam.ac.uk ☆ ☆

● University Collection of Air Photographs

More than 400,000 air photographs taken throughout Great Britain. ☆

THE FITZWILLIAM MUSEUM

University of Cambridge

One of the finest art collections in the UK: antiquities, armour, sculpture, furniture, pottery, paintings, drawings, prints, coins, medals and much more. Temporary exhibitions, gallery talks, concerts and events.

Tuesday - Saturday: 10.00am - 5.00pm
Sunday: 2.15pm - 5.00pm

ADMISSION FREE

Guided Tours for groups telephone 01223 332904

Shop and cafe.

The Fitzwilliam Museum, Trumpington Street, Cambridge CB2 1RB Tel: 01223 332900

Email: fitzmuseum-enquiries@lists.cam.ac.uk
www.fitzmuseum.cam.ac.uk

New Museums Site, Free School Lane. Admission free. Open Monday to Thursday, 9am to 1pm and 2pm to 5pm, Friday 9am to 1pm and 2pm to 4pm. Closed public holidays (01223 334578).

● Museum of Archaeology & Anthropology

Explore civilisations past and present without leaving Cambridge, through the Museum's collections from all parts of the world. Special exhibitions throughout the year. ☆☆

Downing Street, Cambridge. Admission free. Open Monday to Friday from 10am to 5pm and Saturday from 10am to 12.30pm except public holidays (01223 333516) cumaa.archanth.cam.ac.uk

● Museum of Classical Archaeology

A comprehensive gallery of casts of Greek and Roman sculptures still serves its purpose as a great teaching resource, casting light on the ancient world. School groups welcome; call the Museum to book in advance. ☆

Sidgwick Avenue. Admission free. Open Monday to Friday from 9am to 5pm. Closed during Christmas and Easter (01223 335153).

www.classics.cam.ac.uk/ark.html

● Sedgwick Museum of Earth Sciences

Extensive collection of geological specimens. (A refurbishment is underway due for completion in early 2002. In the meantime, parts of the museum may be closed.) ☆

Downing Street. Open Monday to Friday from 9am to 1pm and 2pm to 5pm, Saturdays 10am to 1pm (01223 333456)

www.esc.cam.ac.uk/SedgwickMuseum/museumIndex/

● Whipple Museum of the History of Science

An amazing collection of scientific equipment, from astrolabes to the first programmable computers. Special 'case studies' provide an insight into current research on the history of science at Cambridge. ☆☆

Free School Lane. Admission free. Open Monday to Friday, 1.30pm to 4.30pm except public holidays (01223 330906).

www.hps.cam.ac.uk/Whipple.html

LEISURE

● The University Museum of Zoology

Traces the evolution of life on earth through the Museum's collections of recent and fossilised animals, including specimens brought back by Charles Darwin from the 'Beagle' Voyage. ☆ ☆

Downing Street. Admission free. Open afternoons only in term time, from 2pm to 4.45pm and during the holidays from 10am to 1pm, weekdays only (01223 336650) www.zoo.cam.ac.uk/museum/index.htm

Cambridge historic centre & colleges

Any good guidebook you open will cover the Cambridge centre and colleges (we list some at the end of this chapter), so we will emphasize their great interest and give you a few insider's tips.

A lovely way to appreciate King's College Chapel is to attend Sunday morning services or 5.30pm at evensong (for information call King's College 01223 331447), when you can hear the famous choristers sing. People queue for a day or more to go to the carol service on Christmas Eve, but the Christmas morning service is also impressive and has only short queues.

Many other colleges, such as Clare and Jesus, also have services open to the public with college choirs singing, and some periodically open their gardens and grounds to the public beyond the usual areas open to tourists. Check with Cambridge Tourist Office to find out when the colleges are open. You can also get information from the extensive Cambridge University website *(see 'Key Contacts,' back page)*.

MUSEUMS AROUND CAMBRIDGE

● The Imperial War Museum, Duxford

The home of the planes used by The Few, biplanes, Spitfires, as well as Concorde and Gulf War jets. Tanks and artillery are also on show, displayed in battlefield scenes. ☆ ☆ ☆ *CHILDREN*

Duxford. About 10 miles south of Cambridge off junction 10 on the M11. A free bus service runs from Cambridge city centre and Cambridge Railway Station. Open all year round, except December 24 to 26, from 10am to 6pm in summer, 10am to 4pm in winter. Admission is £7.70 for an adult. Children under16 enter free. (01223 835000) www.iwm.org.uk

● The National Horse-Racing Museum

A collection celebrating the horse and historical horse memorabilia. Try the horse simulator or horse-racing karaoke. Guided tours around Newmarket Stables can be booked. (The horses' swimming pool is fascinating). Newmarket itself is the headquarters of British horse-racing. See the horses working the gallops or strings of horses en route to the rings in early morning before breakfast. ☆ ☆ ☆ *CHILDREN*

99 High Street, Newmarket. Museum is open from April to October from 10am to 5pm daily. Last admission 4pm (01638 667333).

HORSE-RACING

Newmarket has two flat racing courses and Huntingdon has jump racing – both sites are classy and accessible.

Rowley Mile is the big Newmarket track, where from March to October meetings take place about 17 times a year, each with six to eight races (typically between 1pm and 5pm). You can pay for expensive indoor seating at the newly built stands, but the outdoor Grandstand and Paddock Enclosure (Tattersall's), close to the finishing line, are the best value at £12 to £15. Call 01638 663482 for information. In summer, racing at Newmarket's July course, also meeting about 17 times a year, is more informal, with bands and open-air bars. Betting begins at about £2 to £5 a stake.

For hurdling and steeple chasing, try The Huntingdon Race Course, at Brampton along the A14. It holds about 17 meetings a year. The adult entry fee is £10 to £15 per day and it's free for children. Information: 01480 453373.

EXCURSIONS – CLOSE

● **Milton Country Park**

Originally an ancient Roman site, and later a gravel pit and quarry, the park provides a welcome place for a lovely walk very near to the city centre, though the sounds of traffic can intrude. The park has lakes, bridges and woods. It also has an organised programme of activities for children. Café and visitors' centre. ☆ *CHILDREN*

LEISURE

SMALL MUSEUMS NEAR CAMBRIDGE

Manor House Museum, Honey Hill, Bury St Edmunds. A Georgian mansion with displays of costume, rare clocks and watches, paintings, furniture and objets d'art *CHILDREN* (01284 757076).

Ely Museum, The Old Gaol, Market Street. The outline history of the isle of Ely from dinosaur fossils to the 1950s. *CHILDREN* Tours by appointment (01353 666655).

The Cromwell Museum, Grammar School Walk, Huntingdon High Street, Huntingdon. Illustrates the life of Oliver Cromwell (01480 375830).

The Shuttleworth Collection, Old Walden Aerodrome, Biggleswade. One of the few remaining active grass aerodromes left. See the flying machines those magnificent men flew *(01767 627288)*.

Denny Abbey Farmland Museum, Ely Road, Waterbeach. Find out about countesses and fighting monks, country craftsman and farmers. *CHILDREN*. 01223 860988.

Wisbech and Fenland Museum, off The Wisbech Crescent, a Victorian building with a Victorian collection including the manuscript of Charles Dickens' Great Expectations and Napoleon's breakfast service (01945 583817).

CHILFORD HALL

Balsham Road, Linton, Cambridge, CB1 6LE Telephone: 01223 895625
Fax: 01223 895605 • www.chilfordhall.co.uk

Open: 1st Mar to 30th Oct (11am-5.30pm) • 1st Nov to 23rd Dec (11am - 4.30pm)

Shop & Winery, new Vineyard Trails, Vineleaf Restaurant, Award-winning wines.

Lookout for special events in local press. Conference and Banqueting Centre.

Licensed for Civil Weddings.

Milton is just north of Cambridge - follow brown country park signs from the A14/A10 junction, right next to Tesco (01223 420060).

● The American Cemetery

A moving and magnificent tribute to American servicemen who died during the Second World War, this sweeping green contains 3812 gravestones and carries an atmosphere of beauty and deep peace. ☆☆☆

Madingley Road., Coton, Cambridge (01954 210350).

EXCURSIONS – IN THE REGION

The following typically have entrance fees, ranging from £3 to £7, though you can often explore the grounds for free.

● Ely Cathedral

Ely Cathedral has 1300 years of remarkable history. Children can take brass rubbings and count the seven-second echo when they clap in the Lady chapel. There is a brass rubbing centre, a stained glass museum, a restaurant, guided tour and maze. ☆☆☆ *CHILDREN/TEENS*

(01353 667735) www.cathedral.ely.anglican.org

● Wimpole Hall

A magnificent 18th-century country house in vast land-scaped parkland, owned by the National Trust. Stunning views, pleasant café. It has a child-oriented farm where rabbit cuddling, donkey grooming, feeding pigs and milking goats are encouraged. Special half-term activities.
☆☆☆ *CHILDREN*

Opening times of house, park and farm vary, so ring to check. Located 8 miles south west of Cambridge off the A603, junction 12 off the M11 (01223 207257).

● Anglesey Abbey

Another National Trust property with gardens renowned for beauty, statuary and historic interest. A must for anyone passionate about antiques and especially clocks. There is also a working water mill. ☆☆☆ *CHILDREN*

Located six miles northeast of Cambridge off the B1102, just as you enter the village of Lode (01223 811200).

● Audley End House and Gardens

Vast country house owned by English Heritage. Magnificent Jacobean hall and architecture of the 17th, 18th and 19th centuries. The whole house is set out to show how it would have appeared at these times. Beautiful grounds. ☆☆☆ *CHILDREN*

Located 1 mile west of Saffron Walden on the B1383 (M11 exit 8 or 9 on the northbound lane only) (01799 522842).

● Chilford Hall, Linton

A working vineyard where you can see how wines are made. The hall itself is impressive and is set in 18 acres of attractive countryside. Guided tours, restaurant, gift shop. ☆☆

Open from March to December. Located in Linton, 10 miles southeast of Cambridge on the A1307 (01223 895625).

● Mountfitchet Castle, Stansted

A reconstructed Norman village of 1066, with its own motte and bailey castle. The original site is described in the Domesday book. Wander through the village among the animals, surrounded by the castle walls. There's also The House on the Hill Adventure Museum, a strange juxtaposition of toys and rock and roll, plus an 'End of the Pier' show. ☆☆☆ *CHILDREN*

Located at Stansted 2 miles from junction 8 off the M11 (01279 813237).

● Flag Fen, Peterborough

A fascinating 3000-year-old Bronze Age site where archaeologists found, amongst other treasures, Britain's oldest wooden wheel. See how the early people lived, preservation techniques, old varieties of sheep, pigs and wild boar, a Roman garden and road, and gift shop with replica artefacts. ☆☆ *CHILDREN*

Take the Fengate exit from Peterborough and follow signs (01733 313414).

WALKS & OUTDOORS

Several of the above attractions include stunning walks. The following offer a selection specifically for walking.

● Welney Wildfowl and Wetlands Centre

One of the largest and most important conservation areas in Europe, the washland attracts numerous varieties of waterfowl. In winter the Bewick and Whooper swans from the Arctic regions of Greenland and north Russia are a particular attraction. Lovely in summer too. ☆☆*CHILDREN*

In Welney, just north of Ely. (01353 860711).

● Wicken Fen Nature Reserve

The last piece of undrained fenland marsh open to the

LEISURE

general public. An interesting visitor centre, a long, long boardwalk suitable for wheelchairs and huge areas of reedbed which are harvested for thatch and varieties of flora and fauna. ☆ *CHILDREN*

A National Trust site 15 miles north east of Cambridge (01353 720274).

● Fen Rivers Way

A 17-mile walk into the heart of the fens (Cambridge to Ely/ Ely to King's Lynn), with vast open spaces, kingfishers, ducks and geese. The route marked with the distinctive eel logo follows the drained floodbanks of the rivers Cam and Ouse. Walk parts of it or make it a two-day camping trip or overnight in a B&B. Muddy so boots are recommended. ☆ ☆ ☆

Good access by public transport; buses go from Cambridge to Waterbeach, Stretham and Ely (01223 423554 for bus timetables, and 01223 317740 for a free public transport map) and trains go regularly between Cambridge, Waterbeach and Ely (01223 311999 for a timetable). For a really good comprehensive pack on walks on and around the Fen Rivers Way, maps, and its history, phone Cambridgeshire County Council Rural Group on 01223 317445.

● Gog Magog Hills & Wandlebury Fort

An Iron Age ring fort associated with the Iceni tribes and Romans, now a nature reserve and country park with trails and walks. Good views over Cambridge and the cathedral city of Ely can be seen to the north. ☆

Located a few miles south of Cambridge on the A1307 (01223 243830).

● Grantchester Meadows

A pleasurable hour or so-long amble along the river from Newnham in Cambridge to the famous village where English teas can be sampled at the wonderful Orchard Tea Rooms and its rambling orchard, once frequented by the Bloomsbury set. Begin the walk at the end of Grantchester Meadows, a road off Grantchester Street. ☆ ☆ ☆

Tearooms 01223 845788. *See also under Punting.*

● Devil's Dyke

A dry, linear defensive earthwork, about seven miles long, built some time in the Dark Ages. Good views from this chalky, hedged heath path over the black peat fens, but a car is recommended as bus services are rather infrequent to the villages at either end. ☆

The walk goes from the Fen edge at Reach (approximately 12 miles northeast of Cambridge on the B1102) to the woodlands of Suffolk at Wood Ditton, crossing Newmarket Heath and the race course en route.

Punting on the River Cam

To experience Cambridge fully, you must go punting, one of the most pleasurable English pursuits that exist. There are hire points at the Quayside, the bridge on Garret Hostel

Lane, at points around the mill pond at Mill Lane/Silver Street and at the Granta Inn on Newnham Road.

You can punt along the famous Backs, a trip well described by the tourist guides (ending with wine and cheese on the grass at the mill pond, surely) or take the wilder, less populated route through Paradise (that's the name of the nature reserve you pass through) from above the weir. If you're a strong and experienced punter, it's possible to punt all the way to Grantchester for tea at the Orchard. The trip takes about two hours each way.

Expect to pay about £8 per hour for the punt plus a hefty, returnable deposit; however you can avoid the deposit and pay less if you have a Leisurecard, details page 156. ☆☆☆

Animals and fun for children

● Linton Zoo

A small zoo housing a birds, mammals and reptiles including protected species. There are special organised children's activities and an education area. ☆ *CHILDREN*

Located 10 miles southeast of Cambridge in an attractive 16-acre site. Admission: £5 adults, children 2-13 £4. (01223 891308)

● Willers Mill Wildlife Park

The park has a range of wild and domestic animals including tropical birds, wolves and monkeys. Children can feed the milder species such as deer and giant carp, have a pony ride or go on the dodgems. ☆☆ *CHILDREN*

Station Road, Shepreth (09066 800031 or 0891 715522).

● Wood Green Animal Shelters

Rescued cats, dogs and rabbits all waiting to be visited. There is a club which children can join. ☆ *CHILDREN*

www.woodgreen.org.uk (01763 838329). Chishill Road, Heydon (near Royston) and at London Road, Godmanchester (01480 830014).

ANNUAL EVENTS

Cambridge has an annual event almost every week of the year if you count them all. These include a packed programme of City Council children's activities too numerous to list here. The council sends brochures home with the

---

MOSTLY FOR CHILDREN / TEENS – COMMERCIAL FUN

Glaze To Amaze, 54 Burleigh Street, Cambridge. You buy a plain ceramic piece from a vast range of shapes, sizes and prices, and are then taught to glaze it, using paint-on glazes in any way you like. The pieces are then fired for you. *CHILDREN/TEENS*. 01223 319600.

Laser Quest, 13-15 Bradwell's Court, Cambridge. Described as 'the ultimate adventure game for mere humans' this laser-based activity, on the second floor, is open daily from 10.30am to 9pm. £3 on weekdays and £3.50 at weekends. *CHILDREN/TEENS*. 01223 312102.

children from school and they are available from the City Council's Promotions team on 01223 457521 or 01223 463363 or Tourist Information, 01223 322640. Below, we list some of the regular major events.

March events

● University of Cambridge open days

The open days take place from March-July and in September. *TEENS*

Check dates for the different colleges on the Cambridge University website: www.cam.ac.uk or ring the University's Press and Publication Office at 01223 332300.

● University of Cambridge Science Week

This is usually in March (in 2001 it runs from 16th-25th) and is a fantastic range of free events, lectures, activities, talks and tours for all ages. The theme for 2001 is Codes and Puzzles, and areas covered will include astronomy, spies and inventions, sound, music and dance, as well as lectures and a debate for adults. The events, held in various University and museum sites, are free, though for some you will need to book a place. The programme is available from Cambridge University Press Bookshop, 1 Trinity Street, or the Tourist Information Office in Wheeler Street. ☆☆☆ *CHILDREN/TEENS*

For details call the Science Week hotline on 01223 766766.

May events

● The Oxfam sponsored walk

The walk has been scaled down from previous years, but still takes place on a Sunday in May to raise money for the charity. Walkers are famously cheerful whatever the weather. Volunteers are needed to act as stewards and marshalls. *TEENS*

For information call 01223 301317.

June events

● The May Bumps

An intercollegiate rowing race for about 150 crews over several days. They start off at different points on the Cam and when they catch up with each other it is called 'bumping'. The traditions of the bumps date back to the late 1820s. Called the May Bumps but like the May Balls, and The May Week Plays – performed in college gardens and open to the public – it takes place in June. All the May university events celebrate the end of exams. ☆☆

Find out more from the University's Press and Publications office (01223 332300).

● Strawberry Fair

You know summer has arrived when it's time for the fair. It's not a funfair, but it is fun. There is a carnival atmosphere on Midsummer Common with live music, hippy clothes for sale, the smell of incense and other herbal products and plenty of beads and veggie food. Takes place on a Saturday in June. ✰✰ *TEENS*

Contact the Cambridge Tourist Office, 01223 322640, for information.

July events

● The Town Bumps

The townspeople's counterpart to the May bumps. ✰✰

● events on Parker's Piece

Three consecutive, free parties on Parker's Piece are laid on a Friday, Saturday and Sunday, in the middle of July. *Pop in the Park* is a Friday night party starting about 6pm with local and national bands playing live. *The Big Day Out* is an all-day and all-evening event with funfair, market stalls, open air-entertainment and live pop music ending with a firework display. On the Sunday, The *Party on the Piece* is a pop party for teenagers. ✰✰ *TEENS*

For information contact Cambridge City Council Promotions on 01223 457521.

● Cambridge Folk Festival

Held annualy on the last weekend in July at Cherry Hinton Hall since 1965. An international event with all 10,000 tickets sold out every year about a month before it starts. This is the oldest and most famous acoustic music festival in the world. It began as the vision of one man, a Cambridge fireman called Ken Woollard. The first year by noon on the Saturday only four people had turned up. For years Ken organised it virtually from the phone box outside the fire station, then the city council stepped in and paid him to run it. Sadly he has died but the quality of the music, food and friendly atmosphere at the festival is a tribute to his faith in human nature. The festival now runs from the Thursday to the Sunday. Attended by newborn babies, their elderly great-grandmothers, teenagers with beaded hair and absolutely everyone in between. The typical festival-goer has a flagon of beer in one hand and a copy of *The Guardian* in the other. ✰✰✰ *TEENS*

For information, e.g. on camping or where to stay, ring the City's Promotions team, 01223 463363, or Tourist Information, 01223 322640.

● Open Studios art exhibitions

From 11am-6pm on the first four weekends of July, approximately 250 artists in the region open their homes or studios to the public for free. You just wander in wherever there's a yellow flag. To get the most out of this fascinating opportunity, pick up a brochure (distinctively long and quite narrow) in the Tourist Information office on Wheeler Street, or just about any Arts venue, and plan which ones you want to visit by looking at the descriptions, map and photos of the work. The work is hugely varied and almost all for sale. Discovering new roads and villages is nearly as pleasurable as seeing all the paintings, pots, prints, carvings, sculptures and jewellery. ☆☆☆

For information: 01223 561192 or www.camopenstudios.co.uk for more details.

July/August

● concerts & comedians

With July, a series of summer events begin including classical concerts, free jazz concerts and events like a tent on Jesus Green with children's activities in the day and comedians doing one-night shows in the evening.

Call 01223 457521 for details of all of these and look out for leaflets in libraries, theatres and The Grafton Centre.

● Shakespeare festival

Annual festival of Shakespeare's plays performed in Cambridge colleges, mostly in the college gardens. Usually good. Mulled wine is sold in the intervals. Take a picnic and a flask of something hot but also dress for the Russian winter. Even on a warm evening you will start to freeze after the interval, especially if you are sitting on the grass. Nevertheless some memorable performances to be seen. ☆☆

Details from OpenHand on 01223 511139 or e-mail the director David Crilly on dcrilly@bridge.anglia.ac.uk.

Institute of Visual Culture

Cambridge

10D St Edward's Passage
Cambridge CB2 3PJ

Telephone +44(0) 1223 350 533
Facsimile +44(0) 1223 312 188

admin@instituteofvisualculture.org
www.instituteofvisualculture.org

Supported by Eastern Arts Board, Cambridge City Council

November events

● fireworks

Fireworks on Midsummer Common: usually held on November 5 itself and run by the city council. Includes free fireworks display and a giant bonfire. Sponsored by a local business or in recent years, The Grafton Centre. Forget trying to drive there and park unless you go early - best to walk most of the way. The region has public displays in almost every village on the 5th and over the weekend nearest to it. There is a collection at the fireworks for contributions toward the cost of the event. ☆☆ *CHILDREN/TEENS*.

See local press for details or contact the nearest library or your local authority.

December events

With Christmas come the pantomimes at the theatres (see page 170), and on Christmas Eve the King's College Chapel Carol Service (see page 160). Queue by 7am to be sure of getting a place when the service starts at 3pm.

EXHIBITIONS & ART GALLERIES

See also 'Open Studios' under July, above, and 'Original artworks, crafts and framing' in 'Shopping', page 108.

● central Cambridge

Cambridge Darkroom, Dales Brewery, Gwydir Street. Touring exhibitions of photographs. Holds talks, video displays, workshops and discussions. Darkroom facilities and classes available. Magazines and books for sale.

Open Wednesday to Sunday from noon to 5pm. Admission free (01223 566725).

The Fitzwilliam Museum, Trumpington Street.

For details see under Museums page 158.

Kettle's Yard, Castle Street. A University of Cambridge art gallery and exhibition centre in a house built from four 17th- and 18th-century cottages. The house is truly unusual and beautiful, with a feeling of all-pervading peace. The gallery exhibits sculptures, paintings and drawings by leading international, contemporary and 20th-century artists. Some work for sale. Has after-school drawing classes for children and Saturday drawing classes for teenagers and adults as well as holiday workshops, lunchtime talks and educational courses. *CHILDREN/TEENS*

Admission free. The house is open from Tuesday to Sunday and on bank holiday Mondays from 2pm to 4pm. The gallery is open from Tuesday to Sunday and bank holiday Mondays from 11.30am to 5pm. (01223 352124) www.kettlesyard.co.uk

University Library (including Exhibition Centre) has public exhibitions of materials.

01223 333000 and www.lib.cam.ac.uk for information.

● close to Cambridge

Wysing Arts, Fox Road, Bourn. Exhibitions, workshops

with access for everyone, children's activities, a gardening club for people with learning difficulties, courses for all ages, and events. Exhibitions are free. *CHILDREN/TEENS*. (01954 718881). Open Monday to Friday from 11am to 5pm, Saturday and Sunday noon to 5pm. (On the B1046 between Bourn and Longstowe) Website: www.wysing.demon.co.uk

CINEMA

The two main venues for film in Cambridge are the *Arts Picturehouse* (38-39 St Andrew's Street, 01223 504444, website: www.picturehouse-cinemas.co.uk) and *Warner Village* (The Grafton Centre, 01223 460442 for recorded information. www.warnervillage.co.uk). The Arts is arty and offbeat, showing the continental, subtitled and less main-stream as well as the usual, and has a devoted band of fol-lowers. The Warner is a multi-screen complex surrounded by eateries and popcorn vendors and showing all the latest releases.

There are also cinemas at outlying towns such as Huntingdon, Haverhill, Bedford, Ramsey and Royston. Favourites are *The Maltings*, Ely, 01353 662633 (interesting venue and riverside setting which offers a range of other entertainment, concerts and a restaurant) and the *ABC at Bury St Edmund's*, 01284 754477, (after the film try the nice Greek restaurant opposite).

THEATRE & MORE

So many venues offer music and plays that they can't be listed exclusively. So we've put those that do mostly per-formance in this section. The next section lists those most-ly associated with music, and then a further section under 'music' explains where different types of music are per-formed and names additional music-only venues.

ADC Theatre

This is where Cambridge University students perform and it has to be the most relaxed and welcoming theatrical venue in Cambridge. The atmosphere is great because so many people in the audience know the people on stage that you often get off to a cheering start. This is the venue for *The Footlights Club*, which produces the annual student comedy review.

It has a newly refurbished bar. Home of the Amateur Dramatic Club since 1855, you can see classical theatre, Shakespeare and the Greeks but also brand new revues from the latest Cambridge University students showing off budding theatrical talent. There is an annual panto but this is never traditional. After the main evening shows, late night comedy revues and short plays start at 11pm.

This is a small theatre so there are no bad seats. Tickets are usually £5 or less. The theatre is in Park Street, Cambridge, almost next to Park Street multi-storey car park. Book via the Arts Theatre on 01223 503333. www.adctheatre.com

The Arts Theatre

This is traditional, classical theatre done well. Shows here come direct from the West End, often with the original cast. They also come here for their first run before going to the West End. Most of the programme is top-notch professional but local amateur and university groups perform here too. The theatre opened in 1936, with funds from John Maynard Keynes. It was in a poor state by the early 1990s and completely refurbished by a Lottery grant and money raised by the people of Cambridge. At the time eight and a half million pounds seemed an unconscionable amount but post-Dome it seems brilliant value.

LEISURE

MAJOR VENUE BOX OFFICE NUMBERS

Cinema

Arts Picturehouse	01223 504444
Warner Village	01223 460442
The Maltings (Ely)	01353 662633 or 01353 669022
ABC (Bury St Edmunds)	01284 754477

Theatre

ADC Theatre	01223 503333
The Arts Theatre	01223 503333
The Mumford Theatre	01223 352932
The Cambridge Drama Centre	01223 511511

Music Venues

The Cambridge Corn Exchange	01223 357851
The Junction	01223 511511
West Road Concert Hall	01223 335182

Around Cambridge

Theatre Royal (Bury St Edmunds)	01284 769505
Littleport Leisure Centre	01353 860600
Haverhill Town Hall Arts Centre	01440 714140
King's Theatre (Ely)	01638 663337
St Ivo Centre (St Ives)	01480 388500
Angles Theatre (Wisbech)	01945 474447

The theatre has been respected for its Christmas pantomime since the days of 'Dame' Cyril Fletcher in the 1950s. This is still a traditional, glittering show with plenty of audience participation. Recent big names in touring plays have included Helen Mirren, Tom Conti, Alison Steadman, Maureen Lipman and Rik Mayall. The theatre has a restaurant but you have to book in advance if you want to eat after the show. Pantomime teas are available between the matinées and evening performances.

Most shows during the year start at 7.45pm with 2.30pm matinées on Thursdays and Saturdays. There are also some one night shows on Sundays.

The Arts Theatre prides itself on accessibility for all. There are signed performances in British Sign Language and audio-described performances for the visually impaired. There is a Gone to Lunch Club for people over 55. Tickets start at £5 for every show. The theatre has only about 500 seats so you can see well from most of them. Top-price tickets can be £20 but this is still half the price of seeing the same show in the West End months later. The theatre is on Peas Hill, just off market square, close to Lion Yard multi-storey car park. Box office: 01223 503333 and website: www.cambridgeartstheatre.com

The Mumford Theatre

This is the most comfortable theatre in Cambridge with the best rake on the seats so that every seat is a good seat. Some remarkable shows can be seen here too. The theatre is part of Anglia Polytechnic University and has student productions plus some impressive performances from visiting professional and local amateur groups. Recent programmes included a stage version of *Captain Corelli's Mandolin* by Cambridge's Mike Maran who got permission from the author Louis de Bernières to stage the show at the 1999 Edinburgh Festival and then tour with it. Other talent included the poet John Hegley and The Actors of Dionysus, who specialise in the drama of the ancient Greeks, with *The Bacchae* by Euripides. The Mumford has an annual panto performed by students. Some years have been magical, others down to earth with a bump. However, the live music is always good.

The Mumford also has free lunchtime concerts on Fridays during term time, promoted by Anglia's Department of Music. Tickets for stage events range around £8 with concessions for senior citizens and children. The Mumford is just off East Road, Cambridge. There is parking but you need to put a pound coin into the barrier first. Call the box office on 01223 352932.

Cambridge Drama Centre

This small but interesting venue has recently merged with The Junction under one box office. Much of the programme is new and alternative. It examines issues and is thought provoking. Among the regular visitors are the acclaimed CandoCo, the dance company which integrates able-bodied and disabled people. The companies who appear at The Drama Centre tend to have imaginative names like Escape Artists, Hoipolloi, Trading Faces and Indefinite Articles. The Drama Centre is also a centre for local amateur theatre and has an annual summer season of new plays by local groups.

It seats only about 150 people, but new tiered seating means everyone has an excellent view. Tickets are are around £7.50. The Drama Centre is in Covent Garden, a cul-de-sac off Mill Road. Parking is anyone's guess in the little streets nearby, but there is a small car park in Gwydir Street further down Mill Road, and a large car park off East Road in Queen Anne Terrace. (01223 511511) www.dramacentre.co.uk

College, school & community theatre

The colleges at Cambridge University have drama societies which regularly put on plays open to the public. There are usually posters about productions in the foyer of the Arts

ANA LUCIA DE SILVA GARCIA – STUDENT

Coming from Brazil everything is different. By comparison, Cambridge is safe and compact. I like it a lot – it means that it is the best place to be a student.

It doesn't feel dangerous here. This is a student city; everyone is safe and everything is near. I don't have a car or even a bike. I can just walk. In Sao Paulo you wouldn't think of walking the streets.

I can cope with the fact that there aren't the facilities of a big city – although I might go crazy if I had to stay forever! There isn't really any nightlife – but that's how it is. You can't cram everything into Cambridge. Whereas Sao Paulo is a 24-hour city, in Cambridge the pubs close at 11pm! But it all adds to the character of the place. A bigger, 24-hour, Cambridge wouldn't be the same and certainly wouldn't feel as safe.

The real down side is that even though Cambridge is small and compact it is so expensive. Because it is small, because of its location, because it is an attractive place for people to be – that all makes it expensive. But there are always good and bad points to a city. That it is a fun, safe place is what matters overall – especially as a student. Besides, Cambridge makes up for not having the facilities or feel of Sao Paulo in lots of different ways. For example, there is a great mix within the student population which means that it feels international.

Maybe I appreciate Cambridge so much because I know that I am here for such a short time. I know that I am going to leave soon so I'm especially proud to be here.

I think that it is perfect. Well almost perfect - as close to perfect as it could be!

Ana Lucia de Silva Garcia is a Brazilian student at Anglia Polytechnic University.

Theatre. Tickets can usually be booked at the Arts Theatre or bought at the college's porters' lodge. A notable company is *BATS* at Queens' College. They perform in their own, very comfortable Fitzpatrick Theatre. You park along the Backs and enter the theatre from Silver Street.

Secondary Schools in Cambridge are known as village colleges or community colleges and have stages used by pupils and some very polished local amateur companies. Bottisham Village College is the home of the award-winning, young people's *Bikeshed Theatre Company*. Comberton Village College is the home of the *Meridian Theatre Company*. Hills Road Sixth Form College has its own *Robinson Theatre* where students have staged some powerful performances. Coleridge Community College has performed original plays and pantomimes.

MUSIC & MORE

Cambridge Corn Exchange

A vast venue for music, drama and legends seating 1,500 people. It is worth buying top price seats because the cheaper ones, especially in the balcony, are a long way from the stage. Almost the whole hall of showbiz fame has appeared here, bands, comics, actors and international ballet companies. A recent list would include Jools Holland, Harry Hill, Eddie Izzard, Joan Baez, Sheila Ferguson of The Three Degrees, The Fun Loving Criminals and The Moscow City Ballet Company. The venue, owned by the city council, hosts rock concerts, comedy, plays, ballet, opera and musical theatre. Recent new work included Pneumonic, Fever Pitch, and the stage version of A Clockwork Orange. It excels in classical music performances. The programme for the year 2001 included The Czech National Symphony Orchestra, Bournemouth Symphony Orchestra, The Orchestra of the Age of Enlightenment, The National Symphony Orchestra of Ukraine, The City of Birmingham Symphony Orchestra and the Berlin Symphony Orchestra.

Tickets range from £9 to £18.50 with concessions for senior citizens, school groups and parties. The venue tends to have Christmas shows rather than pantomimes, such as Joseph and the Technicolour Dreamcoat or Grease. The Corn Exchange is in Wheeler Street, off the market square and near Lion Yard Car Park. Website: www.cornex.co.uk. Box office: 01223 357851.

The Junction

The Junction is known mainly as a music venue and a major part of the teen scene but also has dance and top-of-the range stand-up comedy. On last season's programme were Rob Newman, Bill Bailey (best stand-up in the 1999 British Comedy Awards) Ed Byrne and Craig Charles. *TEENS*.

The Junction is in Clifton Road, off Cherry Hinton Road. It has its own car park. Box office 01223 511511.

West Road Concert Hall

The site holds a range of music events, mainly classical. It is part of Cambridge University's music department.

For information See Cambridge University Website www.cam.ac.uk or ring 01223 335184.

The Cambridge Fringe

● The Boat Race

A pub in East Road, Cambridge, mainly a music venue, but also host to The Comedy Cupboard, a stand-up comedy night on the last Friday of every month. Doors open at 7.30pm. Tickets on the door or from 01223 508533, The Arts Theatre on 01223 503333 or Cambridge Corn Exchange 01223 357851.

● CB2 Café

An internet café in Norfolk Street, off East Road, Cambridge which has seasons of plays and play readings. Tickets from 01223 508503 or on the door.

● The Playroom

A small, fringe venue in St Edward's Passage, near the Arts Theatre, mainly used by Cambridge University Students for new writing.

Information/booking via Cambridge Arts Theatre on 01223 503333.

THEATRE & MORE IN THE AREA

● Theatre Royal, Bury St Edmund's

A Georgian theatre kept lovingly and without much alteration since it was opened by its first owner, the architect William Wilkins in October 1819. Wilkins also designed the National Gallery in London and Downing College, Cambridge. The theatre is vibrant with a range of performance from comedy and the latest devised productions to traditional acts such as The Bachelors and the Beverley Sisters. It is a venue for Shakespeare, opera and ballet and has one of the best value, glitzy pantomimes in the region.

Tickets for most shows from about £8. Panto tickets start at £2 going up to a top price of £13. The theatre is in Westgate Street, opposite the Greene King brewery. It also shows films. There are car parks nearby. Visit the website on www.TheatreRoyal.org or call the box office on 01284 769505.

● The Maltings, Ely

Venue for theatre, music and film with comfortable, tiered seats and a café. The Maltings is in Ship Lane, Ely on the banks of the Great Ouse River with a car park nearby. Call 01353 662633 or contact ADec (Arts Development in East Cambridgeshire) at Babylon Bridge, Waterside, Ely on 01353 669022.

● Littleport Leisure Centre

The centre has an annual, summer visit from The Royal Shakespeare Company. For details call 01353 860600.

● Haverhill Town Hall Arts Centre

Excellent, comfortable and welcoming venue for drama, music and comedy, with a bar and bistro. It is home to a top-notch amateur group, The Centre Stage Company, part of Haverhill and District Operatic Society, which puts on a glorious rip-roaring musical and a pantomime each year. It always has a most exciting, must-see programme. Last season's included Andrew Sachs, Dillie Keane from Fascinating Aida, The Yardbirds and The Animals. The annual Footlights Revue premieres here before it goes to Cambridge and then to the rest of the country. The centre also has jazz and pensioners' line dancing and shows films. There are art exhibitions in the Bistro. The Arts Centre is in Haverhill High Street with car parks nearby. Call the box office on 01440 714140.

● King's Theatre, Newmarket

Home of Nomads, the Newmarket Operatic, Musical and Amateur Dramatic Society which puts on several sell-out shows a year including a pantomime and has a thriving youth section. Often has free previews for pensioners.

The theatre is in Fitzroy Street. Call the box office on 01638 663337.

● St Ivo Centre, St Ives

This is home to The Centre Theatre Players, an amateur group who for the past 30 years have put on a pantomime so good it is often better than the professional ones. Enormous wit goes into the staging. One year a milk cart turned up on stage, and when the bottles of milk were lifted off, they were all small children... who then did a milk bottle dance. There are other shows through the year.

Call the centre on 01480 388500.

● Angles Theatre, Wisbech

One of the fans of this venue is comedienne Jo Brand who has appeared there several times. Its director Michael Burrell is so dedicated he worked without pay for several months in the late 90s to keep the theatre afloat. It is strong on comedy and community theatre. Home of the Right Angles Theatre Company.

The theatre is in Alexandra Road, Wisbech and also holds art exhibitions. Call the box office on 01945 474447.

MUSIC FOR AFICIONADOS

Cambridge may not have hills but it is alive with music. All the year round at venues large and small there are amateur and professional groups and orchestras playing rock and pop, folk, jazz and classical. Flyers for concerts are found at all the theatrical and music venues as well as libraries. The Cambridge Concert Calendar is produced each term and is available from Cambridge Tourist Information Centre *(see Key Contacts, back page)* or from the music faculty at Cambridge University 01223 335184.

Classical music

A number of Cambridge sites host classical music perform-ances. *The Mumford Theatre* in East Road (page 172), has free lunchtime concerts in term time. *Kettle's Yard* (page 169), the art gallery in Castle Street, holds concerts during term time and *The Fitzwilliam Museum* (page 158) some-times has concerts. Check the *Cambridge Corn Exchange* (page 174) which has its own International Concert Series. Finally, performances at *The West Road Concert Hall* are mainly classical.

● **Haverhill and other venues**

Haverhill, which has its own Sinfonia, holds concerts in Haverhill Town Hall Arts Centre (01440 714140). Classical music is also played in churches, colleges, schools and com-munity centres all over the region. There are concerts somewhere every day. Most, but not all, will be listed in The Cambridge Concert Calendar (see above). Look also for fly-ers left in libraries, theatres and at the information point in The Grafton Centre.

Folk music

● **the folk clubs and venues**

The highlight of the year is the Folk Festival (see page 167 above). Regular folk venues at the time of writing (and they do change, so check before you go) include: *The Portland Arms*, Mitcham's Corner, Cambridge (01223 357268), which hosts the *Cambridge Folk Club* on Fridays, with an emphasis on acoustic music (to be put on the club's list, e-mail: cambridgefolkclub@ryanne.demon.co.uk), and the more traditionally-oriented *The Mayflower Folk Club* on Tuesdays. A Celtic/folk session is held on Monday evenings at *The Boat Race* (see 'The Cambridge Fringe', page 175).

Outside the centre and around the area, the *Fulbourn Folk Club* which meets at the White Hart, Balsham Road, Fulbourn (01223 880264), *The Red Lion Folk Club* meets at The Red Lion Hotel, Whittlesford (01223 832047), *The Cherry Hinton Folk Club* meets at *The Unicorn*, High Street, Cherry Hinton (01223 245872), and *The Ely Folk Club* meets at several venues in Ely and has an annual Folk Weekend (For information, Contact Adec Arts Development in East Cambridgeshire on 01353 669022).

All that Jazz

For jazz events in the region contact Jazzeast by e-mail: Joan@jazzeast.org.uk or www.traditional-jazz.com. Jazzeast events mainly take place at *Sophbeck Sessions*, the jazz club on Tredgold Lane, Cambridge, which has live jazz from Wednesday to Saturday, 6-11pm (bands usually begin around 8.30), and Latin nights with Salsa dancing on Sunday nights (www.sophbecksessions.co.uk and 01223 470257).

LEISURE

Jazz is also often performed at the *Cambridge Corn Exchange*, *The Boat Race* and *The Maltings* in Ely (see listings above). Keep an eye out also for the free open-air performances in the summer at Cherry Hinton Hall, off Cherry Hinton Road, Cambridge and on Jesus Green, Cambridge; Waites Green, St Ives; Grantchester Recreation Ground; Huntingdon Town Park Bandstand and Ely market square.

Regular Cambridge venues include *The Portland Arms* (see 'folk'), meeting place of Cambridge Jazz Co-operative; The *Cricketers,* Prospect Row (01223 516701); *The Elm Tree*, Orchard Street (01223 363005); *The Garden House Hotel*, Mill Lane, (01223 259988); *Pizza Express*, Jesus Lane (01223 324033).

Elsewhere try *The King William IV*, Fenstanton, (01480 462467); *Nelson's Head*, St Ives (01480 463342); *The Crafty Fox* on the road to Somersham in Chatteris, (01945 481765); *The Crown*, Little Walden Road, Saffron Walden (01799 522475); *The King's Arms*, Market Hill, Saffron Walden (01799 522768); and *The Five Miles from Anywhere* in Upware, Ely (01353 721654).

Clubbing

Night clubs in Cambridge are all mentioned in our companion *Best Cafes, Pubs, Clubs and Restaurants in and around Cambridge*, 2001 edition, available in bookshops. See the local media for what the DJ is spinning on a particular night.

ADDITIONAL INFORMATION

● what's on - general

Cambridge Evening News, the region's daily newspaper: www.cambridge-news.co.uk (01223 434434).

Adhoc magazine, a free weekly and website: www.adhoc.co.uk/cambridge/ (01223 568960).

(see 'Key Contacts', back page for further details)

● regional listings

The Guide, What's On in East Cambridgeshire. published by ADec (Arts Development In East Cambridgeshire). For free delivery contact: Babylon Gallery, Babylon Bridge, Waterside, Ely, Cambs CB7 4AU (01353 669022).

What's On: Art Events in South Cambridgeshire. The Arts Unit, South Cambridgeshire District Council, 9-11 Hills Road, Cambridge CB2 1PB (01223 724142).

Huntingdonshire District Council Arts (01223 724142).

What's On, a free listing of University of Cambridge events by Press and Publications Office. Look for it at the tourist office or call 01223 339397 to request a copy.

● music listings

The Cambridge Concert Calendar, published three times a year by the University of Cambridge music faculty termly, and sold for £2 at music shops and at the tourist office. To subscribe call the music faculty 01223 335184.

Jazzeast, lists jazz events across East England: Unit A, Dales Brewery, Gwydir Street, Cambridge (01223 722811) www.jazzeast.co.uk

For more media see 'Household Services' page 68

● tourist guides

Central Cambridge: A Guide to the University and Colleges, by Kevin Taylor (Cambridge University Press) 1994.

Cambridge Official Guide: essential information for visitors, Jarrold Publishing, 2000, a colourful guide for tourists, useful to the stayer. Vetted by the Tourist Information Centre. Text by Janet and Michael Jeacock, Jarrold Publishing

● lifestyle, eating out and other books

Best Cafes, Pubs, Clubs and Restaurants in and around Cambridge, 2001 edition, by Neal E. Robbins, published by the Wavy-Haired Reader (Insider Guides). All you could possibly need, with free vouchers thrown in.

Cambridge Secrets 2 (Wavy-Haired Reader) 2000.

Citizens' Guide. A special annual Cambridge Evening News supplement listing clubs and other organisations in the Cambridge area. £1 where sold. Also available online at www.cambridge-news.co.uk/citizens-guide/

● excursions with children

Let's Go with the Children in Essex and Suffolk, Cube Publications. Useful booklet covering hundreds of activities for children and parents. *CHILDREN*

Days Out With Kids (southeast edition) Janet Bonthron, Bon-Bon publishing. Fun family outings. *CHILDREN*

● walks and outdoor

Walks in South Cambridgeshire, one of a series published by the Cambridge Group of the Ramblers' Association. Twenty-three detailed walks with maps.

Gentle Strolls Around Cambridge/Peterborough, Discovering Cambridgeshire Woodlands and others – a series published by the Rural Group, Cambridgeshire

LEISURE

Photo by Findlay Kember

Cambridge rock singer Ezio performing at the folk festival

County Council, from whom various free leaflets on walks and the countryside can be obtained on 01223 317445.

Footloose and Carfree lists 11 walks using public transport in the Cambridgeshire countryside. Order it from Cambridgeshire County Council, Rural Group, Shire Hall, Cambridge CB3 OAP (01223 317445). Available at the tourist office and libraries.

● cycling

Cycle Cambridge, Barny Hill, White Hart Press, Twelve easy circular rides around the Cambridge area described by an avid cyclist.

● places to visit in the area

The Fens - Places to visit, things to see, by Trevor Bevis. Comprehensive for the fenland area.

20 Interesting Places to Visit from Cambridge, E. Pilmer Burlington Press. Detailed guide.

● punting

A Guide to Punting on the River Cam, is available from Scudamore's Boatyard, Magdalene Bridge 01223 327280/359750. Useful tips and historical information.

● libraries

Central Library Information Service, Lion Yard, (01223 365252) Leaflets galore downstairs, and a reference section upstairs for anything from clarinet lessons to Morris dancing.

Tourist information centres

Cambridge, Wheeler Street (01223 322640). 10am-5.30pm Mon-Fri, 10am-5pm Sat.

www.cambridge.gov.uk/leisure.tourism

Bury St Edmund's, 6 Angel Hill (01284 764667). 10am-4pm Mon-Fri, 10am-1pm Sat.

Ely, Oliver Cromwell's House, 29 Mary's St (01353 662062). (Oct-March) 10am-5pm Mon-Sat, 11am-4pm Sun. Summer 10am-5.30pm daily.

Huntingdon, The Library, Princes St (01480 388588). 10am-5pm Mon-Fri .

Mildenhall (open May to Sept only) (01638 667200). 11am-3pm Mon-Fri.

Newmarket, Palace House, Palace St. (01638 667200). 9am-5pm Mon-Fri, 10am-1pm Sat.

Peterborough, 3 Minster Precincts (01733 452336). 9am-5pm Mon & Wed-Fri, 9.30am-5pm Tue, 10am-4pm Sat.

Royston (01923 471333). (information only - no public office) 8am -8pm weekdays, 9am-4pm Sat.

Saffron Walden, Market Street (01799 510444). Open 10am-5pm Mon-Sat.

St Neots, The Old Court, 8 New St, (01480 388788). Open 9.30am-4.30pm Tue - Sat.

Sandy, Girtford Bdge, London Road (01767 682728). Open 9.30am-4.30pm Mon-Fri, 10am-3pm Sat-Sun .

CHAPTER 9
FAMILIES & CHILDREN

Photo by Neal E. Robbins

Cambridge is a lovely place to bring up children, well provided with support and enrichment. This chapter aims to give new families and families new to Cambridge all the basic information they need. It begins with the basics of birth and pregnancy, with first-hand tips on the local hospitals and after-care, child care and parenting of toddlers. That is followed by tips on bringing up older children and teens – keeping them safe – in their activities and travel to and from school and outings.

Children also need fun and learning. These are covered in Chapter 10, page 195, 'Education'; and Chapter 8, page 155, 'Leisure.' Additional information on help lines and general health can be found in Chapter 6, 'Health', page 123.

PREGNANCY AND CHILDBIRTH

● confirming a pregnancy

If you don't use an over-the-counter pregnancy test, your GP can do the test for you. Cambridge University students can get information about pregnancy and free pregnancy tests through the student union (CUSU) at 11-12 Trumpington Street, 9am-5pm, Monday-Friday.

● choosing where to give birth

Two NHS hospitals have maternity units in the Cambridge area: the Rosie Hospital in Cambridge and Hinchingbrooke Hospital in Huntingdon. For those a bit further afield, the West Suffolk Hospital in Bury St Edmund's also serves nearby Newmarket. Yet further, the hospitals in Peterborough, Harlow and Bedford are choices. It is worth visiting the delivery units of the different hospitals to see which one seems to match your requirements the best. All maternity hospitals offer tours of the delivery units by a member of staff who can answer your questions. Phone the numbers given below to find out when these tours are held. Seek the advice of your GP in making the decision.

The Rosie Hospital

Addenbrooke's NHS Trust, Hills Road, Cambridge CB2 2QQ (01223 245151).

Most people in Cambridge and the immediate area choose 'The Rosie' as it is called. The Rosie, the maternity wing of Addenbrooke's Hospital on the southern edge of Cambridge, is the largest maternity hospital in the area. Mothers from Ely, Royston and Saffron Walden as well as Newmarket and the surrounding area go there to give birth. Over 4,700 babies are born there every year. That's more than 12 a day!

As part of a large teaching hospital, the Rosie is at the forefront of new research and technology. It has more expertise than most hospitals, including a specialist neonatal care unit, and is the obvious choice for anyone expecting a difficult birth or complications. The high-tech facili-

Cover picture: A family on Midsummer Common in Cambridge

ties lead to the impression that the Rosie tends to have a more interventionist approach to delivering babies, with more inductions (the artificial bringing on of labour with hormones), more caesarian sections and more use of anaesthetics. In fact, they take a higher proportion of women who have problem pregnancies and so have to intervene more often. There is an emphasis on midwifery-led care for straightforward pregnancies, where women are encouraged to make their own decisions about how they give birth and to make use of natural methods if they wish.

The Rosie delivery rooms are more like hotel bedrooms! The midwife... let me choose how I wanted to give birth... You also have the reassurance at the Rosie that if there are any complications, there is every facility
Anna Scott, mother

Because the Rosie is so large, it is unlikely that the same midwife you see antenatally will deliver your baby or happen to be on duty when you go into labour. This doesn't seem to matter because most women who have given birth at the Rosie praise it highly, noting the delivery rooms are decorated to give a homely feel, with hospital equipment tucked out of sight. They also praise the flexibility of the midwives, who are open to all sorts of requests, from bean bags and floor mats, to a range of pain relief. There are two large baths available for use during or after labour. However a birthing pool and water births are not an option at the Rosie, as yet.

The booklet *Your Guide to the Rosie Hospital* – available from your GP or the Rosie – gives a comprehensive description of how maternity services work at the Rosie.

Hinchingbrooke Hospital

Hinchingbrooke Park, Huntingdon, PE29 6NT (01480 416416. Ask for Clinic 4, the maternity unit).

The next closest hospital is Hinchingbrooke in Huntingdon, which is much smaller than the Rosie with some 2,300 births per year Hinchingbrooke, and the midwives attached to it in the community, have been seen as champions of natural childbirth. With two large birthing pools available for use during labour, and midwives trained in delivering babies in the water if women choose this, the whole thrust is towards viewing pregnancy and birth as a natural event rather than a medical problem unless there are obvious reasons for this to be so. While Hinchingbrooke is able to handle most birth situa-

At Hinchingbrooke, the midwife who had given me antenatal care stayed with me throughout my labour... I would definitely have known whichever midwife had been on duty. Hinchingbrooke is so small you have the chance to meet all the midwives...
Sue Edwards, mother

FAMILIES / CHILDREN

tions, including planned and emergency Caesarian sections, complicated pregnancies are generally referred to the Rosie.

Midwives attached to Hinchingbrooke encourage women to remain in their own homes for as long as possible during labour and return home as soon as possible after delivery. They also support women who want to give birth at home. Antenatal care for women choosing to give birth at Hinchingbrooke takes place almost exclusively in the community rather than at the hospital, with midwives forming close relationships with the mothers in their care and often delivering their babies themselves.

For information on antenatal services offered by Hinchingbrooke contact the midwifery services manager.

West Suffolk Hospital

Hardwick Lane, Bury St Edmund's, Suffolk IP33 2QZ (01284 713000).

West Suffolk hospital in Bury St Edmund's is seen as treading the middle ground between Hinchingbrooke and the Rosie. It delivers about 2,500 babies a year from Newmarket and other surrounding areas in Suffolk. A two-tier system operates. Mothers with low-risk pregnancies can be cared for by a community midwife during pregnancy who will attend the birth and then return home with the mother afterwards (called the Domino Scheme). Mothers with more complicated pregnancies will be cared for by an obstetrician. There is a special care baby unit which can support babies after 30 weeks gestation. Younger premature babies are referred to the Rosie.

While there is a birthing pool for use during labour, midwives do not encourage mothers to give birth in the water. Some midwives will deliver babies at home if mothers meet certain criteria, but there is not an active policy of encouraging this as there is at Hinchingbrooke.

ANTENATAL CARE

The NHS runs antenatal classes on parenting, breastfeeding and for second or subsequent pregnancies. In the Cambridge area, they are increasingly run in the community rather than at hospitals to make them more accessible. Information about NHS-run classes is available at your GP's health centre or at the antenatal unit of your local hospital.

Cambridge is also alive with alternative antenatal exercise classes, discussion groups, yoga and classes preparing mothers and their partners for labour and birth. Swimming classes are sometimes offered at the community colleges.

● The National Childbirth Trust

The National Childbirth Trust (NCT) runs classes on all aspects of pregnancy and childbirth with an emphasis on natural methods. Cambridge has an active local branch including Newmarket, Saffron Walden, Huntingdon and Royston and Ely. Phone for answer machine information on local representatives, as these change periodically. The classes are good but cost more than some, typically £90 for eight weeks of 2-hour couples classes, with concessions available to students and those on benefits. Hotline 24-hour answer phone 01223 567900, e-mail NCT@nctrust.swinternet.co.uk, website: www.nct-online.org

● the Active Birth Centre

The Active Birth Centre runs antenatal yoga and exercise classes as well as providing birthing pools, aromatherapy oils and other equipment, advice and support on the whole experience of pregnancy and birth. Several representatives work in Cambridge, each offering a variety of classes, including a swimming class and discussion groups. Personnel change from time to time so contact the headquarters (0207 482 5554) or their website, www.active-birthcentre.com, to locate the nearest local representative. Classes typically cost £7-£8 per two-hour session.

● other sources

Romsey Mill Community Centre, Hemingford Road (off Mill Road), Cambridge, CB1 3BZ (01223 213162), offers a free antenatal class run by health visitors for under 25-year olds with an all-round approach, looking at access to information, housing and benefit advice as well as health. Free transport is provided.

Paraphernalia for labour and birth

'What else might I need before I go into labour?'

You can begin to feel overawed with the amount of paraphernalia different people will tell you you need for labour and your new baby. But there are one or two things which really can make a difference and so here are the places to get hold of them in Cambridge.

TENS machines for pain relief during early labour can be hired from the Rosie or Boots the Chemist 28 Petty Cury Cambridge, the latter at 01223 350213.

Birthing balls, aromatherapy oils, maternity bras and *feeding cushions*, are all available from the local active birth representative (see above).

● cotton nappy services

Research suggesting disposable nappies may affect boys' fertility as well as damage the environment have given many people the incentive to use cotton nappies.

Cotton botties (0800 9154195) is an excellent cotton nappy service delivering clean cotton nappies to your door and taking soiled nappies to launder. They also provide covers, a bin and advice. Cost: £30 returnable deposit £45 for a set of seven covers, £7.95/week for the service. *(See page 64 for the nappy recycling rebate from the county council).*

Bambino Mio (01604 883777) is a good source for mail

FAMILIES / CHILDREN

order cotton nappies.

For further information on using real nappies contact: The Real Nappy Association, PO Box 3704, London SE26 4RX or their website at www.realnappy.com.

See Chapter 5, 'Shopping', for other equipment and details on chemists page 103, maternity wear and children's clothing page 111-112.

POSTNATAL SUPPORT

Once you have had your baby and have been discharged from hospital, it is quite common to feel marooned with a tiny alien on your hands, and this is where postnatal support comes in. This section deals with the immediate needs. See also the section on childcare, page 188 below.

Health visitors and support groups

Your GP or community midwife will keep an eye on things for the first few days with home visits usually made every two days up to 10 days after delivery. It is your right to have a midwife visit you for up to 30 days after you give birth, but you can ask for further visits. When your midwife has signed you off, a 'health visitor' – similar to a community nurse with an interest in mothers and babies, will visit you to ensure you are recovering, give advice, and direct you to your local child health clinic where you will go to have your baby weighed, for any further advice and check-ups.

Support groups provide the opportunity to meet other women in the same boat and helplines are your link to wider experience and greater expertise. Local parents have found the following especially helpful:

● support with breastfeeding

The Rosie breastfeeding clinic (01223 217617). Drop in for practical advice on a Friday afternoon 2.30-4pm or phone the emergency support line 01223 217002 between 6pm-10pm for very patient, personal attention.

La Leche League (0207 242 1278). Ask for local representative or obtain advice over the phone. Hugely helpful.

● support with emotional issues

Parentline (freephone 0808 800 2222) is a confidential telephone service offering support in areas such as depression, bad behaviour and sleep problems. All the volunteer call takers are parents trained in dealing with the problems.

Crysis (0207 404 5011) supports families troubled by excessive crying or sleepless babies. Ask for local representative or obtain advice over the phone.

Association for Postnatal Illness (0207 386 0868). Gives telephone support for mothers suffering from postnatal depression.

● support for single parents

Cambridge Gingerbread (01223 321562). A self-help

organisation for one parent families.

Step-families, the national step-family association (0990 168388) and e-mail tnsa@ukonline.co.uk

● **baby massage**

International Association of Infant Massage (0208 591 1399). Phone for details on local classes.

● **other postnatal groups**

Both the *National Childbirth Trust* and the *Active Birth Centre* run postnatal exercise classes locally. The NCT organises postnatal support groups and coffee mornings for new parents, has a pool of breastfeeding counsellors and an 'experiences register' with advice and support from parents on a range of problems. NCT postnatal groups are free but there is a fee for some classes. As above, try the national numbers to find out what is happening locally.

Birthlight, Meadows Community Centre, Arbury, 1 St Catherine's Road, Cambridge (01223 564064 or 362288). Offers a mother and baby yoga class for mothers with babies from 0-4 months or 4-12 months. Costs: postnatal groups £45 for six weeks of 2-hour classes. Single classes £8.50. It also offers mother and baby swimming (for babies from three months) for £45 for six weeks.

The Birth Café (01763 261696) St Paul's Church, Hill's Road. An informal meeting place for new parents that normally takes place on the first Wednesday of every month at 1pm (but phone to confirm times and dates). You can chat and compare notes over a cup of tea.

Romsey Mill Community Centre (see page 185) also runs a new mothers group, including mothers under 25, where they can meet and have a cup of tea and a sandwich. There is sometimes a discussion topic, such as sleep. £1 a session.

● **classes with creches**

Many community colleges, gyms and community centres run classes for adults during the day with creches for babies. Those mentioned below are examples of the type available, but there are many more.

YMCA, Gonville Place, Cambridge (01223 356998) has a creche for babies from 9.45am-noon on Tuesdays and Fridays.

Cambridge Women's Resource Centre, Hooper Street, Cambridge (01223 321148) has a free on-site creche and runs vocational training in computing, accounting, woodwork, English, Maths and English as a second language. It can also give advice on aspects of child rearing such as benefits, paternity rights, housing etc. The centre gives priority to women who want to improve their employment opportunities. Courses are free if you are unemployed or working less than 16 hours a week.

CHILD CARE - YOUNG CHILDREN

Finding good day-time care for young children is a stressful business, as anyone who has been through the process knows. With complex transport and work schedules, so many different options and conflicting pros and cons, making a decision for your unique child is a challenge under any circumstances. The decision is always hard, but the good news is that this area is well served with child care options. The not-so-good news is that you may find the option you want is booked far ahead. So, make arrangements for child care early, even before the birth.

Finding good day-time care for young children is a stressful business... but the good news is that this area is well served with child care options. The not-so-good news is that you may find the option you want is booked far ahead.

This section describes what's available and how to find out more, and, while we cannot recommend any particular option or individual, we do give you some of the views of parents who have been through the process themselves.

Lists of local care choices

We emphasise the value of *Opportunity Links*, a voluntary organisation set up specifically to give free advice on all the issues surrounding childcare and returning to work. It keeps a list of local parent and toddler groups, playgroups and day nurseries for every area, as well as a wealth of other information about child care. It will also advise you on whether you are entitled to any benefits, such as the Working Families Tax credit, Child Care Tax credit, or the Disabled Person's Tax credit, since child care can be a costly business.

For an up-to-date list of childminders or nurseries in Cambridgeshire freephone 0800 298 9121 or check www.opportunity-links.org.uk (for information local to Cambridge) or www.childcarelink.gov.uk (for National information). Click on the area you are interested in. Click on child care. You can then search through childminders or for nursery child care. Click on 'day nurseries' rather than 'nursery schools'.

The telephone directory also has a list of nurseries, which includes LEA (local education authority) nursery classes (under 'nurseries' and also 'County Council'). However, this list is not as comprehensive as the one offered by Opportunity Links.

The information below will help you make a choice.

● University child care

Employees of the University of Cambridge can consult the University Child Care Coordinator at 01223 339905 (or by e-mail: jb242@cam.ac.uk) for information about child care and the 120-place holiday play scheme for children aged 5-

14. The University has a 60-place nursery. For admission contact the staff child care committee secretary at 01223 332320. Apply early! The waiting list is long.

The play scheme is shared with Anglia Polytechnic University, which also has its own 50-place nursery for children of 12 weeks to five years of age. Priority on nursery admission is given to the children of students and staff. For information contact 01223 263271 ext 2202.

Child minders

Child minders look after your children in the child minder's home. Usually parents themselves, they are registered with the local authority and their homes are inspected every year to ensure they are clean, safe, and suitable for young children. They can often be flexible about the hours they work and can take up to three children under the age of five and three children under eight at any one time, including their own children.

Costs: the rate may vary from area to area but will be in the range of £2.50 to £5 an hour.

For an up-to-date list of child minders in your area refer to the sources in Opportunity Links (but choosing cold from them is not recommended). Select a few names, go to visit, take your child, see how the child minder reacts to your child, get a feel, and try to find someone else who knows the person who is going to take care of your child.

A trustworthy child minder will not mind you popping in unannounced on the odd occasion on some pretext or other, but really to ensure your child is happy. It is worth doing the ground work, because if you find a good child minder, they can accompany your child right up to school age and beyond and become part of the fabric of his or her life.

Nannies

Nannies are the most expensive option for child care, but are a popular choice amongst Cambridgeshire residents, as they can be flexible and will often drive your children around to the different clubs and activities they might be engaged in.

Nannies are trained to look after children, either with an NNEB (National Nursery Examining Board), a BTEC, or an NVQ (National Vocational Training) qualification. They tend to be women, usually without their own children. They work in your home or live in.

Nanny salaries in the Cambridge area vary and tend to be linked to house prices, so while a weekly salary in Huntingdon may be in the region of £220 a week, in Cambridge this may go up to £250 and nannies in Royston can charge as much as £300.

Recommending individual nannies is not possible here, but the nanny agencies listed in the box below can to do some of the sifting for you. The agencies interview and vet individual nannies and attempt to match them with suitable families. The agencies charge a fee to register.

Be aware, however, that child care provided by nannies or au pairs is not eligible for Child Care Tax Credit.

Au pairs

There are several au pair agencies in Cambridge. Au pairs are usually overseas students or younger people staying in Britain to learn English. They live in your home and require their own room and board.

They may be asked to provide help in the home and some child care but it is unwise to rely on them to care for children under three unless you are in the home with them as they will have no formal training, and cannot be held responsible if things go wrong. Au pairs need time off and should be treated as members of the family. The typical cost is £45 a week for 25 hours help and au pairs must have two free days and full board and lodging.

Nurseries

This is a really confusing term because it covers such a wide range of child care, including private nurseries – also sometimes called nursery schools or day nurseries, state nursery classes attached to primary schools – sometimes referred to as nursery schools, and creches where children can only be left for short periods of time.

To make things worse, different types of nurseries can also be called kindergarten or pre-school, but what one 'pre-school' offers may be very different to another! Some nurseries offer full-time child care for babies (These are usually listed under 'day nurseries'). Some take children only from age two or three, others only offer part-time education to three and four year-olds!

The common thread, however, is that nurseries are places for children under five years old to play and learn in groups.

● private nurseries

Private nurseries, sometimes called 'day nurseries' or 'nursery schools', are usually (but not always) designed to cater for the children of working parents, many opening from 8.30am to 6pm. They have their own individual philosophies. Expect to pay from £80 to £180 per child per week for a full-time place. Private nurseries usually take children from age two, although some take them younger.

● workplace nurseries

Workplace nurseries are run for the employees of a particular company and are generally organised to fit in with the hours an employee would work. Check with your own employer about whether a nursery is available.

● nursery classes

Nursery classes (not to be confused with private nursery schools) attached to primary schools or Local Education Authority (LEA) nursery schools are run for pre-school children aged from three or from the September before their fourth birthday. Staff are trained teachers and nursery nurses. Classes run from 9am to 11.30pm or 1pm to 3.30pm so are not really an option for working parents. They should be looked upon as offering pre-school experience rather than as child care.

LEA nurseries are like nursery classes but not necessarily attached to a particular school. They give priority to special needs and low-income families but places are available to others. It is advisable to get onto a waiting list. Hours are similar to nursery classes. Nurseries should be registered with their local authority so that premises are inspected to ensure they are safe for children, and staff checked to make sure they are suitable to work with children

There must be one member of staff for every eight children aged three to five, one for every four children aged two to three, and one for every three children under the age of two.

Finding the right nursery can be a challenge because hours do not always quite meet those required by working parents, particularly if there is a journey involved. Only a few nurseries in Cambridge take babies under two years old, so getting a place can be difficult. However, parents

---

NANNY AND AU PAIR AGENCIES: (IN THEIR OWN WORDS)

Nice Nannies, 40 Station Road, Huntingdon (01487 823516) e-mail: nicenannies@hotmail.com. Registration fee £15. A small agency with lots of advice as part of the package. Provides maternity care and general nannies. Operating since 1986.

Cambridge Nannies and Au Pairs, 38 Oxford Road, Cambridge, (01223 576069). Registration £20-£50 fee, includes a substantial information pack. Places au pairs from Europe and full and part-time British nannies. Friendly and supportive of families.

Cambridge Au Pairs, 49 Glisson Road, Cambridge (01223 360373). £15-£20 registration for Cambridge area. Founded in 1988. Personal and friendly. All families personally visited. Au pairs come through personal connections and agencies.

Cambridge Connection Au Pair Agency, Milford House, 134 High Street Cottenham (01954 206489). £12.50 registration. Concentrates on au pair placements, organises au pair tea parties to help with smooth integration of au pairs within their families in Cambridge.

who choose nurseries believe they give their child a structured day, stimulating activities and opportunities to socialise with other children.

Pre-school education

Pre-school education has always been a bit of a patchy affair, although it is now improving.

Not all children have access to a purpose-built local authority nursery class (a pre-school room attached to a primary school) or local authority nursery school and in Cambridgeshire particularly these are thin on the ground. However, all children aged four (that is, for the three terms before they reach the compulsory school age of five) are guaranteed a free, part-time, early education place and the Government is doubling the places for three-year-olds.

In order to meet this pledge, these free places may be offered in a variety of settings in addition to LEA nurseries, such as private nursery schools, pre-schools or playgroups, day nurseries, a group of registered child minders or a reception class in a state primary school (not for three year-olds).

● Ofsted inspection and regulation

Any place offering this free pre-school education will have been inspected by a registered nursery inspector, from the Office for Standards in Education (Ofsted) and must have a qualified teacher involved, who will either lead the group or supervise the people working with the children.

While the inspectorate (Ofsted) attempts to ensure that standards in the different pre-school establishments meet certain critieria, making a decision about the right place for your own child cannot always be based on a set of figures and inspectors' comments.

● play groups

Play groups are often run on a voluntary basis by parents or play group workers. Staff are not trained teachers (as they are

---

TOYS THEY WON'T GET TIRED OF

Toy libraries, where children can try out the toys (and toys for special needs children) are often run in local community centres or libraries. The benefits are that once the child has tired of the toy, which it surely will after a few days, it can be returned to the library, and of course the cost is minimal (usually about 50p-£1 to borrow a toy for two weeks). Toy library locations change, so the best way to find out what's near you is to call the National Association of Toy and Leisure Libraries, 68 Churchway, London NW1 1LT, 0207 387 9592, admin@natll.ukf.net and www.charitynet.org/~NATLL

At last count there were local toy libraries in: Huntingdon, Ramsey, Ely, Papworth Everard, Sandy, Burwell, Somersham, Impington, Bar Hill, Cottenham, Great Shelford, Hardwick, Eynesbury and several sites in Cambridge.

in nursery classes) but will have some playworker training. Not all play groups are registered for pre-school education. Those which are will have been inspected by Ofsted and you are entitled to check their reports. Children can usually attend unaccompanied from age two and a half for part of the day. Play groups usually charge a fee of about £2 a session.

● choosing the right place

There are no hard and fast rules to finding the right nursery. Only you know your child, and only you have the sense of what environment may be best. If you feel your child would be happy in a fairly relaxed, informal atmosphere, a play group may well be right. For a child who requires a more structured setting, look at Montessori nurseries or the High Scope approach. Some nurseries emphasize early education, even with computers, and others combine approaches, offering a character of their own. You just have to ask and observe the nursery to learn which one will be the right one for you.

Out of School clubs (OSCA)

School children aged 4-11 can attend out of school clubs before and after school or in the holidays. Activities range from cooking to crafts and sports. The clubs and staff are currently certified by Social Services, but from September 2001, will be Ofsted inspected. Typically clubs run from 8am until school starts, then after school until 6pm and from 8am-6pm on holidays. A session typically costs around £5. Get information from the school or OSCA at 01223 202308 or through Opportunity Links website.

CHILDREN'S SAFETY OUT & ABOUT

Bringing up children and teenagers in the Cambridge area has many advantages, one of which is the accessibility of Cambridge itself. Most parents of children aged 11 or older feel quite happy about letting them go into Cambridge city itself during the day independently or with a group of friends. The city centre is fairly car-free and compact enough for children to walk around without getting lost.

Cambridge is also a reasonably safe place for teenagers to go out at night, although it is advisable to take the usual common sense precautions of ensuring they let an adult know where they are, that they go out with a friend or in a group rather than alone, and avoid badly lit roads or open spaces at night. If personal safety is a matter of special concern the city offers a self-defense class for 9-13 year-olds that may be of interest.

See page 145 in Chapter 7 'Sport and Fitness'.

Road safety

As with everything, a bit of care, caution and information goes a long way. Ask your school about the following:

● in addition to common sense safety measures – wear-

FAMILIES / CHILDREN

ing a helmet on a bike, and being visible, as well as ensuring the bike is properly maintained – it is a good idea to enroll children who are eligible (10- and 11-year-olds) on a 'Safer Cycling Course'.

- 'Lollipop' School Crossing patrols should be available outside school entrances on busy roads.

- a 'Safer routes to School' project, funded by Cambridgeshire Health Authority works with schools, looking at the ways staff, pupils and parents travel to school and encouraging safer and more sustainable forms of transport. As a result of the project, some schools have set up 'walking buses' (where children meet and walk to school along designated 'safe routes' in a crocodile with two adult leaders), others have set up bike storage facilities, and the villages of Melbourn, Teversham, Barrington, Thorndown and Somersham have identified the need for traffic calming measures in their villages which should be completed early in 2001.

- 'Hedgehogs' is a national child pedestrian safety campaign targeting 8-12 year-olds highlighting safe and unsafe places to cross the road and advising on the best ways to cross. The local Road Safety Officer issues copies of campaign materials such as worksheets to schools in Cambridgeshire to reinforce the cinema and television advertising.

● pre-driving teenagers

For older teenagers, (school years 10,11 & 12) Pre-driver training courses (PDT) prepare young adults for learning to drive and look at issues such as driver attitude, speeding, and drinking and driving with a view to fostering a mature attitude. A new programme was launched in the Autumn of 2000 by the Road Safety Officer.

For further information contact the Road Safety Officer, Environment and Transport, Shire Hall, Cambridge, www.camcnty.gov.uk and 01223 717747.

ADDITIONAL INFORMATION

Cambridge for the Under Fives, by Andrew Kennedy and Elizabeth Walter, Sedgwick Publishing 1999 (PO Box 142 Cambridge, CB1 3GR). A useful guide to living with children in the Cambridge area including activities, days out, antenatal and postnatal care, shopping, support groups.

Kids Direct, A free guide to things to do with children in Cambridge. Issued four times a year, it is available in schools and libraries (01223 860747). e-mail: kidsdirect@ntlworld.com

Birth to Five, a Health Education Authority guide, has a full list of support groups, including those for special needs children and helplines at the back. Your health visitor should give you a copy.

CHAPTER 10
EDUCATION

Photo by Findlay Kember

So many different kinds of school, so many places of further education. It can be a puzzle to people already living here, let alone anyone else. And for people coming from abroad, it's a complete mystery. But this chapter will set you straight. It can't answer all your questions – there isn't room for that – but it'll certainly put you on the right road and tell you what to do next. Whether you're a parent of a child of school age, an undergraduate, an adult interested in continuing education or a pensioner looking to keep your mind occupied, it'll give you an address to write to, a website, or a number to ring to find out more. And where space does permit, it'll fill you in on a few details as well.

The chapter begins with a look at local authority schools. These are financed by the state and are free for everyone, although they all have fund-raising activities to raise cash for extra facilities. They are *not* to be confused with public schools. In England, a public school is a fee-paying school for children aged 13 or more. It can be very grand and expensive, usually hundreds of years old with a list of famous alumni to prove it. A public school is also a private school, since it's not funded by the state. And if that isn't confusing enough, it's an independent school as well. Once you've grasped that though, the rest is easy!

After state and private schools, the chapter deals with schools for children with special needs. It takes a look at the National Curriculum and the exam system, and then moves on to higher education, either at universities nation-wide or at other places of continuing education in the Cambridge area. It looks also at language schools – Cambridge is one of the biggest centres in the country for learning English. And then it finishes with a list of useful contacts not already mentioned elsewhere in the text.

LOCAL AUTHORITY SCHOOLS (State Schools)

These are divided into primary schools for children between five and 11, and secondary schools thereafter. There are several different kinds of primary school (see box 199). In practice, most children attend their nearest one, but they can apply to a school in another catchment area if they wish. Whether they get in or not depends on local demand, because priority is always given to applicants living closest to the school.

Finding a school

The first thing therefore is to identify the nearest school in your catchment area (the area served by each school). Check the maps on page 201-203 and there's a full list on www.schoolsnet.com. You can also contact the Education Information Centre at Castle Court, Shire Hall, Cambridge

Cover picture: Teacher and year-11 students at Coleridge Community Clg

CB3 0AP (01223 717667) or Gazeley House, Huntingdon, PE18 6NS (01480 375518). If you live near the borders of Suffolk, Essex or Hertfordshire, your nearest school may be in another county, in which case contact the appropriate information centre listed at the end of this chapter. All the centres will send you a guide for parents listing the schools in your area (with map) and telling you what the entry procedure is. The guides are full of useful information for people with no previous experience of the system.

● selecting the best school

Once you've identified the school, ring up the head teacher and ask to look round. If you like what you see, ask for the school's SATS results and Ofsted report. The SATS results are tests of the pupils' achievement, telling you what percentage of them meet the standards expected of their age group. The Ofsted report examines the school itself and decides whether it passes muster, but note that the reports are only done every few years, so things may have changed – for better or worse. Ask also how the school compares with others in the performance league tables, or look it up yourself on www.parents.dfee.gov.uk.

When does school begin?

Your children usually go to primary school in the September before their fifth birthday (perhaps not full-time until Christmas, if they're very young), or secondary school in the September before their 11th. They are legally entitled

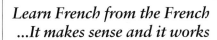

EDUCATION

to a place at their nearest school unless it is oversub-scribed. In that case priority is given to children with med-ical needs, a sibling already at the school, or a long walk to another school. It's no surprise therefore that parents sometimes move house to be near a good school. Property prices, however, are a poor indicator of school quality. Schools vary greatly, depending largely on who is in charge. The best policy is check the SATS, Ofsted reports and trust your own instincts based on a personal visit.

All state schools cater for children with learning diffi-culties or other special needs (see later section). They also cater for the very able, though not always terribly well. If you are from overseas, your children will usually be eligible for a free education, but you must write to the Education Information Centre and get a letter of approval from the Assistant Director (Schools). Your children should be between five and 16 when you apply.

● choosing a secondary school

If you're applying to send them to secondary school, you must complete a form naming up to three schools in order of preference. Do some research first, because although a few secondary schools go on to 18, most stop at 16 and transfer their pupils to a Sixth Form college for the last two years of schooling. Sixth Form colleges are more adult than school (they allow smoking) and point their students firm-ly towards higher education. Entry to the best of them can be competitive.

Appealing a decision

If your child doesn't get in to your chosen school for any reason, you can always appeal against the decision, though this is rarely necessary. Most parents do get the school they want. The Education Information Centre will tell you how. The appeals panel usually consists of three or five people, a mix of lay people and retired teachers advised by a lawyer. They are independent of both the school and the local authority, but their decision is final, so you won't be able to argue the toss any further in that academic year unless there's a significant change in your family's circumstances.

SECONDARY SCHOOLS

The schools in and around Cambridge below come in several different categories. One is a church school, some are community colleges and others are village colleges – a 1930s concept designed to revolutionise rural education. Broadly speaking though, they're all just schools serving their local area, and all co-ed.

Bottisham Village College, Lode Road, Bottisham, Cambridge CB5 9DL (01223 811250). Community school, 949 pupils aged 11-16. Had a disastrous fire a couple of years ago, but is getting over it now. A broad mix of kids, many from professional homes. Busy, happy place, always with plenty of activity and lots going on.

Chesterton Community College, Gilbert Road, Cambridge CB4 3NY (01223 712150). Community school, 962 pupils aged 11-16. Big place with a large social and ethnic mix. Wide range of academic abilities, but a fast track approach for the cleverest means that one or two take as many as 13 subjects at GCSE.

Comberton Village College, West Street, Comberton, Cambridge CB3 7DU (01223 262503). Foundation school

---

A PRIMER ON PRIMARY SCHOOLS

Primary schools take children between five and 11, although some also have a pre-school class for the very young. There are sometimes also infant schools for five to 7 year-olds and junior schools for seven to 11. The schools come in four categories: **Community**, owned and run by the local authority; **Foundation**, formerly grant-maintained, still owned by the governors but now funded by the local authority; **Voluntary-Aided**, owned by a voluntary body, often the Church of England, but mostly funded by the local authority; **Voluntary-Controlled**, owned by a voluntary body, but fully funded by the local authority. In practice the distinctions are minimal and nothing to worry about. A Church of England school, for instance, will certainly teach Christianity, but children of other religions or none can always thrive there perfectly happily.

with 1,005 pupils aged 11-16. Phenomenally successful, very popular with academic parents. A good intake of kids, excellent exam results, high morale all round.

Coleridge Community College, Radegund Road, Cambridge CB1 3RJ (01223 712300). Community school, 435 pupils aged 11-16. Nearly closed a couple of years ago, because of a dramatic fall in numbers. But parents rallied round and demonstrated in its favour. Coleridge has had a stay of execution and is now fighting to pick itself up and start again,

Cottenham Village College, High Street, Cottenham, Cambridge CB4 8UA (01954 288944). Community school, 920 pupils aged 11-16. Wide mix of children including many at its special unit for hearing problems and language disorders. Does better than the national average in some subjects, but not in others.

A QUICK GLANCE AT KEY STAGES/CURRICULUM

General Certificate of Secondary Education (GCSE) Exams are based on the National Curriculum set by the Government. The curriculum is only compulsory in state schools, but most private schools follow it as well. In addition to what is listed below, all schools follow a course of personal, social and health education. Religious education and communal worship are also part of the curriculum, but children needn't attend these lessons (or sex education) if their parents don't want them to.

	Age	Year Group
Key Stage I	5-7	1-2
Key Stage 2	7-11	3-6
Key Stage 3	11-14	7-9
Key Stage 4	14-16	10-11
Post-16	16-19	Sixth Form

Key Stages 1 and 2
Core subjects: English, maths, science.
Non-core foundation subjects: design and technology, geography, history, art and design, music, physical education, information and technology (IT).

Key stage 3
Core subjects: English, maths, science, one foreign language (usually French), *from 2002:* citizenship.
Non-core foundation subjects: As before.

Key stage 4
Core subjects: English, maths, science, design and technology, information and communications technology (ICT), physical education, one foreign language and vocational education.
Other subjects: optional.

Published Standard Attainment Tests (SATS) given at the end of each stage measure how the school is doing in comparison with others nationally.

Impington Village College, New Road, Impington, Cambridge CB4 9LX (01223 200400). Community school, 1,030 pupils aged 11-18. The original village college, one of very few taking pupils all the way to 18. Very highly rated nationally. Some students take the International Baccalaureate exam, a sure sign of a good school.

Linton Village College Cambridge Road, Linton, Cambridge CB1 6JB, (01223 891233). Foundation school, 734 pupils aged 11-16. Mixed intake, but plenty of good work going on. A lot of kids come to Linton from other catchment areas, perhaps because of its relatively low class sizes.

Manor Community College Arbury Road, Cambridge CB4 2JF (01223 508742). Community school, 376 pupils aged 11-16. Small school, with fewer middle class parents than elsewhere. Had a tough reputation in the past, but things are changing and bright kids can do perfectly well here.

Melbourn Village College, The Moor, Melbourn, Royston, Herts SG8 6EF (01763 223400). Community school, 680 pupils aged 11-16. The school is in Hertfordshire, but most of its catchment area is in Cambs. Kids usually go on to Melbourn Community College at 16, rather than anywhere in Cambridge.

Netherhall School, Queen Edith's Way, Cambridge CB1 8NN, (01223 242931). Community school, 1,252 pupils

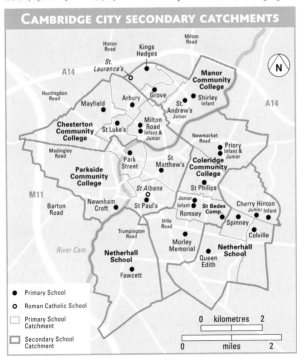

CAMBRIDGE CITY SECONDARY CATCHMENTS

aged 11-16 and another 219 in the Sixth Form (aged 16+). Very large and diverse intake. Some kids from rough areas, but also plenty of high fliers doing well. An impressive number choose to stay after 16, rather than leave for Sixth Form college elsewhere.

Parkside Community College, Parkside, Cambridge CB1 1EH (01223 712600). Community school, 608 pupils aged 11-16. Close to the centre of Cambridge, very popular with academic parents. Good exam results, perky kids, high marks in every department.

Sawston Village College, New Road, Sawston, Cambridge CB2 4BP (01223 712820). Foundation school, 1,085 pupils aged 11-16. Very much a part of the community, with more than 500 adults using the facilities every day. Also plenty of kids with disabilities, who feel safe and valued here.

St Bede's Inter-Church Comprehensive School, Birdwood Road Cambridge CB1 3TD, (01223 568816). Voluntary-aided school, 625 pupils aged 11-16. A joint Anglican and Roman Catholic school, with religion a central feature. Priority given to families whose application is supported by their parish priest. A very popular place, always oversubscribed, taking children from 60 different feeder schools.

Swavesey Village College, Gibraltar Lane, Swavesey,

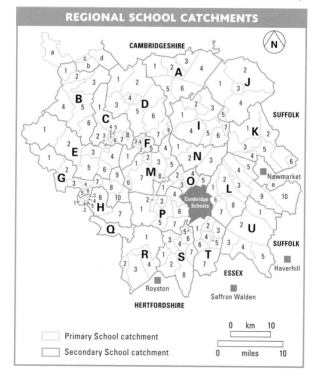

REGIONAL SCHOOL CATCHMENTS

Primary School catchment

Secondary School catchment

0 km 10

0 miles 10

REGIONAL SCHOOL – MAP INDEX

CAMBRIDGESHIRE

FENLAND DISTRICT

A - Cromwell Community College, Chatteris
1. Benwick
2. Lionel Walden
3. Thomas Eaton
4. Manea
5. Burnsfield Infant & King Edward Junior
6. Glebelands

HUNTINGDONSHIRE DISTRICT

B - Sawtry Village College
1. Folksworth
2. Stilton
3. Holme
4. Great Gidding
5. Sawtry Infant & Junior
6. Alconbury
a. Elton
b. Yaxley Infant & William de Yaxley Junior
c. Fourfields
d. Farcet

C - St Peter's School, Huntingdon
1. Abbots Ripton
2. Huntingdon Infant & Junior
3. Stukeley Meadows
4. St John's
5. Thongsley Infant & Junior
6. Hartford Infant & Junior
7. Houghton
8. Wyton

D - Ailwyn Community School, Ramsey
1. Ashbeach
2. Spinning Infant & Ramsey Junior
3. Upwood
4. Bury
5. Warboys
6. Somersham
7. St Helen's
8. Earith

E - Hinchingbrooke School, Huntingdon
1. Brington
2. Spaldwick
3. Brampton Infant & Junior
4. Godmanchester & St Anne's
5. Buckden
6. Offord

F - St Ivo School, St Ives
1. Hemingford Grey
2. Eastfield Infant & Westfield Junior
3. Thorndown Infant & Junior
4. Wheatfields Infant & Junior
5. Holywell

G - Longsands College, St Neots
1. Overhills
2. Great Staughton
3. Priory Park Infant & Priory Junior
4. Little Paxton
5. Crosshall Infant & Junior
6. Priory Park Infant & Priory Junior
7. Holy Trinity
8. Newton
9. Pendragon
10. Newton

H - Ernulf Community School, St Neots
1. Bushmead Infant & Junior
2. Eynesbury
3. St Mary's
4. Winhills
5. Middlefield
6. Eynesbury
7. Barnabas Oley

EAST CAMBRIDGESHIRE DISTRICT

I - Witchford Village College
1. Sutton
2. Mepal & Witcham
3. Rackham
4. Robert Arkenstall
5. Wilburton
6. Stretham
7. Little Thatford

J - City of Ely College
1. Downham Feoffes
2. Littleport
3. Millfield
4. Spring Meadow Infant & St Mary's Junior
5. Ely St John's

K - Soham Village College
1. Weatheralls
2. Isleham
3. St Andrew's
4. Burwell
5. Fordham
6. Kennett

L - Bottisham Village College
1. Fen Ditton
2. Bottisham
3. Swaffham Bulbeck
4. Swaffham Prior
5. Burwell
6. Teversham
7. Fulbourn
8. Great Wilbraham
9. Kettlefields
10. Cheveley
e. Ditton Lodge

SOUTH CAMBRIDGESHIRE DISTRICT

M - Swavesey Village College
1. Fenstanton & Hilton
2. Fen Drayton
3. Swavesey
4. Over
5. Hatton Park
6. Pendragon
7. Elsworth
8. Bar Hill

N - Cottenham Village College
1. Willingham
2. Cottenham
3. Waterbeach

O - Impington Village College
1. Dry Drayton
2. Oakington
3. Girton Glebe
4. Histon & Impington Infants & Junior
5. Milton

P - Comberton Village College
1. Bourn & Monkfield Park
2. Caldecote
3. Hardwick
4. Coton
5. Meridian
6. Barton
7. Haslingfield

Q - Gamlingay Middle

R - Bassingbourn Village College
1. Petersfield
2. Guilden Morden
3. Steeple Morden
4. Bassingbourn

S - Melbourn Village College
1. Meldreth
2. Melbourn
3. Barrington
4. Foxton
5. Harston & Newton
6. Hauxton
7. Thriplow
8. Fowlmere

SOUTH CAMBRIDGESHIRE DISTRICT (continued)

T - Sawston Village College
1. Great & Little Shelford
2. Stapleford
3. Babraham
4. John Falkner Infant & John Paxton Junior
5. Icknield
6. William Westley
7. Duxford

U - Linton Village College
1. Burrough Green
2. Meadow
3. Great Abington
4. Linton Infant & Linton Heights Junior
5. Castle Camps

ESSEX

The Saffron Walden/ Great Dunmow area is served by Uttlesford Distrct 2.
The Halstead/Braintree area by Braintree Distrct 3.
Call Essex Learning Services for information : (01245) 436231

HERTFORDSHIRE

Meridian Upper School fed by Greneway Middle School and Roysia Middle serves the area.
Call the admission officer for Royston and surrounding villages for information : (01462) 704374

SUFFOLK

Newmarket Upper School fed by Scaltback and St Felix Middle Schools, serves Newmarket City.
To the north, Mildenhall is served by Mildenhall Upper School and to the south, Haverhill by Castle Manor and Samuel Ward Upper school.
Call Suffolk Education department for information : (01284) 352000

Indexed by

COUNTY : CAMBRIDGESHIRE, ESSEX, HERTFORDSHIRE, & SUFFOLK,

DISTRICT Cambridgeshire only

Secondary School catchment, A-U (for Cambridgeshire) Listed for other surrounding counties

Primary School catchment Numbered within each Secondary catchment

Note : a,b,c,d & e are Cambridgeshire Primary School catchments falling outside Cambridgeshire Secondary catchments

EDUCATION

SCHOOL TERM TIMES

The academic year in Britain has always been linked to the annual harvest. Students in medieval times spent summer in the fields, making sure the crop was safely in before resuming their studies in the autumn. Their year was divided into three academic terms, with religious names such as Michaelmas, Lent and Easter sometimes still used today.

Most schools however simply call the terms autumn, spring and summer. As a rough guide, they run from 6 September-19 December, 9 January-3 April and 24 April-10 July, but the difference between various schools can sometimes be as much as 10 days.

Cambridge CB4 5RS (01954 230366). Community school, 883 pupils aged 11-16. Part of the 'necklace of education' around Cambridge. Campus-style facilities, firm sense of purpose, high standards, good teaching, always plenty going on.

SIXTH FORM COLLEGES

Hills Road Sixth Form College, Hills Road, Cambridge CB2 2PE (01223 247251), www.hrsfc.ac.uk. A jewel in the state system, taking in 750 pupils at 16 for a two-year course that prepares them for higher education. Last year its pupils received 66 Oxbridge offers, by far the highest total in the country, easily outnumbering anything in the private sector. It's fun too. Mickey Dolenz's daughter, of *The Monkees,* has only just left. And if you've seen *Grease,* Olivia Newton-John's father used to be headmaster.

Long Road Sixth Form College, Long Road, Cambridge CB2 2PX (01223 507400), www.longroad.ac.uk. Takes 800 pupils at 16. Not as academic as Hills Road, but probably better in terms of added value. Hills Road takes kids with good GCSE results and gets them good A levels. Long Road takes kids with less good GCSEs and puts a lot of effort into getting them A level grades that they would never have thought possible.

PRIVATE (Independent) SCHOOLS

If you're looking for a fee-paying school, you won't get much help from the local authority. Your best bet is to consult one of the guides in the library, either the *Independent Schools Yearbook* or the *Sunday Times Schools Yearbook,* or else try www.isis.org.uk, which will give you all the information at a glance. Once you've found something you like, ask the school to send you a prospectus and a copy of the latest Independent Schools Inspectorate report. Ask too if they have any vacancies, because the best private schools are usually full up for years ahead. There's no point applying if the waiting list is long and they've no room anyway.

EDUCATION

An important difference in the independent system is that quite a few students transfer to their secondary school at 13, rather than 11. Before that they are at preparatory school, preparing for the Common Entrance exam to their public school. Most go on to other schools in the Cambridge area, but some move at 13 to boarding schools such as Eton and Winchester in other parts of the country. Girls change at 11 if they're going from one all-girls school to another, although an increasing number now attend mixed schools and move with the boys at 13. Below the leading schools are listed.

The Perse School, Hills Road, Cambridge CB2 2QF (01223 568300, www.perse.co.uk). Highly academic day school for boys, 580 of them aged 11 to 18, but also admits 25 girls to the Sixth Form (aged 16). Always well in the league tables, yet provides plenty of extra-curricular activity as well – sport, music, combined cadet force etc. The top boys' school in Cambridge, fees £7,023 a year, but not quite in the top flight of public schools nationwide.

The Leys School, Trumpington Road, Cambridge CB2 2AD (01223 508900, www.theleys.cambs.uk). Originally a boys' boarding school, but now one third day pupils and co-ed all the way through. There are 333 boys and 187 girls on a splendid site near the city centre. The Leys provides a full public school education and was the model for James

Photo courtesy of The King's School, Ely

King's School (Ely) scholars returning from services at Ely Cathedral

Hilton's novel *Goodbye Mr Chips*. Exam results could be improved, but the school makes a virtue of teaching people of widely differing abilities. Fees £14,505 yearly for boarders, between £6,495 and £10,740 for different categories of day pupil.

The Perse School for Girls, Union Road, Cambridge CB2 1HF (01223 359589, www.perse.cambs.sch.uk). The cleverest girls' day school, featuring regularly in the country's top ten for GCSE results – particularly impressive when the girls take 10 or 11 GCSEs against other schools' nine. But it's a bit of an exam factory. Some girls complain of stress and others find it dull. A huge number leave after GCSE for Hills Road or anywhere else with boys. There are 550 girls in the senior school, fees £6,372 a year. The school treasures a letter from the cartoonist Ronald Searle, naming it as the original for *St Trinian's.*

St Mary's School, Bateman Street, Cambridge CB2 1LY (01223 353253, www.stmarys.cambs.sch.uk). Ostensibly a Catholic girls' day school, but now overwhelmingly Protestant. There are 466 girls from 11, fees £6,180 a year for day girls. A handful are weekly boarders at £11,070 a year, and even fewer now board full-time at £13,650. St Mary's is perceived as less academic than the Perse, but there are bright girls there who prefer it because there's less emphasis on maths and science (a must at the Perse, where all girls are expected to take three separate sciences at GCSE). The school will even take the occasional boy, if Catholic instruction is deemed essential, but he'd have to be pretty brave to apply.

The King's School, Ely, Cambs CB7 4DB (01353 660700, www.kings-ely.cambs.sch.uk). Very old school, tracing its origins to the dawn of Christianity in Britain and still using many of the ancient buildings. Edward the Confessor was a pupil before the Norman Conquest. He entered the school in 1010. King's is now fully co-ed, with 238 boys and 164 girls in the senior school, a quarter of them boarders. Fees are £15,006 a year for boarders, £10,305 for day pupils. Not particularly academic, but a friendly enough place with a pleasant, unassuming product fitting easily into Cambridgeshire life.

Friends' School, Saffron Walden, Essex, CB11 3EB, (01799 525351, www.friends.org.uk). Nominally a Quaker school, although pupils are not Quakers. There are 175 boys and 158 girls from three to 18, 81 of them boarders. Many take the train from Cambridge every morning and are collected from Audley End station in the school bus. Fees are £12,900 a year for boarders, £7,740 for day pupils, of whom Joseph Stalin's granddaughter used to be one.

Private school primary departments

All these schools have junior departments or feeder schools. For younger children, see also King's College School, West Road, Cambridge CB3 9DN (01223 365814) and St John's College School, Grange Road, Cambridge CB3 9AB (01223 353532). Both are tiptop mixed preparatory schools, full of talented kids. The choristers at King's wear top hats and appear on TV at Christmas time, singing in the carol service in the chapel.

SPECIAL NEEDS EDUCATION

Government policy for children with special needs is to keep them in the community wherever possible. Most attend their local school, where a specially trained teacher will cater for their requirements. There's an elaborate support system to identify the children's needs, see that they are met, and keep the parents in touch. Each child is assigned a Named Officer from the local authority to take charge of their case. The Education Information Centres can provide further details.

Among pre-school children, early warning signs of special needs are often picked up by the Health Visitor, who routinely tests all infants in his or her area to see if they can perform certain specified tasks. You will be visited automatically if your child is registered with a doctor, otherwise contact your nearest Health Centre. As soon as a problem is identified, an appropriate educational plan will be arranged. In most cases, children go on to their local school, as normal. But several schools do offer additional specialist support in particular areas, as follows:

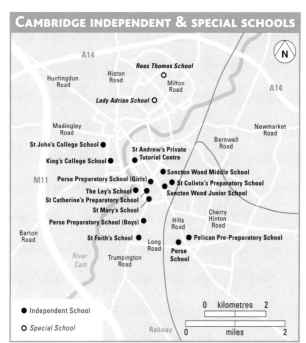

CAMBRIDGE INDEPENDENT & SPECIAL SCHOOLS

- ● Independent School
- O Special School

EDUCATION

● visual impairment

Manor Community College, Cambridge
Eastfield Infant School, St Ives

● hearing impairment

Cottenham Village College
Neale Wade Community College, March
Huntingdon County Infant and Junior Schools
Mayfield Primary School, Cambridge

● physical impairment

Ernulf Community College, St Neots
Impington Village College
The Grove Primary School, Cambridge

● speech and language difficulties

Cottenham Village College
Arbury Primary School, Cambridge
Sedley Infant School, Cambridge

● infants needing assessment

Ely Infant School
Histon and Impington Infant School
Shirley Infant School, Cambridge.

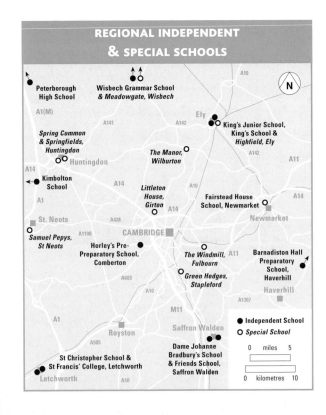

REGIONAL INDEPENDENT & SPECIAL SCHOOLS

Special needs schools

For children with more severe problems, the situation is different. They attend special schools where the facilities are adapted for their particular needs. All children have individual education plans created to address their individual needs and parents are actively involved in their education.

- Green Hedges School, Stapleford - day school for severe learning difficulties.
- Highfield School, Ely - day school for moderate or severe learning difficulties.
- Lady Adrian School, Cambridge - day school for moderate learning difficulties.
- Littleton House School, Girton - residential and day school for emotional or behavioural difficulties.
- The Manor School, Wilburton - residential and day school for emotional or behavioural difficulties.
- Meadowgate School, Wisbech - day school for moderate or severe learning difficulties.
- Meldreth Manor School, nr Royston - residential and day school for severe learning difficulties.
- Rees Thomas School, Cambridge - day school for severe learning difficulties.
- Samuel Pepys School, St Neots - day school for moderate or severe learning difficulties.
- Springfields School, Huntingdon - day school for moderate or severe learning difficulties.
- Spring Common School, Huntingdon - day school for moderate or severe learning difficulties.
- Windmill School, Fulbourn - day school for severe learning difficulties.

HIGHER EDUCATION

For those going to university, the choice in the UK is bewildering. It ranges from world-class institutions like Cambridge – recently voted the best in Europe by its peers – to other places that are far less distinguished.

Approach with care, therefore. All the universities and their courses, good and bad, are listed in the Universities and College Admissions Service handbook, obtainable from UCAS, Rosehill, New Barn Lane, Cheltenham, Gloucestershire GL52 3LZ, 01242 227788, www.ucas.com. *The Times Good University Guide* or the *Which Guide to University* are also helpful. It's very important to remember that you can only apply to six universities in any one year, so they need to be the right six. A study of the guides, together with the entry requirements for each course, will tell you what kind of place you're dealing with.

Gap-year opportunities

Once they've secured a university place, many students take a gap year beforehand, either to earn the money to finance their studies, or else to see the world. About 30% go abroad, some on working holidays, others on lavish expeditions arranged by professional organisers who charge for their services. The choice is huge – the world really is their oyster – and often confusing. All major libraries have a boxful of brochures to browse through, but you can also consult *Opportunities in the Gap Year* (ISCO Publications, 12A Princess Way, Camberley, Surrey, GU15 3SP, www.info@isco.org.uk), *The Gap Year Guidebook* (Peridot Press, 2 Blenheim Crescent, London W11 1NN, www.gap-

---

A QUICK GLANCE AT THE EXAM SYSTEM

General Certificate of Secondary Education (GCSE)

An exam for 16-year-olds, taking anything between five and 11 academic subjects. The results are graded A* to E. An average result should include at least five passes graded C or above.

General National Vocational Qualification (GNVQ)

Less academic and more work-related than GCSEs. Design, business, health care, rather than Latin, physics or history. See also National Vocational Qualifications (NVQs) which are usually acquired in the workplace after leaving school.

General Certificate of Education Advanced Subsidiary Level (GCE AS Level)

A new idea for 17-year-olds, designed to bring them into line with the International Baccalaureate so popular abroad. They study five subjects in their first year in the Sixth Form (instead of only three, as previously) and are examined on them at AS Level.

General Certificate of Education Advanced Level (GCE A2 Level)

An exam in three subjects (or exceptionally four) continued in greater depth from AS Level and taken by 18 year-olds in their last year at school. The results are graded A to E and university admission depends on them.

year.com) or *Taking a Gap Year* (Vacation Work, 9 Park End Street, Oxford, www.vacationwork.co.uk).

CONTINUING EDUCATION

For those not going anywhere, but ready to continue their education, there are plenty of local options available. If you're looking for a vocational qualification, or simply enjoy learning for its own sake, you're bound to find something you like at one of these:

The Open University, Cintra House, 12 Hills Road, Cambridge CB2 1PF (01223 361650 www.open.ac.uk). Part-time distance learning for adults. No entrance requirements for most courses. Students work from home, accumulating credits for a degree, or in some cases a certificate or diploma. There are tutors, so you won't feel entirely alone, but of course working at home in front of a screen is a very different experience to actually going somewhere, attending lectures.

Anglia Polytechnic University, East Road, Cambridge CB1 1PT (01223 363271 www.apu.ac.uk). Has vocational courses of immediate practical use. Law, construction, business, nursing, community care etc. APU has close links with the region's business and industrial community and specialises in turning out highly skilled people to meet local demand. Courses are very flexible and tailored to specific needs. Student placements and management consultancy services keep APU in touch with the real world, with a strong emphasis on continuing professional development.

EDUCATION

Cambridge University Board of Continuing Education, Madingley Hall, Madingley, Cambridge CB3 8AQ (01954 280399, www.cont-ed.cam.ac.uk). These are short courses – typically 10 or 20 lectures – run by the university and offered to the public at venues all over East Anglia. Everything from Dark Age Archaeology to Ornithology to the Poetry of the Elizabethans. A complicated system of credits can lead to Certificates of Continuing or Higher Education, worth either half or a full year towards a university degree.

For more on training and education see Chapter 11, 'Employment' page 226.

National Extension College (NEC), The Michael Young Centre, Purbeck Road, CB2 2HN (01223 450500). A non profit-making trust providing education for adults through open or distance learning. Teaches everything from basic numeracy and literacy to GCSEs, A levels and vocational

Cambridge Students in degree ceremony at Senate House

Photo by Findlay Kember

courses in accounting, computing, book-keeping etc.

University of the Third Age (U3A), The Old Warehouse, 33 Bridge Street, Cambridge CB2 1UW (01223 321587). For retired people, or those no longer in full-time work. Runs more than 200 weekday courses, everything from arts and crafts to music, philosophy and science. No qualifications needed, but there's a small charge for some courses. U3A organises day trips as well, and a variety of leisure activities for those keen to get involved. *(See also box page 215)*

Village/Community/Regional/Sixth Form Colleges. Except for Regional Colleges, which also take adults, these are all just schools under another name. As their names suggest though, they are very much a part of the local community. They provide all sorts of courses for adults in the evenings, and at weekends. The courses are very cheap and usually good value.

ENGLISH AS A FOREIGN LANGUAGE

There have been foreigners in Cambridge ever since the Dutch humanist Desiderius Erasmus taught at the university 500 years ago. He complained of the cold wind and dreadful beer and thought Cambridge was a pretty awful place to be. The wind is still cold and the beer still dreadful, but Cambridge has picked up in other ways. It is now a major centre for learning English, with several dozen language schools in the area, all touting for business in a highly competitive market.

EDUCATION

WHO PAYS UNIVERSITY FEES

Most people's university tuition fees are heavily subsidised by the Government. In 2000-01 the fees were set at £1,050 a year for British or European Union citizens. That is the amount students have to find themselves unless they're poor, in which case the local authority will help. Students from elsewhere usually have to pay the full whack – anything from £7,500 for arts subjects to £9,800 for science or £18,500 for clinical subjects – unless they have lived here for three years, in which case they pay the same as the British.

On top of that, there is also board and lodging. As a rough guide, the Government calculates the cost of going away to university at £4,590 a year for London, £3,725 elsewhere. It will lend the full amount to poor students (subject to a means test) or 75% to those with better-off parents. The loan does not have to be repaid until students have graduated and are in gainful employment. For further details, click on www.dfee.gov.uk, phone 0800 731 9133 for the free booklet *Financial Support for Higher Education Students*, or contact the Student Awards Service, Box ELH 1112, Cambs County Council, Castle Court, Shire Hall, Cambs CB3 0AP (01223 717942).

> ### DEGREES FOR CONTINUING LEARNERS
>
> CATS is adult education's Credit Accumulation and Transfer Scheme, which enables you to accumulate points towards a Certificate of Continuing or Higher Education, equivalent to the first year of a degree. It's intended for continuing learners, often without formal qualifications, rather than full-time undergraduates. Cambridge University's Board of Continuing Education (see above, page 212) has a booklet explaining the procedure in greater detail.

Business is the operative word. Some language schools are non profit-making trusts, but most are money-making businesses. The best provide an excellent service, sending customers home with fluent English and a recognised certificate to prove it. A few, however, are more interested in taking the cash than actually teaching anything. Buyers should investigate very carefully before committing themselves. You get what you pay for in the language business and cheapest isn't always best.

● Cambridge Advisory Service

Your first port of call should be the Cambridge Advisory Service, Rectory Lane, Kingston, Cambridge CB3 7NL (01223 264089). They know all about the language schools and will tell you what is best for your personal requirements. Customers for language tuition vary hugely – everything from rich bankers brushing up their business English, to school and university students from Brazil. Tell the advisory service who you are and what you want. They will do their best to point you in the right direction.

What to look for in a language school

Once you've found a school, have a look round and see what kind of place it is. Some are very plush, with all the comforts that businessmen expect and pay for. Others are less lavish, concentrating instead on the bare essentials. Chat to the staff and students. If you are doing an exam course, ask which exam syllabus you will be following – Oxford, Cambridge, the British Council and others all award certificates for various levels of proficiency in English. Check that the school has been recognised by the British Council, which inspects and certifies the schools. A good indicator of quality is membership of any of these professional bodies: FIRST (Quality English Language Services), ARELS (Association for Recognised English Language Teaching Establishments) or IALC (International Association of Language Centres).

To get you started, we print a selection of language schools below. It would be invidious to compare them in any detail, but you ought to find something here that you like. A much longer list is available from CambsTEC or the Central Library (addresses at the end of the chapter). If money is a problem, it's perhaps worth mentioning that most regional and community colleges run English courses for a fraction of the cost of a professional language school. But whatever you choose, make sure you know exactly what you're paying for before parting with any cash.

- Anglia Polytechnic University, East Road, Cambridge CB1 1PT, 01223 363271.
- Anglo-World Cambridge, 75 Barton Road, Cambridge CB3 9LJ, 01223 357702.
- Bell School of Languages, 1 Red Cross Lane, Cambridge, 01223 247242.
- Cambridge Academy of English, 65 High Street, Girton, Cambridge CB3 0QD, 01223 277320.
- Cambridge Centre for Languages, Sawston Hall, Sawston, Cambridge CB2 4JR, 01223 835099.
- Cambridge School of Languages, 119 Mill Road, Cambridge CB1 2AZ, 01223 312333.
- EF Language School, 222 Hills Road, Cambridge CB2 2RW, 01223 240020.
- International Language Academy, 12/13 Regent Terrace, Cambridge CB2 1AA, 01223 350519.
- Language Studies International, 41 Tenison Road, Cambridge CB1 2DG, 01223 361783.
- New School of English Ltd, 52 Bateman Street, Cambridge CB2 1LR, 01223 358089.
- Newnham Language Centre, 8 Grange Road, Cambridge CB3 9DU, 01223 311344.

UNIVERSITY OF THE 3RD AGE
A CAMBRIDGE STORY

The **U3A**, as it is known, or locally the **U3AC** (University of the 3rd Age in Cambridge), takes place mostly in people's homes, in church halls and other public venues. The teachers are the students and vice versa. Any member with a special area of competence or bright idea can offer a class. The 200 choices on the Cambridge timetable alone range from embroidery to dream sharing to Russian and computing. All activities have a social element, drawing together people in later life to learn as well as enjoy one another's company.

Photo by Perry Hastings

Peter Laslett, U3A founder

The organisation, with a following in Australia, New Zealand and elsewhere, and over 350 branches in the UK alone, started in Cambridge. In 1981 Cambridge academic Peter Laslett led a group at Trinity College in planning for the needs of the growing proportion of the population in retirement from active work. Out of these discussions, U3A was founded.

Photo courtesy of Cambridgeshire Collection

The way it was – St Matthews School, Cambridge 1919

- OISE-Cambridge – Cambridge Intensive School of English, 81/83 Hills Road, Cambridge CB2 1PG, 01223 320184.
- Studio School of English, 6 Salisbury Villas, Station Road, Cambridge CB1 2JF, 01223 369701.

ADDITIONAL INFORMATION

● school website

edweb.camcnty.gov.uk – information about schools in Cambridgeshire

● educational bodies

Essex Education Information Centre, PO Box 47, Chelmsford, CM2 4WN (01245 436231).

Hertfordshire Education Information Centre: County Hall, Hertford, SG13 8DF (01992 555827).

Suffolk Education Information Centre, St Andrew's House, County Hall, Ipswich IP4 1LJ (01473 583000).

Student Loans Company, 100 Bothwell Street, Glasgow G2 7TD, (0800 405 010, www.slc.co.uk).

Ofsted, Alexandra House, 33 Kingsway, London WC2B 6SE, (020 7421 6744, www.ofsted.gov.uk).

● gap-year websites

gapyear.com, lonelyplanet.com, roughguides.com, doh.gov.uk/traveladvice, ticltd.co.uk, trailfinders.co.uk, workandtravel.com

● other

Cambridge Central Library, Tourist Information Centre and other sources (see 'Key Contacts' back page).

CambsTEC:The Business centre, Histon, Cambridge CB4 9LQ (01345 882255, www.cambstec.co.uk). Career guidance, developing skills, setting up a business etc.

CHAPTER 11
EMPLOYMENT

Photo courtesy of University of Cambridge

Considering a career move or simply looking for a job when moving to the area? This chapter describes where to find work, highlights regional growth sectors and discusses opportunities for commuting to work. The best and most comprehensive sources of vacancies and careers advice are detailed and sources of further information listed at the end of the section. In short, it gives you a picture of the job scene and an understanding of the resources you may want to use in finding the right job.

JOB PROSPECTS

Job prospects in East Anglia are generally very good. Within this broad region, unemployment is 2.4%, much lower than the national average of 3.5% and figures from the National Office of Statistics show that unemployment in the region fell slightly faster than the nation as a whole between 1997 and 2000. Things look even better in Cambridgeshire and again in Cambridge itself, where unemployment in 2000 was 1.8% and 1.4% respectively, as demand for labour continues to exceed supply.

Highly skilled, especially high-tech professionals and unskilled workers, will find lots of opportunity, but demand varies more in the mid-range. Skilled trades, like carpenters and electricians, along with teachers, nurses and care workers are in severe short supply. Demand in other fields depends on the size, activity and nature of the local industry or commerce. But prospects for all fields are much improved over the wider commuting area including several larger cities. The Cambridge area has excellent transport links to these markets, particularly to London (under 50 minutes train ride away) where many of the UK's best jobs are based.

in Cambridgeshire and again in Cambridge itself... unemployment in 2000 was 1.8% and 1.4% respectively, as demand for labour continues to exceed supply

JOB SEARCH STRATEGIES

Which job search strategy you use will depend on the kind of work you want. Highly skilled, unskilled work and some semi-skilled areas are better served by agencies and websites, as are certain specialities, like teaching and nursing. Other areas will find these much less helpful, and are better advised to locate and approach employers directly through networking and speculative contacts. Below we give you information about using these various tools.

Networking

Networking has been and will continue to be a powerful tool for those who are skilled in building up personal con-

Cover picture: Worker at King's College, Cambridge.

tacts. Newcomers to the area may find that they have lost a number of their connections and be unsure of how to develop their personal network again. Here are some starting points:

Try business and professional groups, of which Cambridge has a wide range – from Junior Chamber of Commerce to Probus and more. Cambrige also has the relatively new Cambridge Network. This organisation was established by a number of prestigious and local businesses and organisations including the University of Cambridge to provide an opening to a whole host of resources and contacts, and its members can attend its regular meetings and meet a range of professional business men and women.

● **contact information**

- The Cambridge Network. POB 362, Unit 56, St John's Innovation Centre, Cambridge, CB4 0WS (01223 422362), (website: www.cambridgenetwork.co.uk, e-mail: office@cambridgenetwork.co.uk). Company members also advertise vacancies on www.cambridgenetwork.co.uk/jobs and you can receive the available vacancies by weekly e-mail.

- The many business and professional groups are listed in the Citizen's Guide (see 'Key Contacts' on the back page).

Speculative approaches

As the number of new firms increases within the area, a speculative application may clinch you a job opening before the vacancy is even advertised. Keep your eye on the local media for reports on firms that may be moving into the area (see news media listed page 68). You will also benefit from being considered without competition. In any

---

TEACHERS IN BIG DEMAND

Looking for a real challenge? Teaching is worth considering.

The shortage of teachers is serious. The number of vacancies for teaching professionals in East Anglia far exceeds the number of qualified teachers, especially in mathematics, science subjects, modern languages and technology. The demand has driven up salaries and spurred the government to offer incentives to those willing to join the field.

Check with the **Teaching Information Line** (0845 6000 991 or the website www.canteach.gov.uk) for details of courses available, eligibility for grants and further information. Teaching vacancies can be found in the *Times Educational Supplement* (www.tes.co.uk) and *The Guardian* on Mondays. www.jobs.ac.uk is a recruitment website dedicated to advertising academic and research vacancies in all sectors. **Timeplan** (0800 358 8040, www.timeplan.com) provides details of both full-time and part-time teaching vacancies. The average weekly salary that workers in education can expect is approximately £420.

case, your CV will probably be kept on file and you may be the first to hear about a vacancy.

www.countyweb.com or *www.cambweb.co.uk* are excellent websites for directories and information on businesses within Cambridgeshire or other surrounding counties, and their associated website *www.joblocator.co.uk* has a number of searchable vacancies. Your local reference library will also be able to assist you and it should hold copies of local business directories. Your careers office (*see page 229 below*) may also know of local companies where opportunities may exist. Jobcentres (*see next section*) can also provide lists of companies in your field. Ensure that you keep good records of all the applications you make and keep the details easily to hand along with a copy of your CV, so that you can reply confidently to return calls from employers.

JOBCENTRES

Jobcentres do not often have openings or vacancies advertised for professionals or executives, nor can they help, as they once did, with National Insurance numbers for overseas students (which should be obtained from the Department of Social Security). But for most other areas, the government network of offices dedicated to promoting employment and aiding the unemployed will be many jobseekers' first port of call.

Its functions are mainly to advertise local (and many national) vacancies for those out of work or looking for work, and to assess jobseekers' entitlement to benefits. The Jobcentre office format varies, but often vacancies are set out on boards and are colour-sticker classified into full-time, part-time, temporary and contract jobs to allow easy identification. Computer terminals are also being introduced into centres to allow jobseekers to carry out searches of the vacancies. A selected number of Cambridge Jobcentre's vacancies are also advertised in the Wednesday and Friday editions of the *Cambridge Evening News*.

As well as turning up in person at your local jobcentre, you can use Employment Service Direct's telephone service (0845 6060234). Both are staffed by qualified job advisers who will endeavour to match a vacancy to your requirements. If you find a suitable position then they will either send you the employer's application form or arrange an interview on your behalf. The service will also be increasingly available via the Employment Service's website www.employmentservice.gov.uk. These are the local Jobcentres:

Cambridge Jobcentre, Henry Giles House, 73 Chesterton Road, Cambridge, Cambridgeshire, CB4 3BG (01223 545000).

Ely Jobcentre, 52 Market Street, Ely, Cambridgeshire, CB7 4LS (01353 605400).

COMMUTING TO EMPLOYMENT NEARBY

The main advantage to commuting is the increased choice and availability of work, and better career prospects if the ideal vacancies are not available locally.

The most obvious and largest choice is, of course, London. The employment market there is huge; finance, media, law, civil service and innumerable other industries in the UK have tended to concentrate there. Salaries are often higher (the average is £543 per week in April 1999 compared to £414 per week in East Anglia). A 'London-weighting' allowance is also made in many jobs to compensate for the increased cost of living in or travelling into the city. And London will forever be the city that offers so much. 'When a man is tired of London he is tired of life; for there is in London all that life can afford,' Samuel Johnson said in 1777. It's still true.

But there are a number of disadvantages these days. Car commuting is expensive and subject to traffic delays. Although the journey into London by train can be a reasonable and comfortable commute, there is the inevitable certainty of train delays, time required for travel to and from the nearest train station and, occasionally, lack of seating at peak times! Commuting is also not inexpensive. A yearly rail ticket, for example, costs over £3,000. Many people in Cambridge have commuted happily to London for years, but others find a regular commute rather too demanding and avoid it.

Cambridge is also within commuting range of a number of centres of industry and business, including Stevenage, Peterborough, Norwich, Ipswich, Milton Keynes, Northampton and Chelmsford.

(For more on transport to London and other regional cities see Chapter 4, 'Transport', page 71.)

Photo courtesy of WAGN Railway

Trains arriving at Cambridge station

Huntingdon Jobcentre, 2-6 Hartford Road, Huntingdon, Cambridgeshire, PE18 6PB (01480 322000).

Newmarket Jobcentre, Wellington Street, Newmarket, Suffolk, CB8 0HT (01638 683500).

Peterborough Jobcentre, Frobisher House, 72 Westgate, Peterborough, Cambridgeshire, PE1 1RR (01733 415500).

EMPLOYMENT AGENCIES

We list many below, covering a wide range of jobs including both temporary, part-time, contract and permanent jobs. Although some have websites with vacancies that you can apply for online, it is generally best to either telephone or visit in person to discuss the application. You will also have a better chance to explain your skills set and experience more thoroughly. With the number of agencies on the market it is worth checking to see if each one is a member of the *Federation of Recruitment and Employment Services*, 36-38 Mortimer Street, London, W1W 7RG (0207 462 3260) e-mail: info@rec.uk.com, www.rec.uk.com. Members of FRES will only forward your details to an employer with your agreement. A consideration to be aware of when dealing with agencies is that agencies receive their commission or payments for each candidate they successfully place in a position. So beware the occasional agent who may try to put you forward for positions for which you may find you are not fully suited.

Finding high-tech jobs

At the heart of the 'Silicon Fen', with its conglomeration of biotech, electronic and pharmaceutical companies, Cambridge continues to expand in the high-tech sector. The big names are companies like Microsoft and ARM Ltd, but the range of enterprise is vast. (To get a feel for the technologies thriving in the area, take a look at the list of companies on the Cambridge Science Park available on www.cambridge-science-park.com.) Due to the shortage of skills in this sector, expect above average salaries and lots of openings. If you are looking for high-tech jobs, start with the many agencies and websites specialising in recruiting skilled and technical staff. Here are a few:

Technical Recruitment 12 King's Parade, Cambridge, CB2 1SJ, 01223 464411, e-mail: jobs@technical-recruitment.co.uk, www.technical-recruitment.co.uk. Established since 1969, this company matches skilled information technology professionals with permanent positions for companies in Cambridgeshire and adjacent counties – Bedfordshire, Hertfordshire and Suffolk.

Connect IT Recruitment, Suite 35, Newton Hall, Newton, Cambridge, CB2 5PE, 01223 874481, e-mail: info@cirltd.co.uk, specialises in information technology and office support roles and encourages you to send your CV in by e-mail to opportunities@cirltd.co.uk (for IT) or connect.resourcing@virgin.net (for office support).

Other useful sources are websites such as *www.job-site.co.uk* which can send you daily e-mail notices about new technical positions and *www.camjob.co.uk* which lists links to companies that have vacancies for programmers.

Finding the un/semi-skilled job

As wealth flows into the area, many service and retailing industries have expanded rapidly. This means jobs for security staff, shop and store assistants and hotel and catering staff. The construction industry is also very busy, pushing up the demand for building trades workers. Demand is such in and around Cambridge that traditionally low-paying jobs in retail and hospitality are commanding higher salaries. Businesses face shortages of workers even in unskilled jobs, like security staff, where the only requirement is a checkable work history.

To fill these positions, employers are finding they must be more flexible, allowing workers increasingly to set their own times of work. A number of retailers have begun to pay their workers at the higher London rates of pay. This is promising news for those employed in this sector, though it should be balanced against the fact that the cost of living is also higher in Cambridgeshire than in many other parts and is nearly on a level with costs in London.

> **Demand is such in and around Cambridge that traditionally low-paying jobs in retail and hospitality are commanding higher salaries.**

The best source of this type of vacancies is the local

A bus worker at the Downing Street bus station in Cambridge

Photo by Dan Porter

JOBS AT THE UNIVERSITY OF CAMBRIDGE

The University employs approximately 3,000 non-academic staff in administrative and service jobs, within the colleges, departments or central administration. Departmental vacancies are advertised in many places, including the Wednesday jobs edition of the *Cambridge Evening News*. A list of online vacancies is also available on the University's server at: www.admin.cam.ac.uk/audience/jobs.html .

If you wish to investigate positions within particular departments, then a list of these and links to their websites are available at www.cam.ac.uk/UnivInfoRes.html. Job seekers should also consider searching each college's web page for vacancies that may be available. A list of colleges and contact details and web addresses for these is available at: www.cam.ac.uk/CambUniv/Finding/Addresses/college.html

Temporary positions for skilled office staff, with a minimum of two years' experience are managed by the University's own **Temporary Employment Service** (TES) at 25 Trumpington Street, Cambridge CB2 1QA (01223 332348). Anyone on the Temporary Staff Register has the chance to work anywhere within the University's 100 departments and colleges. For those skilled in the use of newsgroups, then ucam.jobs.offered is updated regularly with local university jobs and www.cam.ac.uk/CambUniv/AnnEvNG.html also provides links to other relevant news servers.

Opportunities for domestic cleaners, serving staff and porters are many, thanks to the large number of colleges that each require their own set of service staff to maintain the colleges' accommodation, ground and catering facilities.

The weekly University of Cambridge publication, The Reporter (an online edition can be found at www.admin.cam.ac.uk/reporter/) publishes academic posts available in the University. Typically, they are also published in the relevant professional publications and often the Times Higher Education Supplement www.thes.co.uk .

Photo courtesy of University of Cambridge

Jobcentre which can have up to or over 1,000 positions available at any one time. Here are major commercial recruiters:

Hays Montrose, 10 Downing Street, Cambridge (01223 361496). An agency with a number of manual labour positions available.

Blue Arrow is a good agency for service and catering jobs. It has offices at: 40 St Andrew's Street, Cambridge, CB2 3AR (01223 324433); 7 Chequers Court, Huntingdon, PE18 6NB (01480 41123); 8a Church Street, Peterborough, PE1 1XB (01733 342766).

Nicholas Andrews & Temps Financial specialises in recruiting personnel into financial and accountancy roles. They have an excellent search function available on their website www.natf.co.uk, with which you can define your location, salary, job type and keywords. The East Anglia branches are: Compass House, 80 Newmarket Road, Cambridge CB5 8DZ (01223 346800); and Trinity Court, Trinity Street, Peterborough PE1 1DN (01733 565488)

AIC Analysts, Sheraton House, Castle Park, Cambridge, CB3 0AX (01223 500055). An agency specialising in computing and IT positions.

Cambridge High-Tech Recruitment, 108 Gilbert Road, Cambridge, CB4 3PD (01223 467724). Has positions within electronics, computer and high-tech industries.

Part-time work opportunities

Temping agencies are the best source of vacancies if you are looking for part-time work, and good positions can be found for secretarial and other office roles. On the Internet, you will find that www.eplace.co.uk is a very good site that brings together all agency vacancies in East Anglia. For your own list of vacancies in the area, then the local Jobcentre can provide you with a full list, including advice on which are the best to use for you.

The best general agencies are listed below.

Brook Street has a number of branches in East Anglia which you can contact and you may be able to check their website www.brookstreet.co.uk for vacancies. They have particular experience in placing staff in secretarial, office and industrial positions as either temporary, permanent or contract staff. The offices are: 1st Floor, 22 Church Street, Peterborough, PE1 1XF (01733 310855, e-mail: Peterborough@brookstreet.co.uk); 6-7 Guildhall Hill, Norwich, NR2 1JG (01603 628931, e-mail: Norwich@brookstreet.co.uk); 52 Regent Street, Cambridge, CB2 1DP (01223 355700, e-mail: Cambridge@brookstreet.co.uk).

Select Appointments is a nationwide agency with a number of franchises in East Anglia and concentrates principally on temporary employment in office-based jobs, including customer service and call centres. The offices are: 9 Thurlow Street, Bedford, MK40 1LR (01234 269111); 50 Regent Street, Cambridge, CB2 1DP (01223 324744); 1st Floor Exchange House, 12 - 14 Exchange Street, Norwich, NR2 4AU (01603 615511); Britannic

House, 11/ 13 Cowgate, Peterborough, PE1 1LZ (01733 346496); 13 Queensway, Stevenage, Hertfordshire, SG1 1DA (01438 740077)

Office Angels, 53/54 Sidney Street, Cambridge, CB2 3HX (01223 365165, www.office-angels.com, e-mail cambridge@office-angels.com) recruits on behalf of many blue-chip companies to fill both temporary and permanent vacancies.

Manpower, 50 St Andrew's Street, Cambridge, CB23AH (01223 354247). Has many office and industrial part-time vacancies.

Human Resources, 49-53 Regent Street, Cambridge, CB2 1AB (01223 460626, e-mail: info@hrl-cam.co.uk, www.hrl-cam.co.uk). A Cambridge-based agency with a number of permanent, temporary and contract positions in a number of local businesses and companies.

General employment agencies

Here are some of the major agencies with Cambridge and area offices:

Cooper Lomaz Recruitment, St Edmund's House, Lower Baxter Street, Bury St Edmund's, Suffolk, IP33 1ET (01284 701302, www.cooperlomaz.co.uk).

Reed Employment, 8 Bradwells Court, Cambridge, CB1 1NH (01223 462872, www.reed.co.uk).

Alfred Marks Recruitment, Parker House, 44 Regent Street, Cambridge, CB2 1DP (01223 324747).

Character Recruitment, 52 Burleigh Street, Cambridge, CB1 1DJ (01223 517215).

Newmarket Recruitment Agency, 10A Old Station Road, Newmarket, Suffolk (01638 561065).

PIR Group, Suites 1-2, Meadow Lane Business Park, St Ives, PE17 4LG (01480 493344).

Travail Employment Group, 1 Wellington Court, Wellington Street, Cambridge, CB1 1HZ (01223 462908).

TRAINING FOR A BETTER JOB

If you find you lack the skills you need, you may wish to consider re-training or gaining experience in other ways. Voluntary work offers good opportunities to learn new skills in preparation for applying for better positions and you can get that extra experience and fresh references. For other kinds of opportunities, try:

The Prince's Trust (0800 842842, www.princes-trust.org.uk). Helps young people aged 15 to 30 improve a wide variety of skills on challenging projects.

Youth Action Cambridge, Shaftesbury House, 22 Godesdone Road, Cambridge, CB3 8HR (01223 316105). A similar local organisation.

Individual Learning Accounts (ILA), 0800 072 4949. You start an account with £25 to get up to £150 towards training courses. For anyone over 19 and not in full-time education or another training scheme.

Photo courtesy of Wood Green

EMPLOYMENT

Other local training centres and courses include:

UK Online (www.ukonline.org.uk). Gives free online computer training from and is available to anyone unemployed and receiving benefits. Contact them on 01223 410611 to enrol on e-mail, Internet and web page design courses.

Cambridge WEA, 95 Richmond Road, Cambridge, CB4 3PS (01223 322710). Has a wide range of courses ranging from developing your assertiveness to local and international history classes. Both morning and evening courses are run at various local community centres in Cambridge and again those receiving benefit

Wood Green Animal Shelter worker

may be entitled to a full or partial subsidy towards the course fees.

Brickworks, The Creative Studies Centre, Manor Community College, Arbury Road, Cambridge, CB4 2JF (01223 508748). Concentrates on part-time artistic and craft training programmes, such as fashion design, sewing and painting.

For more courses see Chapter 10, 'Education'. For more on voluntary opportunities, see Chapter 12, 'Community'

Always check with the local Jobcentre, as paid voluntary work may affect your entitlement to benefits, though unpaid work usually does not. Generally as long as you continue to seek paid employment and are available to attend interviews, you should be eligible for benefits. Information from the Jobcentre can also provide you with details of training courses accessed through the *Training and Enterprise Council* (for your nearest see www.tec.co.uk).

A FIRST JOB FOR GRADUATES

The demise of the 'graduate job' (jobs reserved for graduates only) over recent years has put graduates on a more equal footing with other jobseekers. Many employers now consider a degree a prerequisite for many jobs previously only aimed at school leavers. However, with the gradual re-emergence of the 'milk round' – big employers visiting university campuses to advertise their companies and to tempt students into applying for their graduate traineeships – university students can expect greater attention from many of the country's top employers.

● **websites for graduates**

A whole host of Internet sites have sprung up to cater for this lucrative market:

www.reedgraduates.co.uk
www.topcareers.net
www.graduatebase.com
www.doctorjob.co.uk
www.the-ladder.com
www.get.co.uk
www.bestofthebest.co.uk
www.majorplayers.co.uk
www.graduate-register.co.uk
www.graduate-recruitment.co.uk
www.topjobs.co.uk
www.gradunet.co.uk

These allow students to post their CVs on their site, receive updates and new jobs by e-mail. They also give plenty of advice on each employment sector and they list many of the top UK graduate employers.

ALTERNATIVE: SET UP YOUR OWN BUSINESS

Looking for a real job change? Why not set up your own business? You may have built up a wealth of expertise and skills – enough to establish yourself as a freelancer or independent consultant – or create a small ongoing concern. For those considering this alternative, Cambridgeshire is indeed a great area in which to carry out such a venture. There is plenty of encouragement and support networks available to budding entrepreneurs.

For anyone starting a small business of any kind the first stop should be **The Cambridge Enterprise Agency** (71a Lensfield Road, Cambridge CB2 1EN, 01223 323553. e-mail: info@cambsenterprise.demon.co.uk and www.cambsenterprise.demon.co.uk). A not-for-profit agency, this organisation really goes the extra mile to help small business – mainly for free.

Services start with a half-day seminar on key aspects of starting on your own. You get one-to one advice from business specialists and workshops on everything from marketing to finances. They also host a local owner/manager network, great for meeting other small business managers/owners and finding service providers.

Similar to the latter is **The Cambridge Network** (see above, page 219), an excellent place to make contact with similar-minded individuals and private local consultancies that can help you organise and put your business plan into effect successfully.

Also you can call **The Inland Revenue** (01223 442400) to ask for a business start-up pack.

● **student careers services offices**

Students also have the opportunity to meet directly with recruiters at employers' presentations and careers fairs in the city and will find details of these at either Cambridge University Careers Service, 6 Mill Lane, Cambridge CB2 1XE (01223 338288, www.careers.cam.ac.uk) or Anglia Polytechnic University Careers Service (www.anglia.ac.uk/students/career.shtml).

They hold extensive information on companies, as well as feedback from past applicants/students who have secured a job and can describe from their own experience exactly what the job entails. The service is only available to past and present members of each respective university.

A hard-copy publication that all graduates should get hold of is *The Prospects Directory*. It is usually available at your local careers service (*see next section*), and an excellent online version, *Prospects Direct*, is also available at www.prospects.csu.ac.uk. If you register, you can receive e-mails to remind you of job openings, deadlines and company presentations in Cambridge. Milkround Online at *www.milkround.co.uk* is similar to Prospects Direct.

A specialist recruitment agency that can place graduates in a role locally is *Cambridge Graduate Recruitment*, Compass House, Vision Park, Chivers Way, Histon, Cambridge, CB4 9AD (01223 257745).

CAREERS GUIDANCE OFFICES

Careers Guidance, a now privatised government agency, serves anyone, whether a school leaver or a mid-career changer, though wage earners may need to pay a small fee for services. It has materials to research the exact career path you have in mind or simply assistance and guidance from an expert advisor. Daily newspapers, employer files, computer databases and reference materials are all available, and staff will be able to advise you on anything from interview technique and psychometric, verbal and numerical testing to assessment centre testing. You should also find Standard Application Forms (SAFs) available which you may have to fill in to apply for certain jobs. Help with these forms and especially with the areas that require you to elaborate or explain your skill set is available from the careers advisor. It can also help with training.

Cambridgeshire Careers Guidance (CCG) will be the first choice for anyone who needs help in making their next move or simply for those looking to use the extensive information libraries. Professional advice and guidance is on hand for a wide range of areas: career decisions and plans, educational courses and training opportunities, job searches, skills assessments and testing, counselling and help for those with special needs. The CCG libraries hold large collections of reference information, including books, prospectuses and databases of jobs, local and national employer information, and training organisations and courses. The area CCG website is:

www.cambscareers.org.uk and the offices are:

Central Library, 3rd floor, Lion Yard, Cambridge, CB3 3QD (01223 712800).

Huntingdon Library, Princes Street, Huntingdon, PE29 2PH (01480 376000).

Cavell Court, 9-11 Lincoln Road, Peterborough, PE1 2RQ (01733 311094).

Ely Library, 6 The Cloisters, Ely, Cambs, CB7 4ZH (01353 669099).

The Library, Priory Lane, St Neots, PE19 2BH (01480 367000) - Part time office.

CCG Administrative Centres:

7 The Meadow, Meadow Lane, St Ives, Cambs, PE17 4LG (01480 376000) and Trust Court, Vision Park, Histon, Cambridge CB4 4PW (01223 712800).

● commercial careers guidance

Cambridge Career Consultants, 10 Gower Road, Royston, Herts, SG8 5DU (01763 236352, website www.cambridge-career-consultants.co.uk) offers career guidance and job search coaching for a fee to working professionals and anyone else who needs it.

NEWS MEDIA JOB LISTINGS

Local newspapers advertise a range of jobs and, in Cambridge, sometimes high-tech listings, but generally few professional positions, even when they are local. These tend to be advertised in the national newspapers.

Local news media

Cambridge Evening News, Winship Road, Milton, Cambridge, CB4 6PP (01223 434434, website www.cambridge-news.co.uk/jobfinder/)

Adhoc magazine, a free weekly and website: www.adhoc.co.uk/cambridge/ (01223 568960)

Peterborough Evening Telegraph (www.peterboroughet.co.uk)

For more local media listings see 'Household Services' page 68

National newspapers

The Independent, 1 Canada Square, Canary Wharf, London, E14 5DL (see www.independent.co.uk/advancement/Career/ for careers advice).

Evening Standard, 60 Charlotte Street, London, W1P 2AX,. Lists jobs in London and surroundings (www.bigbluedog.co.uk is its online job finder).

The Times, News International Syndication, PO Box 481, London E98 1SY (www.revolver.com lists all its vacancies and includes a CV submittal service and careers advice).

The Guardian, 119 Farringdon Road, London, EC1R 3ER

(www.jobsunlimited.co.uk is its jobs and careers website).

The Daily Telegraph, 1 Canada Square, Canary Wharf, London E14 5DT (www.appointments-plus.com to search its job listings).

ADDITIONAL INFORMATION

● general interest job websites

www.stepstone.co.uk is a superb site with thousands of jobs available. It also has a powerful search facility, allowing you to select various locations, job sectors and keywords and have new jobs sent every day to you by e-mail.

www.totaljobs.com, *www.monster.co.uk* and *www.wcn.co.uk* are comprehensive sites, which can store your CV, answer your career questions and update you with suitable jobs by e-mail.

● speciality websites

www.netjobs.co.uk includes a directory of the UK's 100 leading online recruitment agencies.

www.nurserve.co.uk is a dedicated nursing professionals site, listing vacancies and training courses, as well as a CV creator service.

Photo by Dan Porter

At the Crowne Plaza Hotel

www.foodjobs.co.uk is an easy to navigate site listing all vacancies within food manufacturing nationally. Post your CV on the website for employers to look at.

www.job-world.com covers IT, financial and accountancy posts.

www.newmonday.com offers free career advice and a listing of over 25,000 searchable jobs, updated on a daily basis.

www.shldirect.com/uk/ and *www.keirsey.com* offer invaluable help and practise tests for those preparing for psychometric, verbal and numerical exercises.

● business information

Cambridge and District Chamber of Commerce (01223 237414) www.cambridgechamber.co.uk For financial information e-mail:

info@finance.camcnty.gov.uk

● related agencies

Cambridge Independent Advice Centre, 41 Mill Road,

photo by Neal E. Robbins

Postal delivery in Cambridge

Cambridge, CB1 2AW (01223 712222, e-mail: ciac@gn.apc.org). An organisation that offers free specialist advice on both employment and unemployment issues.

Opportunity Links, Trust Court, The Vision Park, Histon, Cambridge, CB4 4PW (01223 566522, e-mail: opportunity-links@dial.pipex.com, www.opportunity-links.org.uk). An organisation supported by various local councils. It is a free service with details on jobs, benefits, training and recruitment agencies.

Cambridge TAP (Training Access Point) Central Library, 7 Lion Yard, Cambridge CB2 3QD (01223 712009, www.serif.org.uk). A database of 6,500 training opportunities in the Cambridge area.

CambsTEC: The Business centre, Histon, Cambridge CB4 9LQ (01345 882255, www.cambstec.co.uk). Helps with career guidance, developing skills, business set up etc.

● citizens advice bureaus

*Citizens Advice Bureau*s offer legal advice on any issues that may arise at work, such as pay and conditions, discrimination, contracts, redundancy, training, tribunals and harassment, as well as information relating to benefits for unemployment:

Cambridge and District Citizens Advice Bureau: 72/74 Newmarket Road, Cambridge, CB5 8DZ (Advice line: 08701 264010) can be e-mailed at:
advice@Cambridge-cab.demon.co.uk

Ely: 70 Market Street, CB7 4LS (01353 661416)

Newmarket: Foley Gate, Wellington St CB3 OHY (01638 661694)

Royston: Town Hall SGS RDA (01763 241356) *Saffron Walden*: Barnards Yard, Essex CB11 4EB (01799 526582)

● books and references

Getting that Job: The complete Job-Finder's handbook by Joan Fletcher (Northcote Books, 1991).

Finding a Job on the Internet by Brenden Murphy (Internet Handbooks, Plymouth, 1999).

The Yearbook of Recruitment and Employment Services (a reference available at libraries).

CHAPTER 12
COMMUNITY

photo by API student

This chapter concentrates on starting points for getting involved in voluntary activity and gives contact details for other aspects of community life. These include local charities, political parties, religious groups and advocacy organisations. We have also listed contacts where possible for local branches of national and international volunteer groups and charities. This list is by no means exhaustive. There is a wealth of community and charitable activity in Cambridge and the surrounding area. The Citizen's Guide, an annual listing by the Cambridge Evening News (See 'Key Contacts', back page), highlights 14 charity shops, 23 environmental groups, 53 voluntary bodies, 104 help groups, 111 churches and religious organisations, and 10 political groups/parties but even this does not cover the full range for the whole area! We have listed those we know to be currently seeking support from volunteers, plus contact details for other key community-based activities where possible.

WHY BOTHER?

Getting involved in a local cause or group is a fantastic way to get to know this area better. You'll be surprised at who is involved! Of course, you get to meet new people and have the quiet contentment that helping others or following your beliefs can bring. But to have a good experience as a volunteer, you need to know what you want to get out of the volunteering and to have a realistic understanding of what you can offer. Community activity can bring you the chance to learn new skills or use existing ones in a different environment. Whichever it is, you should be able to find a group that will welcome your commitment – however time-limited – with open arms.

What needs doing?

Most of the local charities and local branches of national organisations face the same key problems: funding and staff. When considering getting involved ask:

- Do I want to support a particular cause by raising money for them, for instance running a special event, doing retail work or recruiting new members?
- Would I prefer to contribute a skill, such as IT support, administrative back-up or experience with children?
- Would I like to do something practical and 'hands-on' such as driving, visiting people, maintenance work or delivery of newsletters?

Do I have a particular type of organisation or group of people I would like to help? Am I motivated to fight for a particular cause or am I concerned about specific health issues? Or do I just want to find a way in which to do something that makes a difference to someone else and makes me feel a part of the community?

Cover picture: Collecting for charity on Market Hill, Cambridge

VOLUNTEERING

Most groups are keen to find people who are patient and willing to learn, not necessarily with any particular experience. However, there will be some ground rules. Many groups very much appreciate people who can commit a reliable, if not regular, contribution of time. In other words, say what you're prepared to do and do it, whether that is a one-off effort for fund raising or a weekly commitment of several hours. Also bear in mind that there are certain legal criteria governing some activities. For example, many youth organisations need to run police checks for security. So don't be put off – it's for everyone's good that both parties know what's expected.

Finding the right charity

If you have no particular idea of what you might want to do then an excellent starting point is to approach the volunteer councils or bureaus in each area. These will have a good idea of what sort of organisations are active where you are and their current needs. Try the following:

● **volunteering in and near Cambridge**

The following operate from Llandaff Chambers, 2 Regent Street, Cambridge, CB2 1AX:

Cambridge Council for Voluntary Service (01223 464696). Supports voluntary organisations throughout Cambridge. Open on Mondays to Fridays 9.30am to 5pm.

Cambridge Volunteer Centre (01223 365549). Helps locate volunteers and provides a starting point for those who would like to volunteer. Open noon-5pm, Monday to Thursday. For a list of volunteer opportunities locally see www.cam-volunteer.org.uk.

Student Community Action (SCA) (01223 350365). Puts students from University of Cambridge and Anglia Polytechnic University in touch with dozens of good causes that need volunteers.

FOR MATURE AUDIENCES ONLY

If you're a more senior volunteer, then in addition to these other organisations, contact one of the following groups, which specialise in finding volunteer positions for older people:

RSVP (Retired and Senior Volunteer Programme), c/o CSV, 237 Pentonville Road, London, N1 9NJ. (0207 278 6601) or e-mail: Joan@RSVPHQ.ssnet.co.uk. The organisation's website is: www.rsvpuk.freeserve.co.uk.

REACH, Bear Wharf, 27 Bankside, SE1 9DP. (0207 928 1452) e-mail: Volwork@btinternet.com. This group specialises in volunteer work for retired professionals and executives. Take a look at their website at www.volwork.org.uk

● volunteering around the region

For support and information about volunteering in the local community:

Ely and District Volunteer Bureau, 41 Forehill, Ely, CB7 4AA (01353 666556).

Huntingdon Volunteer Bureau, Nursery Road, Huntingdon (01480 415145).

Uttlesford Volunteer Bureau, Saffron Walden Community Hospital, Radwinper Road, Saffron Walden, Essex CB11 3HY (01799 513626).

Royston & District Volunteer Bureau, Royston Hospital, London Road, Royston. (01763 243020).

● volunteering and the workplace

Is your workplace involved in a regular charity appeal? Many local businesses are involved in 'Business in the Community', or support national fund raising initiatives. Some even run their own charitable foundations or appeals.

Does your local school need support? There have been recent shortages of school governors and members for Parent-Teacher or 'Friends' associations.

What do the local media suggest? Your parish magazine or newsletter and the local papers and radio often feature fundraising events or groups needing volunteers.

Finally, many villages have Community Centres which are frequently the focal point for local activity.

IF YOU WANT TO DO FUND RAISING

Check out the media and other contacts suggested above. Many smaller local organisations will have sub-committees who are responsible for fund raising to keep their groups going. You should also look out for local fêtes and carnivals whose committees are often trying to raise money for their own community and are frequently short-handed! The same is sometimes true of community sports clubs, especially youth teams (see 'Sport' page 143). The larger organisations often have supporters helping with fund raising, as do local branches of national organisations. There are also many charity shops in the area making a vital contribution to fund raising. A number of groups, such as Oxfam, employ retail managers but depend upon volunteer shop assistants.

Fund raising groups - local

The following all rely on charitable donations and are involved in major local fund raising campaigns:

Arthur Rank Hospice Charity, Brookfields Hospital, Mill Road, Cambridge (01223 723110). A hospice and day centre for cancer patients. Volunteers help organise events or can volunteer in the hospice.

East Anglian Children's Hospice (EACH) Quidenham, Norwich NR16 2PH (01953 888603). Runs hospices in Cambridge, Ipswich and Norfolk for terminally ill children.

> ## THE ANNUAL RAG
>
> Students: watch out for the Annual Rag – this raises many thousands of pounds each year, distributed to local causes. Cambridge Students' Rag Appeal, 01223 330286. The office is staffed throughout the year, with the main Rag week happening around the last weekend in February.

Addenbrooke's - The Friends of Addenbrooke's, Box 126, Addenbrooke's NHS Hospital Trust, Hills Road, Cambridge, CB2 2QQ (01223 217757). Funds go to equipment, staffing and refurbishment of any ward/department.

Wintercomfort for the Homeless - Friends & Volunteer co-ordinator, Overstream House, Victoria Avenue, Cambridge, CB4 1EG (01223 518148).

Fund raising groups - national

These have regular fund raising needing local support:

British Red Cross - Community Fund raiser, 2 Shaftesbury Road, Cambridge, CB2 2BW (01223 272804).

British Heart Foundation - Regional Administrator, 2 Kiln House Yard, Royston, SG8 5AY (01763 242414).

MacMillan Cancer Research - 32 St Andrew's Street Cambridge CB2 3AR. Contact fund raising manager (01223 577020).

Helping out in charity shops

Association of Charity Shops, 224 Shoreditch High Street, London, E1 6PJ. (0207 422 8620). E-mail: charityshops@talk21.com. No particular skills are needed to help out in a charity shop; you will learn on the job. So if you fancy working on the till, making window displays or serving customers, contact this organisation for a list of their members in your area.

IF YOU WANT TO 'DO SOMETHING'

This is a selection of organisations (some local, some branches of national or international groups) who welcome volunteers. It is impossible to list all the area voluntary groups, as there are so many. Consult the sources at the end of this chapter for information on how to find the many other worthy groups we are unable to list here.

Helping those with special needs

Camread, The General Secretary, 167 Green End Road, Cambridge, CB4 1R. (01223 424220). Read to visually impaired people on a regular basis (either reading in their homes or onto a tape in your own home) or fund raise.

'Good Night' Child Sitting Service, The Co-ordinator, Alex Wood Hall, Norfolk Street, Cambridge, CB1 2LD (01223 519220). If you are over 16 years of age, have at least one evening a month to spare and want to help children with special needs and their parents, then contact 'Good Night'.

Riding for the Disabled, Weston Colville Hall, Cambridge, CB1 5PE. (01223 290807). Volunteers help children (and occasionally adults) in horse riding.

Bridge Summer Camps, 11-12 Trumpington Street, Cambridge, CB2 1QA. (01223 321690). The group's summer camps provide Cambridgeshire's mentally and physically disabled adults, as well as underprivileged children, with adventure holidays. The camps are run by volunteers.

Working with animals

The Blue Cross Animal Shelter, 20 Garlic Row, Cambridge, CB5 8HW (01223 350153). Volunteers feed, clean and look after the cats and other animals.

Wood Green Animal Shelters, King's Bush Farm, London Road, Godmanchester PE29 2NH (01480 830014). Volunteers walk dogs and help clean and feed dogs, horses, pigs and other domestic animals here or at a site in Heydon, near Royston, specialising in small animals and cats.

Royal Society for the Prevention of Cruelty to Animals (RSPCA), Edgington Clinic, Edgington Road, Cambridge (01223 247986). Volunteers can act as administrators in the Cambridge Great Eastern Street clinic, dog walkers, home visitors and in other capacities.

Hospitals and First Aid

Addenbrooke's NHS Trust Hospitals (Addenbrooke's Acute, Rosie Hospital, & Fulbourn), Voluntary Services Manager, Voluntary Services Department, Box 214, Addenbrooke's NHS Trust, Hills Road, Cambridge, CB2 2QQ (01223 217356). Volunteers able to offer time on a regular basis are needed for the newspaper service, flower service, as guides, group therapy helpers, visitors and drivers and to help at Radio Addenbrooke's. Full training is given where required.

Princess of Wales Hospital, Ely and *Brookfields Hospital*, Cambridge, among others (see 'Health page 130-132 for more sites) use volunteers. If interested contact the Voluntary Services Co-ordinator, Lifespan Healthcare NHS Trust, Brookfields Hospital, 351 Mill Road, Cambridge, CB1 3DF (01223 723013).

St John Ambulance, Cambridgeshire Headquarters, 3 Barton Road, Cambridge, CB3 9JZ. (01223 355334) or e-mail: St_John_Cambs@compuserve.com. Help St John Ambulance provide first aid at public events, care in the community or in their hospital library service.

Sharing time with the elderly

Age Concern, County Office, 2 Victoria Street, Chatteris, Cambridgeshire, PE16 6AP.(01354 696677) or e-mail: ACCambs@aol.com. Local Office, The Cherry Trees Club, St Matthews Street, Cambridge, CB1 2LT (01223 506002). The Visiting Scheme requires a volunteer to spend an hour each week visiting an older person.

CONTACT, The Student Visiting Service for the Elderly and Housebound in Cambridge, 11-12 Trumpington Street, Cambridge, CB2 1QA (01223 360441) e-mail: contact@cusu.cam.ac.uk. University students volunteer to visit and chat with an elderly person on a weekly basis, usually for about one hour. CONTACT is supported by donations from Cambridge colleges, Cambridgeshire County Council, Cambridge City Council and by fund raising.

Providing support and advice

Basic Skills Service, Cambridge Regional College, Newmarket Road, Cambridge, CB5 8EG (01223 532287). Gives adults the chance to improve their grasp of the three R's in groups led by volunteers and a group tutor. The Service is looking for volunteers who are flexible and willing to undertake Induction Training before they start.

CAM-MIND (Cambridgeshire Mental Welfare Association), Barrere House, 100 Chesterton Road, Cambridge, CB4 1ER (01223 311320). Offers various ways to help those in need, through befriending, housing, and caring, as well as office work.

Cambridge AIDS Action, Office B, Dales Brewery, Gwydir Street, Cambridge, CB1 2LJ (01223 508805). Provides support for those living with HIV or AIDS. Activities include counselling, buddies (one-to-one support), and outreach through promotion of awareness and understanding of HIV and AIDS.

Cambridge Rape Crisis, Box R, 12 Mill Road, Cambridge, CB1 2AD (01223 358314). If you can offer a minimum of three hours a week (Wednesday evenings and/or Saturday daytimes), a non-judgemental attitude and are willing to learn, then Cambridge Rape Crisis can provide you with the necessary training to help women coping with the aftermath of rape.

Cambridge Victim Support, The Bath House, Gwydir Street, Cambridge, CB1 2LW (01223 329000). This national charity aids victims of crime. Volunteers are trained to offer victims free and confidential advice and support following the trauma of crime. Volunteers help by visiting victims, aiding victims in court and in publicity and fund raising.

Linkline, 17 St Edward's Passage, Cambridge, CB2 3PJ (01223 367575). The confidential and non-judgemental Cambridge University nightline run by students for students in the city. If you're interested in manning the lines, then contact the above address for information. Open during term-time from 7pm-8am.

The Samaritans, 4 Emmanuel Road, Cambridge, CB1 1JW (01223 364455). If you are over 17, a good listener and able to commit to a regular weekly shift, then you could have what it takes to be a Samaritan. Volunteers receive preparation and training.

Working with young people

Cambridge YMCA, Queen Anne House, Gonville Place, Cambridge, CB1 1ND (01223 356998). Needs volunteers to help in a variety of projects such as Youthwise (providing leisure activities for eight to 16 year olds in Cambridge and South and East Cambridgeshire), the befriending scheme and creche, as well as volunteer drivers. Contact the volunteer co-ordinator on the above number if interested.

YOMP (Youth Mentoring Project), Mentoring Co-ordinator, YOMP, Greshams, Owen Webb House, 1 Gresham Road, Cambridge, CB1 2ER (01223 369273). If you possess patience, a sense of humour and common sense, then you could be what YOMP is looking for. As a volunteer, you would receive training in order to be able to support and guide a young person in various ways, meeting him/her for an hour and a half a week for about six months or more.

Environmental tasks

Cambridge/Ely Conservation Volunteers. Contact Mark Easton (01223 510019) or Annette Copping (01223 513372). A local team of green-thinking volunteers. No previous experience is necessary and the group goes out most Sundays to visit sites of wildlife interest and take part in practical environmental improvement tasks, such as scrub management and footpath construction. For Ely contact Sandra Hodkinson (01223 571421).

Cultural interests

Many cultural sites need volunteer help. The Cambridge Museum of Technology, Friends of Kettle's Yard and Friends of the Fitzwilliam Museum are, among many others, examples. See Leisure, page 155, for names of many other sites.

RELIGIOUS GROUPS

Cambridge and its surrounding communities offer a range of ways in which to contemplate matters of faith and spirit. Contacts are comprehensively listed in telephone directories under 'Places of Worship'. However, some of the groups are particularly active in outreach to their local community and beyond, supporting voluntary projects, mission work and spiritual teaching. The following is a selection across the faiths. These have been chosen just from the City Centre area.

Christian

● **Roman Catholic**

Fisher House, Guildhall Street, Cambridge, CB2 3NH (01223 350018), www.fisherhouse.org.uk. The Cambridge University Catholic Chaplaincy has daily masses, a library, social events, a Bible study group, a folk choir and a Latin choir, and CAFOD (Catholic Fund for Overseas Development) among its activities.

Our Lady and the English Martyrs, Hills Road,

Cambridge, CB2 1JR, England. (01223 350787), e-mail: olem@dial.pipex.com, web: www.olem.freeuk.com/ . The church's groups include Lourdes Pilgrimage, flower arrangers, Noah's Ark playgroup, bell ringers, St Vincent de Paul and Latin Choir.

● Methodist

Wesley Church, Christ's Pieces, Cambridge. (01223 352115). Promotes social events ranging from a New Year Party and annual quiz, to special dinners at volunteers' homes. It has a play group, luncheon clubs for the retired, a ramblers club, speakers nights and debates. House groups promote Bible study and the Cambridge Methodist Society.

● Church of England

Abbey Church and Christ Church, Newmarket Road, Cambridge (01223 353794). Christ Church (established in 1839). A local parish church using the historic 13th-century Abbey Church for its services. The church supports the local community near the Grafton Centre and has strong link to missionary groups, particularly in Romania.

Great St Mary's, market square, Cambridge (01223 741716) (9am-5pm daily). This is both a parish church and the church of the University of Cambridge. As well as services, Great St Mary's Church also has a Bible study group, a healing group and various committees, such as the 'Worship and Education' Committee.

Holy Trinity Church, Market Street (opposite Woolworths), Cambridge (01223 355397). Historically a 'town and gown' church ministering to students and city people for over 250 years. Has a balance of worship, groups and teaching and a chaplaincy for city shops and offices.

Little St Mary's, Trumpington Street, Cambridge (01223 366202). Runs a Mission Link Group to provide support, assistance and contact to church and charity work overseas, particularly Papua New Guinea, Borneo and Zambia.

St Martin's Church, Suez Road, Cambridge CB1 3QD. (01223 508080). Runs a centre to provide support for elderly people with hot lunches, and activities .

St Matthew's Church, St Matthew's Street, Cambridge (01223 363545). Has a sound-proofed creche, an electronic induction loop for those with hearing difficulties, organises projects, such as missionary support for the lonely, and music, youth and Christian nurture groups.

● various

Emmanuel United Reformed Church, Trumpington Street (01223 351174). Hosts a Mencap café run by the disabled, a Fair Trade Shop (see page101) and many cultural and other activities.

St Andrew's St Baptist Church, St Andrew's St, Cambridge (diagonally opposite the University Arms Hotel) (01223 506343). A family-based church that hosts a range of youth activities and groups and the Living Stones coffee shop as outreach.

The Society of Friends has three meetings in Cambridge at 12 Jesus Lane (01223 357535), 91-93 Hartington Grove (01223 214438) and Oast House, Pembroke College. All meet at 10.30am Sundays, and one at 1.15pm on Wednesdays on Jesus Lane. The Quakers do a lot of outreach, lending their facilities out for all sorts of groups.

Moslem

Cambridge Moslem Welfare Society, Islamic Centre and Mosque, Mawson Road, Cambridge. (01223 411695). Holds regular services and prayer meetings.

Jewish

Cambridge Traditional Jewish Congregation, The Synagogue, 3 Thompson's Lane, Cambridge, CB5 8AQ. (01223 368346). An orthodox synagogue that holds services every Friday, Saturday and Sunday of the year. Services are also held every day during the university term.

Beth Shalom Synagogue, Cockcroft Hall, Cockcroft Place, Clarkson Road, Cambridge (01223 365614). Services are on every Saturday and festival day.

Buddhist

Cambridge Buddhist Centre, 36-38 Newmarket Road, Cambridge, CB5 8DT. (01223 577553), e-mail: cambudcen@cwcom.net, www.cambridgebuddhistcentre.com. The centre forms part of the Friends of the Western Buddhist Order (FWBO) which has 50 major global centres aiming to make Buddhist teachings more accessible to the West. The centre offers classes, regular weekly meetings, festivals, weekend retreats and events.

Other religious groups

Cambridge Inter-Faith Group, contact the secretary at 45 Walpole Road, Cambridge CB1 3TH (01223 510442) www.rainbownet.fsnet.co.uk/interfaith/. Aims to provide a forum where people of different religions can meet and share their experiences. The Cambridge Group is part of the Inter-Faith Network UK (0207 388 0008).

● **websites for further information**

Check following website for more churches:
www.ely.anglican.org/parishes/index.html
www.cam.net.uk./home/aaa315/spirit/SPIRIT.HTM#church

The Citizen's Guide has a further list of churches and other religious groups (see 'Key Contacts', back page).

ADVOCACY GROUPS

If you feel particularly strongly about a certain issue, then chances are that there are other people who feel exactly the same way. Below is a list of just some of the major locally active organisations. More information is available from

Anglia Action which produces packs on social, health, and community topics to supplement items on Anglia TV's community service announcements. Contact: Anglia TV, Hubbard House, Civic Drive, Ipswich, IP1 2QA (01473 217363) e-mail: anglia.action@angliatv4demon.co.uk

Social issues

Amnesty International. AI promotes human rights throughout the world. The Cambridge group meets at 7.45pm on the second Thursday of the month (except in August) at the Friends Meeting House, Jesus Lane. Contact:

ROBIN GILES – BAPTIST MINISTER

My interaction with Cambridge is mainly through the churches. As a part-time industrial chaplain, I visit companies in and around Cambridge, so I have contact with people at work and

with clergy and church leaders across the denominations. This gives me some insight into the differences in the way the church functions in the city and in surrounding areas.

Photo by Ian Gilbert

The city centre churches tend to draw their congregations from a very wide area, which means the membership tends to be more diffuse, larger and better resourced than village or small town churches. The people in the city congregations generally know each other less well, while the villages and smaller towns have more of a sense of belonging to the community and a more committed church membership.

But villages are changing. Due to the increase in high-tech industry in the area, they are becoming dormitories for commuters from Cambridge and further afield. It is getting harder for ministers to encourage people to become involved in the life of their local church. Of course, people today are under more pressure to work longer hours. That leaves less time to participate too.

Although Landbeach and Waterbeach have five churches and strong links between the two places, we tend to suffer from depleted resources. On a good Sunday, my own church has an attendance of only about 50 people. As a convinced ecumenist, I believe the churches need to stand and work together to fulfill their mission in today's world.

Robin Giles is the Minister of Waterbeach Baptist Church and part of the Cambridge Chaplains to People at Work group, which visits people in the workplace to offer pastoral support.

Jean Sell (01223 880335). For Saffron Walden ring 01799 522891. You can also take a look at www.amnesty.org.uk.

Cambridge Council for Racial Equality, c/o 86 Peverel Road, Cambridge, CB5 8RH. This voluntary organisation works to eradicate racial discrimination and promote equality.

Cambridgeshire Against Refugee Detention (CARD), c/o CUSU, 11-12 Trumpington Street, Cambridge, CB2 1QA. (07989 453208), www.card.freewire.co.uk/, e-mail: card@zensearch.net. Campaigns against the imprisonment of refugees.

POLITICAL GROUPS

In the first chapter, pages 28-31, local and regional constituencies and government bodies are listed. If you want to get involved in politics, you first port of call will be these entities. www.ukpol.co.uk would be a useful website to consult. Also consider:

Cambridgeshire Make Votes Count, 10 Pye Terrace, Cambridge, CB4 1DX, e-mail: cmvc@the-hug.org. The local contact for the national organisation 'Make Votes Count' which promotes the benefits of a proportional voting system.

The Institute for Citizenship, 62 Marylebone High Street, London W1M 3AF. (0207 935 4777), www.citizen.org.uk. Seeks to increase active debate and participation in society and encourages 'Speak out!' campaigns particularly directed to dispel apathy among young people and to promote discussion in the community.

www.citizensconnection.net is an excellent website which gives advice on how to gain influence and attention, help and make a difference within the community, and it explains clearly how national and local government works and the opportunities that exist to make changes.

ADDITIONAL INFORMATION

Cambridge Central Library (see 'Key Contacts', back page) has noticeboards and leaflets on all sorts of events and activities, including voluntary work.

Also check the Thomson Local directory under 'Charities and Voluntary Organisations', and 'Youth Organisations' and the Yellow Pages starting with 'Charitable and Voluntary Organisations'. *(see 'Key Contacts', back page, for how to get directories)*

Citizens' Guide. (see 'Key Contacts', back page)

Cambridge Online City, www.colc.co.uk/index.html – details of all manner of organisations, religious, charitable, voluntary, and advocacy.

One World, for details on volunteering opportunities in global, social, and environmental issues, can be found at: www.oneworld.net/action/volunteers/index.html

@Work With You, a directory of Cambridge church activities. Call 01223 423177 and ask for Alison Boddington.

USER'S GUIDE
INDEX

INDEX

INDEX

Cambridge railway station, 1904

On the London Road in Trumpington, Cambridge, 1880s

INDEX

INDEX

Spectators at a River Cam boat race, probably near Fen Ditton, 1880s

About the authors

Nicholas Best is a freelance writer. Raised in Kenya, he has lived in Cambridge for the past 18 years.

Jane Bower is a primary teacher, artist, actress and writer travelling countrywide teaching art, drama and dance. Her passions include food and competitions.

Kate Burdett worked as press and radio journalist for over 10 years. She has recently set up her own public relations and media consultancy based in Stamford, Lincolnshire.

John Gaskell left the Cambridge Evening News in 1982 for Fleet Street where he joined the staff of the Daily Telegraph and Sunday Telegraph. He has been freelance since 2000.

Jan Gilbert BA (Hons), MPhil (Cantab) an experienced editor and writer for new and traditional media, is currently writing her PhD thesis and translating a Spanish novel.

Penny Hancock is a freelance writer, specializsing in education and issues affecting parents and children. She also writes fiction and materials for English students and children.

Collette Nicholls is a journalist who has worked on both local and national newspapers and magazines. Her specialist fields include theatre, film, television and education.

Neal E. Robbins, publisher and editor of the Wavy-Haired Reader guides, has lived in Cambridge for six years.

Edward Yoxall (BA Hons) studied Modern and Medieval Languages at Cambridge University, and is a freelance writer and translator in English, Spanish, Portuguese and Catalan.

LIBRARIES

The Cambridge Central Library, 7 Lion Yard, Cambridge CB2 3QD (01223 712000) 9am-7pm Mon-Fri, Sat 9am-5.30pm, www.cambridgeshire.gov.uk/library

For a full list of libraries see the map indexes.

NEWS MEDIA / PUBLICATIONS

Cambridge Evening News, Winship Road, Milton CB4 6PP (01223 434434) www.cambridge-news.co.uk

Citizens' Guide, A special annual *Cambridge Evening News* publication listing clubs and other organisations. Sold at the reference section of the library or with the newspaper. Available online: www.cambridge-news.co.uk/citizens-guide/

Adhoc City. A free weekly what's on. Janus House, 46-48 St Andrew's St, Cambridge CB2 3BH (01223 568960), www.adhoc.co.uk/cambridge/

Yellow Pages, (0800 671444) and Thomson's Directory (01252 555555). Usually arrives free, or visit www.yell.com or www.thomweb.co.uk. If you need a copy, call.

For more media see page 68. For listings see page 178-180.

MAIN TOURIST INFORMATION CENTRES

Cambridge, The Old Library, Wheeler Street, Cambridge CB2 3QB, 10am-5.30pm Mon-Fri, Sat 10am-5pm (01223 322640 for information 01223 457574 for group tours), www.tourismcambridge.com

Ely, Oliver Cromwell's House, 29 Mary's St (01353 662062) (Oct-March) Mon-Sat 10-5, Sun 11-4. Summer 10am-5.30pm daily.

Huntingdon, The Library, Princes St (01480 388588) Mon-Fri-10am-5pm.

Newmarket, Palace House, Palace St. (01638 667200). 9am-5pm Mon-Fri, 10am-1pm Sat.

Saffron Walden, Market Street (01799 510444) Open 10am-5pm Mon-Sat.

For a full list of Tourist Information Centres see page180.

GOVERNMENT SOURCES

Cambridge City Council, *Guildhall, Cambridge CB2 3QJ (01223 457000) www.cambridge.gov.uk and Cambridge On-Line City: www.colc.co.uk and e-mails to: Guildhall.Reception@cambridge.gov.uk*

Cambridgeshire County Council, *Shire Hall, Castle Hill, Cambridge CB3 OAP. (01223 717111):*
www.cambridgeshire.gov.uk

South Cambridgeshire District Council, *9/11 Hills Road, Cambridge CB2 1PB (01223 443000)*
www.scambs.gov.uk
For a full list of District Councils see page 65.

UNIVERSITY SOURCES

University of Cambridge, *central number: 01223 337733. For information about the University itself: www.cam.ac.uk and for general local area information:*
www.cam.ac.uk/CambArea/index.html